D0251276

# BEAUTY *and the* SOUL

ALSO BY PIERO FERRUCCI

*The Power of Kindness*

*What We May Be*

*Inevitable Grace*

*What Our Children Teach Us*

*The Child of Your Dreams* (with Laura Huxley)

JEREMY P. TARCHER/PENGUIN

a member of Penguin Group (USA) Inc.

New York

# BEAUTY
## *and the* SOUL

### THE EXTRAORDINARY POWER
### OF EVERYDAY BEAUTY
### TO HEAL YOUR LIFE

## PIERO FERRUCCI

Translated by Vivien Reid Ferrucci

JEREMY P. TARCHER/PENGUIN
Published by the Penguin Group
Penguin Group (USA) Inc., 375 Hudson Street, New York, New York 10014, USA •
Penguin Group (Canada), 90 Eglinton Avenue East, Suite 700, Toronto, Ontario M4P 2Y3, Canada
(a division of Pearson Canada Inc.) • Penguin Books Ltd, 80 Strand, London WC2R 0RL, England •
Penguin Ireland, 25 St Stephen's Green, Dublin 2, Ireland (a division of Penguin Books Ltd) •
Penguin Group (Australia), 250 Camberwell Road, Camberwell, Victoria 3124, Australia
(a division of Pearson Australia Group Pty Ltd) • Penguin Books India Pvt Ltd, 11 Community Centre,
Panchsheel Park, New Delhi–110 017, India • Penguin Group (NZ), 67 Apollo Drive, Rosedale,
North Shore 0632, New Zealand (a division of Pearson New Zealand Ltd) • Penguin Books
(South Africa) (Pty) Ltd, 24 Sturdee Avenue, Rosebank, Johannesburg 2196, South Africa

Penguin Books Ltd, Registered Offices: 80 Strand, London WC2R 0RL, England

Most Tarcher/Penguin books are available at special quantity discounts for bulk purchase for sales
promotions, premiums, fund-raising, and educational needs. Special books or book excerpts also
can be created to fit specific needs. For details, write Penguin Group (USA) Inc. Special Markets,
375 Hudson Street, New York, NY 10014.

Library of Congress Cataloging-in-Publication Data

Ferruci, Piero.
Beauty and the soul : the extraordinary power of everyday beauty to heal your life / Piero Ferrucci;
translated by Vivien Reid Ferrucci.
p.      cm.
ISBN 978-1-58542-707-9
1. Aesthetics.   2. Healing.   3. Aesthetics—Religious aspects.   I. Title.
BH39.F47713      2009                   2009017816
111'.85—dc22

Printed in the United States of America
1   3   5   7   9   10   8   6   4   2

BOOK DESIGN BY AMANDA DEWEY

While the author has made every effort to provide accurate telephone numbers and Internet addresses at the time
of publication, neither the publisher nor the author assumes any responsibility for errors, or for changes that
occur after publication. Further, the publisher does not have any control over and does not assume any
responsibility for author or third-party websites or their content.

# Acknowledgments

Writing this book has been an inspiring adventure, but not an easy one. It has been a journey into unexpected terrain, where I have at times felt unsure and lost. The subject of beauty is elusive and mysterious. I have done my best. The difficulty in this work is one more reason to be grateful to all who helped me: First, my interviewees, who generously opened the doors to the inner world of their experience; they are both the many I quoted in the text, and the much greater number I did not quote but who were useful anyway. I want to thank my wife, Vivien, who not only translated this text into English, but, in reading the manuscript, gave me lots of valuable suggestions; Linda Michaels, my agent, who encouraged me from the start and, as always, helped me in many ways; and the editors at Tarcher/Penguin, Mitch Horowitz and Gabrielle Moss.

# Contents

# Introduction

Let us start with an African story. Once upon a time there was a normal family: mother, father, children. It was normal in every respect except one: Rather than of flesh and bones, the children were made of wax.

This was a serious problem. The children could never go outside in the sunlight, because if they did, they would melt. They had to live at nighttime and could not see what the world was like. By day they stayed inside a windowless hut, where they were protected from the heat. "We will never know what the world is like," they would say. Yet they were good children and got along with one another. Besides, being made of wax, they had the advantage of not feeling pain. If, say, a needle pricked them, they would not even notice.

All went well. But one of them, Ngwabi, was very curious. He wanted to explore the wonders of the world, as he had heard about them and often dreamt of them. He wanted to see the clouds and the sky, the great river, the zebras, lions, and giraffes. He wanted to see the trees moving in the wind and wander in the vast savannas.

He was tired of staying at home and just staring at the wall: He wished to see the many faces of beauty.

So one day at dawn he decided to go out and set off on a journey of discovery. "Do not go," his parents told him. They were afraid he would melt. "Do not go," his brothers and sisters begged him. But out he went, into the light.

His trip did not last long. He managed to see the glory of dawn, the delicate pinks and mauves of the clouds, the cheetahs in their magnificent race. Everything seemed marvelous to him. But shortly the sun came up and beamed more intensely. He began to melt. Soon he was nothing more than a pool of colored wax on the dusty ground.

At nightfall, his brothers and sisters looked for him, found him, and cried. Their tears fell upon the remains of their brother. With their parents, they took the wax and molded it into a bird. They made wings out of palm leaves so the wax would be protected from the sun. Then they put the wax bird on top of a hill near their home, and waited inside their hut, watching through a crack.

At dawn, the wax bird took the color of fire. He seemed to breathe. His eyes opened. He began to fly. His parents, brothers and sisters watched in awe. He was now a noble bird of many colors. He circled once above their heads, as if to greet and thank them. Then he flew away, far away, ready to explore and enjoy, happy at last.

The theme of this story is death and rebirth. At its highest, beauty not only makes us happy: It shakes us, confronts us, transforms us. Its grandeur and intensity can be too much for us as we presently are. Our obsolete beliefs vanish, our timeworn blocks melt. Our old self dies, the new one comes to light.

Sometimes in our life, a door opens. We enter, and a landscape appears in front of us—a scene that is new, vaster and more striking than anything we have ever been used to. Before, we were contained in a small, safe place. We did not imagine this door existed. But once we open it, we find bright, beautiful views, hills and valleys, sunlit rivers, mists like embroidery, wide spaces. Our life will never be the same.

Let us imagine a person, say a thirty-year-old woman. She has the usual concerns: her love life, her career, her chances of having a family, how to make ends meet, staying fit, and so on. She is not particularly interested in beauty, in the aesthetic experience. She has too much on her mind.

Then one day, as if by a spell, the door opens for her—onto a world whose existence she scarcely suspected. And this woman starts to perceive beauty everywhere, around and inside her: in the shape of clouds, in birdsong, reflections in a puddle, a car-wreck dumped in a field of weeds, an act of unconditional kindness, the adagio of Mozart's K488 piano concerto, the memory of an encounter many years before, an autumn leaf against the sunlight, a brilliantly played goal in a soccer match, a letter expressing gratitude, the magic of dance, the skyline of a big city, the veins of a freshly cut onion, the colors of a landscape at sunset, the sound of waves breaking on the shore, a discolored half-ripped billboard, the hues on a beetle's back, a walk through the streets of town on a clear night, a Rembrandt etching, an elegantly worn garment, mountain air on a summer morning, the perfectly measured words of a poem, the perfume of a flower, Gershwin's *Summertime,* moonlight cast over the countryside, the look in a child's eyes, the patterns on a shell, a dream, the starry sky. Just to mention a few examples.

Now suddenly this person is able to perceive beauty. So the question is: How does her life change? How does *our* life change when we open to beauty? The answer to that question is the theme of this book.

## A Primary Need

Some would say that beauty is an extra because it is not useful or practical and life can go on without it in more or less the same way. I disagree. In our example, we would be dealing with a new person, someone with a different character, a far more intense love of life, an inner world immensely richer and more varied, a more vital connection to feelings, a greater ease in relationship with others, a stronger identity and more solid self-esteem, a greater competence in making choices and moving through everyday life, a deeper understanding of existence.

This is the first vital point in looking at the aesthetic experience. Beauty is not like a distant satellite, but like a sun that gives life and light to all areas of our life. In workshops I conduct on this subject, at the end participants often tell me that they used to think beauty was a specific, occasional experience, like enjoying a painting or a piece of music, but they now see that it is a central factor that concerns all aspects of their existence and goes straight to the heart of who they are.

## Benefits

For many years I have been running courses on this subject and dealt with it in psychotherapy sessions. I have also interviewed people on the effects beauty has had on them. In studying the subject, I have cast aside all theoretical preconceptions. As far as possible, I have looked at each experience in an open way, letting it teach me what it had to teach, never using it to prove a point of view. I drew my conclusions afterward.

Furthermore, in conducting these interviews, and generally in all of this study, I followed a basic principle: There is no fixed norm for beauty. I did not decide beforehand what I would or would not regard as beautiful. Whatever anybody regarded as beautiful, I accepted without reservations. In my line of work you do not quarrel with experience. You make of it your starting point.

As I proceeded in my research, I increasingly saw the extraordinary effects of beauty on our personality and all its unsuspected branchings that touch many other sectors, even those which seem to have nothing to do with it: "I forget all my fears," "I understand so many things," "I glimpse happiness," "I feel relieved and fulfilled," "I am grateful to be alive."

Feelings are paramount here. In this digital age—an age of loud emotions, unrelenting stress, and stimuli galore, of fake desires and exposed intimacy, frenetic pace and mass-media bombardment—an age in which our society assaults, haunts, seduces, or paralyzes us—what has happened to our true feelings? We risk losing ourselves in a host of emotions that are not ours, or worse, being stranded in a vast, anonymous void of the heart, maybe without even realizing it. The encounter with beauty takes us easily back to the pure spring of our spontaneous emotional life.

It was surprising that not a single person in this study asked me what I meant by "beautiful." They all knew straightaway, as if I had asked them what is "blue" or "sweet." Their *relationship* with beauty was another matter. For some it was full and direct, for others more difficult and tormented: the same as with other basic realities in our life—food, for example, or sex, money, death. There may be attraction, fear, embarrassment, ambivalence, repression. Each of us approaches beauty in a way that is unique and which in some way represents our entire personality.

We should not miss here another essential point: The experience of beauty is *multidimensional.* When it happens, we usually feel it to be a homogeneous and unitary event. What produces the experience, however, is a variety of independent, and at times coincidental, factors. For instance, I see a Greek temple, I am moved and overcome by a sense of harmony and perfection. What causes this feeling? Is it the perfect proportion of the temple, the Golden Mean—that code of proportion which for classical Greece was the core of all beauty? Or is it the reds and yellows of the poppies and brooms, the fragrance of the sea, the clear air and staggeringly beautiful landscape all around the temple, which are part of my experience? If, instead, I see the temple on a November morning, as it mysteriously emerges from the fog, perhaps it is precisely this gradual revelation that makes it beautiful for me. Or maybe it is the echo of Greek mythology: In this temple I feel the numinous presence of the gods, or I am reminded of Greek and Roman classical poetry. Or perhaps what moves me is the rough texture of ancient stone, the special fascination of ruins, and if I were to look at a brand new copy of the same temple I would be indifferent. Last but not least: I am looking at the temple with the person I love and that makes this moment intense and memorable. What if, instead, I were with a group of coarse tourists, who make loud remarks, carve their names on the columns, and throw their trash around?

### The Poverty of the Affluent

In this project I have followed the original idea of Roberto Assagioli, an Italian psychiatrist and the founder of psychosynthesis. He was the first to emphasize the importance of beauty in the field of psychology. Assagioli often asked his patients and students what their favorite films were, and what books, paintings, and statues had affected them most. For him beauty was a sine qua non.

Assagioli was a precursor: His ideas are relevant and more useful now than ever. At this time in our history, in Western society, our situation is both promising and terrifying. On the one hand, we are in contact with the whole world, our knowledge is multiplying immeasurably, barriers are falling, the miracles of technology are turning fairy tales into everyday reality. On the other hand, we are risking impoverishment: We are becoming slaves dashing from one errand to the next, or trapped in the suffocating city traffic; zombies, consuming and wandering in vacuous shopping malls; ghosts in our relations, because we are submerged by so many stimuli, and we end up too distracted, to the point of being absent. This is the poverty of the affluent: the painful lack of meaning, values, beauty. This is the wasteland of the soul: We think we can have everything, but, in the last analysis, we feel that we are nothing.

In this amazing and frightening era, institutions are losing their force and can no longer help us. The values of justice, freedom, and love are becoming abstract and distant, outshone by the lure of a thousand seductive promises. In such a critical situation, beauty can be a lifesaver—because it is all around us, if we know how to find it. It is beyond any dogma. It answers a deep need. It is immediate and spontaneous. It can be the way back to ourselves.

In my interviews I have seen again and again that beauty is not a whim, but a vital need. Often, however, we are not aware of this need. It can be compared to thirst: Many people are thirsty without knowing it. They do not drink enough, their body desperately needs water and becomes dehydrated, and they feel some kind of malaise. Yet they are not aware of thirst. It is often like that with beauty. Not satisfying our need for beauty can generate depression, restlessness, a profound sense of futility, inexplicable aggressiveness, pathologies of all kinds.

### Resistance to Beauty

The trouble is that the need for beauty, however strong and vital, is easily pushed aside by the distractions and thoughts that everyday life brings us. In the story *The Door in the Wall* by H. G. Wells, a child finds a mysterious door, opens it, and enters a marvelous garden, so beautiful that spending even a short time there makes him overwhelmingly happy. The next day he looks for the door but cannot find it. Later the door appears again, but in difficult moments, when he is busy with other matters, such as when he is on his way to the very first day of school. The child grows, and in rare moments he remembers the wondrous garden and seeks the door without finding it. But when by chance he does find it, he is caught in some commitment he is not able to postpone. He cannot find the time for beauty. Only in death is he to enter the garden again.

We, too, are distracted, too busy and hurried. And we often forget about beauty. This is a tragedy, because without beauty we die. It is a long agony, full of grayness and squalor, hardship and oppression. Without beauty we lose contact with our feelings, the world appears harsh or banal to us, others do not interest us, and life loses its bright colors. We move heavily from one day to the next, without knowing what we are here for, what life is all about.

Why, then, if beauty is so vital and available all around us, do we so often end up ignoring it? There are several answers to this question.

First of all, like the protagonist of the H. G. Wells story, we are too busy and worried about what we have to do. Beauty is right there, but we are occupied elsewhere. After all, haven't we been taught since childhood to be this way? We were not allowed to look out the window at the birds flying, or to be caught daydreaming, instead of paying attention to our lessons. Often—too often— beauty is taken as a synonym for frivolity.

Or it is seen as useless. Beauty is free. A screwdriver, a pen, a missile, a banknote: They are all useful objects. A piece of poetry, a sonata, a dry leaf, a dragonfly: All apparently useless. Beauty is not useful for anything. So why waste our time with futility?

What is more, some of us feel they do not *deserve* beauty. Life gives us an extraordinary gift, and we believe we are not worthy of it. To be happy while others are in strife seems a selfish pastime. A luxury we should not afford.

Or else we are convinced that we need to be highly educated to appreciate beauty. Be well-read. Possess some special competence. Collect antiques. Be part of an elite. But this, too, is a mistake. While it is true that some reading and studying at times helps us understand and enjoy beauty, it is also true that beauty is free, available to everyone in many ways and forms. Beauty is democratic.

Yet others find beauty frightening. They instinctively know that to appreciate it, they have to lower their defenses, become more vulnerable, more open. This state spells danger. They are afraid they will be overwhelmed, exposed, and hurt. Past memories of defenselessness and trauma, perhaps, have made them more cautious and rigid. They are too scared to surrender.

A further obstacle, similar but even deeper, is the fear of disintegration. It is a fear that, if we appreciate beauty, if we really let ourselves go, our personality will change forever. As in the African story, we are afraid that beauty will be intolerably strong and upsetting, that it will make us die. And in a way we are right. But we forget the essential point: After death comes rebirth.

### Ugliness

Meanwhile, ugliness marches on and invades our lives. Just as beauty heals, stimulates, and inspires, ugliness in all its forms has a destructive effect on the human psyche. It depresses and harms us, upsets our inner world, creates disharmony and chaos. It disorients and impoverishes us, makes us feel weak and incapable. It rips us apart.

James Hillman, one of the few psychologists who has emphasized the importance of beauty and the tragedy of its repression, asks what is the cost of ugliness: "What does it cost in absenteeism; in sexual obsession, school drop-out rates, overeating and short attention span; in pharmaceutical remedies and the gigantic escapism industries of wasteful shopping, chemical dependency, sports violence, and the disguised colonialism of tourism? Could the causes of major social, political, and economic issues of our time also be found in the repression of beauty?"

As beauty is so often not acknowledged, neither is the evil power of ugliness. Thus we are invaded by it. At some point in my workshops on beauty I invite participants to think about ugliness and its effects on them. They come up with examples: violent video games, animals killed in the slaughterhouse, the spoiling of nature, the horrors of war, land mines that murder the innocent, child abuse. The atmosphere grows heavy, as each sees how astonishingly destructive ugliness can be. This is a part of the seminar I have difficulty in facing, because I know the participants suffer to some degree. And yet to understand beauty fully, we have to meet ugliness face-to-face and acknowledge its power. Otherwise beauty will remain a sentimental and superficial concept.

### Aesthetic Intelligence

Luckily we then go back to beauty. And the question which naturally arises is: How can we stimulate and deepen our perception of it? We need to see that we are endowed with a capacity to appreciate beauty, a kind of intelligence. In the last decades, psychologists have studied various forms of intelligence—mathematical and linguistic intelligence, emotional intelligence, kinetic intelligence, verbal intelligence, and so forth. To these I will add *aesthetic intelligence*: the faculty of perceiving the beautiful. Where one sees a dump, another sees an enchanted castle. The sounds that one person finds boring may make another's heart leap. In any situation, one person may sense beauty and another may not.

Aesthetic intelligence has various aspects. First, the aesthetic *range*. Those who have a wider aesthetic range will be able to experience beauty in many more situations. Instead of finding it, for instance, only in a Beethoven symphony, they can also find it in poetry, understand it in the inner qualities of people, feel it in a book, a film, a landscape, the way a home is decorated, the sound of the rain on the roof, and the thousand banal situations of everyday life.

Second, the *depth* of experience varies. Some people are just barely touched by beauty. They notice it, but are not really moved. It remains an external and temporary fact. Some, on the other hand, feel that beauty penetrates them. They can feel that beauty, at least in that moment, pervades their whole being, moves them, perhaps even overwhelms them.

Third, the *capacity to integrate* beauty also varies. If I appreciate the beauty in a piece of music, or a poem, for instance, I can let this beauty not only touch me, but also change me: It alters my thinking, continues to work inside me, influences my way of relating to others, of acting in the world, even my relationship to the planet I inhabit. I see and feel the connections that an experience of beauty makes in all sectors of my life.

## The Exploitation of Beauty

Meanwhile, however, our society does not recognize our need for beauty. Or rather, it recognizes it only to exploit it. The beauty and fashion industries are bent on convincing us that they can sell us beauty and that we can possess it. But we can possess it only if *we* are beautiful. And we are beautiful only if we use such and such a cream, wear certain clothes, buy that gadget or those fashionable sunglasses or this sports car. Beauty is a product you can buy. Buy that product—and beauty is yours, you will be happy. But unless you buy the product, you will not be beautiful. And you will not take part in a rich, dazzling, almost divine world, with which the media seduce us every day.

It is a paradoxical situation, because, in fact, beauty has never been as accessible as it is now. Just enter a large bookstore and you find all the great literary and artistic masterpieces of humankind. Or go to a travel agent and, at a cost affordable by many, you can buy a ticket to some of the most exquisitely beautiful places on Earth. Not to mention the Internet, from which you can download sonatas and symphonies that only a century ago you could only hear in exceptional circumstances. Exhibitions and shows abound and timeless masterpieces are flown to your city for you to enjoy. Even television commercials are beautiful, sometimes.

This is an extraordinary development of our civilization, although the risk of making everything too easy—and therefore banal—surely lurks. Moreover, for beauty to be transformed into products available at the supermarket, its essential aspect must be removed. We are made to forget that beauty is not an object but a way of being. Although marvels of nature and art masterpieces are more accessible than they ever used to be, we can still be blind to beauty.

Nearly all of us, if we look honestly at ourselves, will find that there could be more beauty in our lives—not simply the beauty of exotic holidays or works of art, but the beauty of people and of the most ordinary objects and events.

## Beauty and Evolution

Our mental equipment is often likened by evolutionary psychology to a Swiss Army Knife—a multifunctional device comprising many skills and intelligences we have developed in the course of our long evolution. Look closely at a Swiss Army Knife and you will find aesthetic intelligence; it is perhaps not immediately evident, but it is nevertheless well-developed and vital.

Aesthetic intelligence is present in every human social group, every tradition. It is an ancient faculty which we have developed in the course of millennia. We know it was active at the dawn of human evolution, and that it is also present in the animal world. Darwin himself spoke of the sense of beauty as a determining element in natural selection.

Certainly the most elementary forms of aesthetic enjoyment is that based on sexual attraction and the tenderness we feel toward small children. These are adaptive emotions which have allowed us to win in the struggle for life. Those who did not have them, did not survive. But the enjoyment of beauty does not stop here. We do not know when a human being first felt awe under the starry sky, or pleasure at a rhythmic sound, or happiness in the lushness of nature. We know that the first explicit expressions of beauty began at the time of the great evolutionary leap, about forty thousand years ago. That was when the first decorated utensils appeared, the first cave paintings, bodily ornaments, music, and songs.

In my work as psychotherapist, when I encounter the aesthetic sentiment in a client, I feel the same force inherent in all primary and ancient emotions, emotions like anger at some affront, or a parent's love for a child, or the fear of death. These emotions have branched into countless forms, but their roots reach deep down in our evolutionary history.

### Brain Imaging and Neuroaesthetics

The aesthetic experience activates specific areas in the human brain. Thanks to new techniques of brain imaging, which promptly visualize brain activity, we know which specific parts of the brain respond to beauty. For example, in an elegant experiment at the University of Parma, subjects were shown images of the *Doryphoros of Polykleitos,* a statue which, perhaps more than any other, incarnates the Golden Mean of proportion and thus represents the classical Greek ideal of beauty. The subjects were shown images of the same statue, but slightly changed: longer chest and shorter legs or else shorter chest and longer legs. When the subjects were looking at the original image, certain cerebral areas lit up, and thus showed an aesthetic response, but when they looked at the altered images there was no response. In another experiment, conducted at the Wellcome Department of Imaging Neuroscience in the University

College of London, subjects were shown images that they themselves had previously classified as beautiful, ugly, or neutral. In this case, too, the same response to beautiful images of a specific brain area (the orbitofrontal part of the cortex) was clearly noted.

An even more recent study shows the importance of empathy in the perception of art. The authors, David Freedberg of Columbia University and Vittorio Gallese of Parma University, show the way in which our appreciation of visual artworks is often empathetic and kinesthetic. The subjects, looking at one of Michelangelo's *Prigioni* (*Prisoners*)—human figures that seem to be struggling to extricate themselves from matter—felt the activation of the same muscles that are apparently at work in the statue itself. Indeed the muscle tensions were consonant with the sculpture. Similarly, those who looked at a painting by Jackson Pollock felt a bodily involvement with the painter's dynamic brushmarks. This is all due to the presence in certain areas of our brain of mirror neurons, which, when we observe an action, simulate the same responses that we would have if we ourselves had to perform that action. Mirror neurons are the basis of empathy, and empathy plays a part in the aesthetic experience.

The fact that some areas of the brain respond to beauty is in favor of the hypothesis that an aesthetic intelligence is at work in us. The new science of neuroaesthetics, as the English neurobiologist Semir Zeki called it, is yet in its dawning stage, but has a promising future.

### Plan of the Book

In this book we will examine one at a time the effects beauty produces on our psyche, plus the ways in which aesthetic intelligence works. Knowing how it works can help us develop it.

Part I talks about how beauty is a potent tonic: It gives us hope and strengthens our connection with the world. Beauty makes us love life.

In Part II we will see that beauty can stimulate the development of personal taste and the sense of identity. Much insecurity disappears once we know how to fully enjoy beauty in our own way. Also, beauty is spontaneous and unpredictable: It teaches us to live in the here and now, to catch the fleeting moment.

Part III shows how beauty generates physical and mental health. It heals our wounds and gives us a sense of well-being. It responds to the pain of the soul and redeems it.

The subject of Part IV is the inner beauty of people and their actions. Aesthetic intelligence is essential for having good relationships with others. We will see how beauty is actually born in the context of relationship.

Part V describes the knowledge factor in beauty. The beautiful not only evokes emotion in us, it opens our mind. It helps us think differently and make more enlightened decisions.

In Part VI we will see how beauty can promote respect for the environment and peace between peoples. It helps us to see the absurdity of war and to respect the magnificent planet we inhabit.

That is what the book is about. The underlying theme is the universal impact of beauty, its pervasive and determing influence over every aspect of our lives. Two images from two very different cultures—traditional Chinese culture and the Italian Renaissance—will help us understand.

In the famous drawing of Universal Man by Leonardo da Vinci—which has been reproduced in thousands of company logos, coins, book covers, film posters, etc.—a man at the center of a circle and a square has arms and legs wide apart, as if to touch the cosmos. For Leonardo, it represented the harmony and supreme beauty of the human being, the microcosmos, which contains in itself the beauty of the universe.

The other image is very different, but also similar. It is the Chinese ideogram representing beauty: 美. At its base is represented, again, a human being with arms and legs wide apart as though opening to the whole world, as if to touch the Earth, its flowers and trees, its rivers and seas; and also the air surrounding us, the sky and the stars. Crossing this ideogram are four lines. The bottom three represent the three levels: Earth, the human world, and the divine world. The topmost line is the energy that pervades the universe.

Both images—Western and Eastern, one more abstract, the other more concrete—remind us of a fundamental fact which ought to accompany us in the reading of this book: Beauty is a primary principle that touches all parts and functions of our being. It opens us to the world and brings harmony to our relation with others and with nature; it helps us reach out and touch the entire universe.

ONE

~~~

# THE FORM OF HAPPINESS

# Affirmation

*Così la neve al sol si disigilla, così la neve al sol si disigilla* . . . This verse of Dante's kept coming into my mind, and I did not know why. We have all had that experience: a musical theme, a poetic phrase occurs to us and then starts haunting us. I recalled that these verses are from Canto 33, the last one of the *Paradiso*. I looked up the entire strophe:

> *Così la neve al sol si disigilla,*
> *così al vento nelle foglie levi*
> > *si perdea la sentenza di Sibilla.*

> *Thus does the snow in sunshine break open,*
> *thus with the wind in the light leaves*
> *was Sybil's sentence lost.*

I find these verses extraordinarily beautiful. Dante has just had a full-blown illumination, and confesses he is unable to hold the complete memory of it, though a trace remains, "the sweetness that is born of it." He is telling us here how precarious and how fleeting the spiritual experience is (and that includes beauty). He compares his vision with the melting snow or the prophetic answer the oracle (the Sybil) would write on leaves, then disperse in the wind.

What is it that makes these verses so beautiful? Perhaps it is the rhythm, the elegant flow of words punctuated by rhyme. Perhaps it is the metaphors, melting snow and leaves in the wind, which give the perfect idea of how evanescent our most profound visions can be, how uncertain and vulnerable our destiny. People went to the Sybil for answers to basic questions about their lives. She would write them on leaves, which she then surrendered to the wind. This made their interpretation harder and more doubtful: They would watch their destiny blow away in the wind. Perhaps what makes these verses so striking is each word's rightness— each word indispensably does the work it must do in the sentence, just as each column of a Greek temple has its place and function. But explanations will not carry us very far. Ultimately beauty is inexplicable.

I remember the dry leaves of another great verse:

*Si sta come*
*d'autunno*
*sugli alberi*
*le foglie.*


*We are as*
*in autumn*
*on the trees*
*are the leaves.*

Giuseppe Ungaretti is a soldier in the First World War and feels that his life is like the leaves barely attached to the branches of a tree. Here, too, we have precariousness, but the verse is not a continuous flow as is Dante's, in fact, it is made of four segments: We are as / in autumn / on the trees / are the leaves. We are obliged to stop at each one, and the rhythm, instead of flowing, is syncopated. It is a short and halting pace, and reminds us of how tragically insecure life is in the trenches.

My reaction to these verses, both Dante's and Ungaretti's, as often happens when I read poetry, is that of incredulity: I cannot understand how words, arranged in this way or that, can have such a powerful effect on me, why they can contain so much beauty. This is of course a common prejudice. We are used to thinking of poetry as weak and insubstantial and of poets as ineffectual people who live in fantasyland. Yet words forge our very lives, and poets are the champions of words. Their verses can speak to our hearts and shape the minds of entire generations.

For many people, the words of poetry have the power to evoke beauty. But this is just one of countless situations in which the aesthetic experience arises. People meet beauty in the most unpredictable circumstances. And yet in the enormous variety of instances there almost always are recurring themes, which may perhaps be summed up in one phrase: Beauty is the affirmation of life.

## Joy

In order to study and understand the experience of beauty and its effects, I have been interviewing many people for several years. As they talk, I notice consistent reactions at the moment they evoke an aesthetic experience: Their eyes light up, they smile, their faces relax, their voices become lower and calmer, their breathing deeper, their posture more open. The most common effects they mention is that beauty has made them happy, has soothed them when they were distressed, has been an invisible ally during critical phases of their life, has reassured them when they were scared, given them strength when they felt weak. In those moments, a feeling of relief came over them—a relief of which I, listening to them speak, hear an echo. They talk about it as a benefit that is still precious to them today. And often, one way or another, they reach the same conclusion: Now that I have had this experience, I know life is worth living.

These are often everyday experiences. For example, a woman tells me: "I stopped in front of a tree in the countryside. It was just the skeleton of a tree with a few red leaves attached. Bare trees are beautiful, too, because you can see their structure. Suddenly the wind blew and the leaves all fell, and I found myself covered with them. It was a wonderful moment."

Francesca, twenty-eight years old, recalls an experience of complicity and wonder that happened many years before, at summer camp with some girlfriends: "One night we ran off and carried out a plan we had prepared during the day. We went into the middle of a soccer field, lay down, and watched the sky. At that moment, I understood the expression: celestial vault. My heart overflowed with joy. It was marvelous to share this experience with the others. And later it remained a positive memory I could come back to. It left a powerful trace in my life."

It is hard work to describe the essence of the aesthetic experience—subtle and imponderable as it is. Luckily mythology comes to our help. Think of Orpheus, for instance. His music reached everyone and everywhere and touched all. At times it was sad, at times happy, but always unspeakably beautiful. The birds, forgetting the joys of the sky, flew down in flocks and gathered, silent, around Orpheus and his lyre. They did not want to miss a single note. The river, too, was stunned by the melodies and deviated as far as it could, flooding the fields, woods, and crags, desperately trying to get as close as possible to this music. The plants were saying farewell to the world in the late autumn. They were dying. But, touched by the miraculous sound, they regenerated instantly. For them it was spring once again.

Beauty enchants us, renews us, and conquers death. This is the story of Orpheus, the great musician. It is a famous myth: Orpheus loses Eurydice, the woman he loves, when she is bitten by an asp and dies. To save her, Orpheus manages to reach the place where no living human has ever trodden before—the ghastly Kingdom of the Dead.

How can he be permitted to venture into a place which is protected by absolute forbiddance? His secret is beauty. Orpheus's music is so wonderful, it persuades the King of the Underworld to fling the gates open just for him—but on one condition: Orpheus must refrain from looking at Eurydice until they are out, because this is the law of Hell. The judges of hell, hearing his lyre, are moved to tears, the monstrous beasts in that dark world are bewitched by his magic, infernal torture is suspended. The souls of the dead gather around Orpheus, the only human alive in the land of the dead. Among them is Eurydice, who slowly approaches, still in pain from the snake wound. They walk toward the world of the living. But when salvation is near, Orpheus yields to temptation and turns to look at Eurydice. Immediately she is called back to the darkness of death. Forever. Thunder seals the drama, echoing three times: The voice of immutable Fate.

The story ends tragically. Orpheus has failed. But what concerns us here is that he had succeeded, at least for a short time, to conquer death. Thus beauty lets us glimpse an alternative even to the most tragic situation. It may not change our destiny, but it makes us feel, even if for a moment, that we can overcome adversity and once more be in love with life.

### The Enigma of Existence

Life, as we well know, is not easy. Here we are, on this planet. We must try to get along with others, make a living, accomplish something worthwhile—but we are not sure what we are here for. Our body is fragile and imperfect. It may get sick; inevitably it ages. Disappointment, betrayal, frustration and suffering punctuate our existence—big and small deaths before the final one, toward which we are all galloping. Not easy.

Despite the difficulties, we keep hoping, perhaps deluding ourselves. And over the millennia, we have developed ways to make life more tolerable. Some are simple distractions: We try not to think about the difficulties awaiting us day after day. During the last century this system of distractions has become a huge source of profit. We have developed many ingenious means of avoiding reality's threats and hardships: We yield to the myths of well-being and the dreams of television, the unlikely mirages of advertising and the sirens of consumerism, which we hope will help defend us from all discomforts. Shop till you drop, smoke and drink, watch a movie or TV, eat all you can, surf the Net, spend money, have fun, enjoy and forget.

Other approaches, on the contrary, try to face facts squarely and honestly. These are the more or less successful attempts to make sense of suffering, unfulfillment and the mystery of our existence.

They are the great religions and philosophies, which have always maintained that life is not senseless chaos, that salvation or liberation is possible, that it is right to be ethical (or perhaps they state there is no sense at all, but this, too, can help us take a stand). And all that gives us hope, helps us live, or at least allows us, more humbly, to understand and accept our limitations.

One element, more than any other, and more strongly and directly, can support us in our predicament and persuade us that life is worth living, that happiness is possible: Beauty in all its forms.

Beauty is an extraordinary tonic. It revives us when we feel depressed. With great ease it pulls us out of the big and small frustrations of life. It accompanies and nourishes us on our way. Sometimes it leads us to finding sense in our lives. It feeds our hopes and helps us dream. Like the music of Orpheus, it does not make us immortal, yet has the potential to transform us.

## The Eclipse of Beauty

We should perhaps ask ourselves what life becomes without beauty: It is the denial of a vital need. We do not know anymore how to be happy. Without beauty we become arid, furious, and desperate. And yet, in one way or another, we would have the chance to give ourselves this missing vitamin. I have found this to be true in my work as psychotherapist. To lose touch with beauty can cause several pathologies. To discover what is beautiful for us, and to enjoy it, is a potent aid, usually accessible if we stop resisting and just try—or if somebody reminds us. We all find our own way, often in nature, or art, but also through some kind of self-expression, through relationships with others, in everyday life, and even, as we will see, in the most banal situations.

In my interviews, I have regularly noticed that those who felt most at home with beauty were also more in touch with their feelings, had a rich inner life and were more capable of using their own resources, were stronger when in difficulty, and more adaptable in changing strategy when they faced a variety of predicaments. They were not invulnerable, but when they met crisis they could cope more competently.

### Expansion of Consciousness

Sometimes it is beauty which finds us. Alberto, forty years old, once received an unexpected visit from Mozart. It all began with a mistake. He was eight years old when a parcel arrived. It was not addressed to him, but since no one knew who had sent it or for whom it was intended, he opened it. Inside was a recording of a Mozart concerto for horn and orchestra. He listened to it and was immediately captivated. His interest deepened. He asked his father for violin lessons. He enrolled in the conservatorium and became a good violinist, though he does not play professionally. He says: "To play the violin, alone or with others, is like giving voice to the soul. It gives me great joy."

Sometimes you find beauty in the secret folds of memory: a memory of past times that comforts us, gives warmth, and helps us find ourselves and our own history again. Martina received a gift from her grandmother, some stereoscopic photographic plates, photos taken using a bygone technique, offering high resolution on glass plates. The plates are inserted in a wooden viewer with ebony eye-pieces and then three-dimensional scenes appear. The photographs, meticulously dated between 1890 and 1935, depict a Rome that no longer exists: The grand avenues and the network of lanes were beautiful because you would come out of a lane and suddenly see the Colosseum, the Capitol, or St. Peter's. There are many views of Rome, the solemn processions of olden times, such as that of Good Friday, with the paraments and all the sumptuous liturgical forms that do not exist anymore. And then there are family photos, the holidays, the ladies of the twenties or thirties, with shiny silk stockings and long strings of pearls, children with embroidered collars. One is of New Year's eve: a giant *panettone*, about a meter diameter, surrounded by children. Then there are everyday life situations: Craftsmen, the traveling fruit vendor, the baker, and so on: "When I see these plates my heart opens, because it is a rediscovery of times past, of beauty, of things that no longer exist. It is a huge emotion, as if all that these people had experienced also existed in me. Beautiful images are the way for me to be truly in contact with myself. I find myself again only in beauty."

For Gaia, about thirty years old, it is Chagall's paintings which evoke beauty—one painting especially, the one with the lovers flying among the clouds: "Chagall enchants me. His blues, reds, and whites take me to a world of dreams and freedom. These villages, these flying figures, communicate happiness to me, they remind me of joy, and take me to a place unencumbered with structures. To stay with these positive feelings helps me in difficult moments."

We could see it in the way Assagioli did: The house of the human psyche contains not only a cellar crawling with rats and cockroaches, an unconscious filled with our anguish and our wounds. It also comprises the higher stories and a terrace from which we can see the stars, a higher unconscious, the source of intuitions, inspirations, creative ideas, expansion of consciousness. And beauty.

## Tyranny vs. Freedom

Yet we often live only in a tiny room of the house, forgetful of all the rest. Beauty makes us conscious of these new possibilities. Without its perspective, everything seems inadequate, perhaps senseless. Without beauty the soul dies. From a documentary about a trip made by the great pianist Glenn Gould to the USSR, we can understand what the deprivation of beauty may mean. When Glenn Gould arrived in the Soviet Union, he was still an unknown artist. The regime used to prohibit access to great Western artists—in their eyes it was too dangerous—but at that time Gould was not yet famous, so he was allowed. Bach, too, was frowned upon, because he was considered a church composer. When Gould started playing pieces from the *Well-Tempered Clavier,* the audience was small. Very soon, however, they realized the caliber of this artist. During the concert people ran outside to call friends and acquaintances, and let them know that something extraordinary was happening. They had to move fast. And in fact, before the end of the concert, the hall was packed. People had crowded to hear the music of freedom.

All dictatorships harbor great suspicion of beauty. And this should tell us a lot about its nature. Beauty means freedom of feeling, expression of life without impediment or arbitrary control. The easiest way to see this fact is to look at the statues of totalitarian regimes—almost always, they look rigid and impassive. They stand there, cold and distant, chest thrust out, all emotion imploded. Look instead at any of the great classical statues, say, the *Charioteer of Delphi* or the *Venus de Milo* or Michelangelo's *Pietà* (just about any other example is valid). They are a fusion of body and soul. Sensual and expressive, they are alive and speak to you. And even when they show pain and dismay, they are fully in their skin.

Why are dictatorships so hostile to the free expression of beauty? For the same reasons that rigid, neurotic people are afraid of it. Because with its vital energy beauty subverts the established order. It unhinges our structures and our blocks, immerses us in the flow of life, it challenges and involves us. And this is why it can even frighten us.

### Beauty Is a Guide

But beauty makes us insecure only when we deny it. Its direct effect is life-giving. A colleague of mine gives counseling sessions to immigrants, people uprooted from their homes and backgrounds. They must adapt to our culture, which they feel to be alien, often hostile. My colleague counsels using poetry. Not the poetry of our tradition, which would have little meaning for these people. When she works with someone, she looks for the poetry of their country of origin. If the client is Ethiopian, she finds an Ethiopian poet, if Rumanian, she will look for a Rumanian poet.

She chooses a poem that has something to do with that person's situation. And the effects are often hopeful. When they hear verses from their homeland, their hearts warm; they hear a friendly voice, and, though they felt lost before, they can find themselves again.

Poetry is just that—a guide. Indeed we could say beauty in all its forms is a guide, a lighthouse in a dark and threatening night. Newspapers and TV keep reporting human evil, war, terrorism, injustice, as well as imminent disasters, the melting of the poles, epidemics, floods and earthquakes, the threat of extreme cold, hunger, thirst, pollution, poverty, bombs, crime, corruption. Meanwhile, daily life moves on amid hardships and dangers. We seem to be in a nightmare. Until we come across beauty. Which reminds us that harmony lies hidden, that even in the darkest, most difficult condition, hope abides.

So beauty lifts our spirits, sometimes resuscitates us. Happiness, albeit temporary, may be just around the corner. Do we take advantage of this opportunity? Do we work on the inner and outer obstacles that prevent us from doing so? Do we seek beauty in its countless forms?

For most of us, the answer is a clear and resounding no.

# Beauty Is Everywhere

In the short story "The Things Her Husband Did Not Do," by Yasunari Kawabata, the main character recalls an episode of his life: One day, by chance, he touches a prostitute's earlobes. His reaction is overwhelming. That tactile sensation conveys to him the beauty of life. He feels that the purity of the woman, all her virtues, are conserved there (even though she is irritated by his strange insistence). "It was like touching the spirit of an enchanting creature."

We never know where and when we will find beauty. If we look for it where we have been told to, if we already know, or believe we know, where to find it, the search becomes a predictable ritual. But if we are ready to discover it in the most unexpected moments, if our attitude is such that we have no preconceived idea of when the decisive moment will be, then the range of our possibilities becomes immeasurable.

## Aesthetic Range

We often think of the aesthetic experience as a state evoked by nature or art. But it can be generated by any situation. Some see beauty in a flower or a sunset, some in a theatrical performance or a musical theme. But others see it in a person, as inner beauty, or in an act of courage or kindness. Others still see beauty in common objects and situations, even in trash and monstrosities. All these experiences resemble one another, just as people in a family look like one another. We have the perception of harmony, of a grace, or a magic appeal that is sometimes evident, and sometimes secret, and which no label, no theory can define. For some people this family of aesthetic experiences is small and closed, for others it is huge and keeps acquiring new members.

Aesthetic intelligence is about where and how well we are able to perceive beauty. It is a capacity akin to tuning in. Imagine two radios. One can barely pick up two or three stations. Another can pick up hundreds—it receives a variety of broadcasts in all languages, traffic reports and weather forecasts, classical music or golden oldies, political debates or talk-shows, sports news or stock-market commentaries, news or publicity, and so on. It is the same with the aesthetic experience: Some people can see beauty almost anywhere, others stay anchored to familiar, reassuring experiences, which then turn into aesthetic habits.

The difference is clear. Those with a limited aesthetic range have not only a more restricted world, but also a personality which is less rich and flexible. Their relationship with beauty may be rigid, limited, even troubled. They live with a fear of upsetting their own inner balance. They look with suspicion upon the new and have little wish to change. But those with a wide aesthetic range are more elastic and adaptable. They allow themselves to be moved, can embrace new ideas and perspectives, can marvel, and are ready to learn. They live in a much richer world.

I know an elderly lady who never wants to throw out garbage.

Not that she is mad—at most, a bit eccentric. She looks at the fine skin of the onion, at celery stalks, at the wonderful avocado pit, so smooth and round, and at the red, orange, purple, and yellow peels of fruits and vegetables. They are such a beautiful collection, it is a pity to get rid of them. So for a few days she leaves this stuff in a transparent glass jar with water. And she places the jar on the windowsill in the kitchen.

These bits of garbage gradually form themselves into spires, floating clouds, pleasant lines, unbelievable colors, abstract shapes. At sunset, against the light, the whole mass becomes incandescent. At other times I have seen in her house a clear glass jar full of peach pits or white eggshells: the image of elegant simplicity. Yes, even garbage can be beautiful.

## *Universality*

Our aesthetic range can in turn influence our relationships. Those with a vaster aesthetic range will have a greater capacity to understand others and adapt to their way of thinking. They know how to move in an increasingly multicultural world. Those who love only the poets they studied at school, for example, or postcard scenery, are psychologically not as rich and well-equipped as those who appreciate, say, African masks and cool jazz, reflections in glass and modern poetry, Sardinian crafts and the urban landscape, asymmetrical faces and wrought-iron sculptures. The latter people have assimilated more ways of being, have traveled into other worlds, and will have a greater capacity to understand the people they meet. In fact, several studies have shown that even a brief contact with literature and art increases our capacity for empathy.

The aesthetic range is a crucial factor because it guards against narrow-mindedness. People anchored in the same aesthetic realities risk hardening. Their world remains small and provincial, their attitudes suspicious and xenophobic. Aesthetic racism can be an extension of a more general racism. To have a wide aesthetic range is a safeguard against any type of prejudice, because it reminds us that other ways of thinking and perceiving exist and are as valid as ours.

Some time ago I looked at a drawing my son Jonathan was preparing for high school. It was a very precise pencil sketch of a Greek temple with Doric columns. Looking at it, I said to him, "You are drawing the foundation of our entire civilization. This is not just a building: It is our way of thinking and being in the Western world." Then I thought how wonderful it would be if our schools had students study and draw not only the classics from Greek art to the Renaissance at the basis of our civilization, but also forms from other cultures: Australian aboriginal art, Islamic patterns, Chinese landscapes, Nigerian wood statues, Japanese bamboo baskets. And the same for music: Not just Bach and Mozart (if they include them at all), but also Indian drums, Japanese melodies, Indonesian chants, African rhythms, and so on.

That way, cultivating a beauty that is foreign to our culture, schools would help the students' minds to think in many ways, acquire a wide and varied sensibility, understand different cultures and other ways of seeing life. The world around us is full of various and contrasting points of view: To gain cognitive flexibility, open to other ways of living and being, has never been as urgent as it is now. Beauty can be an easy way to promote a universal outlook beyond provincialism and parochialism.

The seventeenth-century English poet Thomas Traherne adeptly described the gifts of a wide aesthetic range. When he was a child, the world was for him "a mirror of infinite beauty." Traherne remembered how he perceived the world in a fresh, pure, ecstatic way: The dust and the stones on the street were as precious as gold, seeing the trees made his heart jump, people were angels, the children playing in the street were jewels. "Eternity was manifest in the light of day." But then little by little the miracle ended, because, as he grew up, he had to learn the "dirty devices of the world." His sensitivity lessened, the aesthetic range shrank—but not enough to prevent a vivid memory. Traherne told the story of the Egyptian king Amasis, who asked the wise men of Greece what was the most beautiful thing in the world. They answered: "The world," because if we were to see it only once it would fill us with wonder, whereas, dealing with it every day, we have grown so used to it we are incapable of seeing its splendor.

### Beauty and Banality

Sometimes people find beauty even in what is normally considered neutral or downright ugly. One day a man admitted to me, with some embarrassment, that he liked squashed tin cans—not the new ones, but those you see in the streets, flattened after hundreds of cars have driven over them. He also liked crumbling houses, old factories in ruins, unused mines, rusty metal structures, decrepit wall surfaces with scraped-off paint, abandoned gas stations overgrown with weeds: "I can't explain why I like all this stuff. For that matter, who can ever explain why they like anything? But I can say that the tin cans, their lines and patterns, just fascinate me. I like the fact that they are used, old, squashed. And then, no two are ever squashed in the same way. Their shape is determined by chance. I would like to collect them, but then I think they look better, stained and wasted, exactly where they are—on the asphalt." So these tin cans are almost a memory of themselves, an archaeological discovery of our times. An icon of the transitory in our society of obsolescence. This is just what evokes beauty for him.

Similarly, a thirty-year-old man remembers how he found an enchanted world in a banal context: "Once, as a child, I was walking alongside the river near my home, and reached a spot two or three hundred meters away. I found some vegetation that blocked the sunlight, then made my way through it to a small waterfall in the sun, and saw its reflection. I expressed all this in a word I invented: *iuaʒ*. For me it was a portrayal of heaven. If you were to see it, you would find just a typical city viaduct made of cement, filled with rubbish and detergent; the vegetation that struck me, you would see as just a few ugly shrubs. In itself it had nothing beautiful to show, but the fact that I got there myself, and found my way through thick vegetation, gave me an unforgettable experience, full of wonder, surprise, of 'heaven.' I was ten years old."

When the aesthetic range is poor, instead, possibilities are limited. I used to know a man who loved only Federico Fellini's *8½*. He had seen it scores of times and was still enthusiastic. He liked no other film by this great director; in fact, he liked no other film. Maybe he liked nothing else at all. I knew another man who found beauty in only one beach on the Adriatic Sea. He really loved it and probably could find in it a charm nobody else was able to see. But he could find beauty in nothing else. If you mentioned some other beautiful place, the Dolomites for instance, or the Greek islands, or something entirely different, like a French cathedral or Aztec earrings, he would promptly say: "Yes, but nothing in the world is as beautiful as the Adriatic!" This extreme aesthetic exclusivity, accompanied often by chauvinism or hostility to the beauty others perceive, is a form of fetishism. A person's whole eros is concentrated and fixated on one object only. Nothing else counts.

On the other hand, we can learn to extend our range. For example, sport can be a huge source of aesthetic emotion: "I love soccer," an interviewee tells me, "a brilliant move, a fantastic pass, a goal that's a work of art, can make me ecstatic." It often happens, however, that those sensitive to the beauty of sports find other kinds boring. And vice versa, those who enjoy beauty in art find enthusiasm at the stadium vulgar. To be able to appreciate the sublime harmony of Olympic dives and of madrigals, the elegance of a pole-vaulter and of a mathematical theorem—that is the secret of a broad aesthetic range.

### Consumerism

Our consumer society may shrink or extend our aesthetic range in a powerful way. Aesthetic production in human society has never been so plentiful and available to so many as it is now. I would not be surprised if, in a few centuries, our epoch will be seen as a new Renaissance. Just think of the design of cell phones, cars, watches; advertising commercials; elegant and visionary software; the unique and extraordinary form of certain buildings; of clothes and all the personal accessories, to name a few examples. You cannot deny that, alongside the garish or banal products, you find much that is original and beautiful. The new technologies are able to multiply our aesthetic potentialities.

But we must bear in mind some features of this aesthetic. What is offered is seen as perfect, polished, sparkling: We seem to be in Toyland. Does beauty always have to be so slick? Also, the mass products of our era push us to possession; they are linked with our comfort and social prestige. All that has little to do with beauty. In urging us to possess, this way of seeing beauty forces us to wastefulness. We are driven to accumulate without thinking, to throw away without caring.

### Wabi Sabi: Imperfection and Poverty

For these reasons, our consumer society can be a bad teacher. Perhaps we should all do a total immersion course in *wabi sabi*. In Japanese, *wabi* means rustic and *sabi* has to do with the difficulty of a solitary and poor life in nature. Together these two words mean a particular aesthetic attitude, for which the poor, simple, and imperfect is beautiful. Implicit in it is the Buddhist principle of impermanence: Everything changes, nothing lasts forever, and nothing can give us perennial satisfaction. *Wabi sabi* is also to do with looking for beauty where you usually wouldn't think to find it, and with the conviction (contrary to contemporary tenet) that material poverty goes hand-in-hand with spiritual richness. In this view, a mended piece of clothing, a worn tool, repaired shoes, a chipped vase, a well-trodden stone pavement may be beautiful. All that is new is not yet beautiful; it acquires beauty little by little, as it is gradually used and the patina of time gives it a unique appeal.

### Possessiveness

Depending on the amplitude of our aesthetic range, our attachment and sense of possession will vary. In a way, we are all fetishists: We all tend to be seduced by the physical appearance of certain people and objects. But how big, or how small, is our range? The more we tend to see beauty in a single item—a house, a car, a piece of jewelry or clothing, a person—the more possessive we will be, because that object or that person, for us, will be our sole access to the priceless treasure of beauty. We want to possess that treasure forever, and will fight desperately to prevent anyone who wants to take it away from us. We know too well that the thirst for possession has brought about social envy, division, and crime in the history of humanity.

The remedy for possessiveness is to widen our aesthetic range. If we can see beauty at every street corner, we will be far less concerned with ownership, because we will know that beauty is a nonmaterial and renewable good, ever ready to appear and surprise us in daily life.

A thirty-year-old woman collects terra-cotta whistles: "It all began by chance, when my mother, half-serious, half-joking, gave me a whistle the day I went to live on my own. Later I found, in a market stall, other whistles in the shapes of a clown, an owl, a black cat. One was a cow with legs in the air and mouth open in a startled expression. Yesterday I found one of a smiling mouse in a ball shape, with a lady beetle on its back. I like only the ones that remind me of folk tradition. I have collected more than a hundred."

This woman also sees beauty in landscape, people, paintings. When she thought of the whistles, she smiled. For a moment she hesitated, as it seemed strange placing them in the same category as other, apparently more profound, experiences. Then she decided that these, too, were experiences of beauty.

Beauty is everywhere. Leonardo da Vinci saw beauty in old women's throats—a theme of his drawings. Rembrandt painted

the play of light on a slaughtered ox. Goya, with his *Caprichos*—
etchings full of witches and monsters showing the dark side of
human nature—scoffed at the society in which he lived. Monet
liked to paint not only water lilies or cathedrals in the mist, but also
the steam from trains. Georgia O'Keeffe was fascinated by coyote
skeletons in the desert. Diane Arbus took photos of circus freaks,
midgets and giants, children handling guns, transvestites and
crackpots—anything departing from what is regarded as normal
and respectable. For her, misfits were the true aristocracy. She saw
them as the character in a fable that gives you a puzzle you have to
solve—the enigma of life. All these artists and many others have
opened our eyes. They have helped us extend our concept of what
is beautiful.

### Expanding the Range

Can we expand our aesthetic range, or are we stuck with what
we have? I am convinced that our aesthetic range can become
vaster. Any aspect of ourselves to which we give attention in time
will grow and develop. This is true of our immature and pathological aspects, as well as of the creative ones, such as aesthetic
sensibility. One method for exercising our aesthetic intelligence,
and thus broadening its range, is to keep a diary of beauty. In a
notebook, jot down big and small aesthetic experiences; describe
not only your experience, but also its effects, immediate and delayed, its deeper ramifications in your personality, the changes of
perspective and the echoes in your mind that the experience produces. Journaling in this way activates our aesthetic awareness and
creates an aesthetic field, an inner space where beauty is not just a
possible encounter, but a close friend.

## Plato's Ladder

The idea of aesthetic range is implicit in Plato's *Symposium*. In a famous passage, the priestess Diotima describes the ladder of beauty. It is possible, she says, to perceive beauty in itself, beyond any of its ephemeral manifestations. But to reach this goal, we have to learn to see it everywhere. First in the visible world of bodies and objects, then in the moral world of inner qualities, then in philosophical and mathematical ideas: an ever-subtler beauty, getting closer and closer to absolute beauty.

Plato gives a hierarchy to experiences of beauty. Here, we will be more democratic, accepting each experience for what it is, without ranking or comparing. That in no way detracts from Plato's idea. It has enormous educational value, and if we follow it, our aesthetic sensibility will reach a deeper level and a wider vision.

It is always a matter of becoming more aware and more flexible, without falling into the usual traps of possessiveness and exclusivity. According to legend, Charlemagne, when he was already old, fell madly in love with a young woman—an embarrassing and difficult situation. The Holy Roman Emperor was losing his imperial dignity. Then suddenly the young woman died. Was the problem solved? No, on the contrary, it was still more embarassing, because Charlemagne kept being in love with her. He had her embalmed and spent his days in adoration beside her body. The archbishop of Reims, Turpino, suspected bewitchment, and indeed found that the girl had a magic ring under her tongue. Clearly the ring had the power to make its owner irresistibly lovable. The archbishop took possession of it, and sure enough, Charlemagne fell in love with *him*. The archbishop was not in the least interested, so he ran away from the emperor and threw the ring into Lake Constance. You can guess what happened to Char-lemagne: He fell in love with the lake and ended his days tenderly contemplating it.

Beauty is like that magic ring. We desire a person, a house, a car, a place, an object, because in some way we are sure it is the best container of beauty. We apparently want the container—solid and visible. In reality we long for an element far more fleeting and subtle—true beauty, which no one can pin down or possess forever.

# Love of Life

In a story from the Jewish tradition, the human soul before birth roams about the universe, collects a great deal of knowledge, sees much beauty, and thus is endowed with great wisdom. But just as birth is drawing near, the angel of death approaches and with his sword touches the soul on the forehead. At that moment, when the soul incarnates into the mass of nerves, organs, and muscles which make up what we are, the drama takes place: The baby being born forgets all it knows. Yet an inkling remains, a vague feeling of what is lost. This, the story tells us, is why human beings are born crying, and why they seek, everywhere and all their lives, in confusion and desperation, a beauty they feel they have lost.

Is there really a soul before birth? I cannot say. And I do not know if we have a past life on other planes or in other worlds. But what interests me here is the experience of this life and this world. The Jewish myth seems to allude to a feeling many, perhaps all of us have: the impression of not belonging to this world. The feeling that makes us wonder "What am I doing here?" Like the alien in the film *The Man Who Fell to Earth*, who came to our planet from a faraway star and landed in an amusement park, we find the world around us strange and bizarre, at times absurd. And perhaps, like him, we feel homesick—for a cleaner, simpler, brighter world.

Luckily we can see the opposite of what the Jewish story tells is also true when we observe children. Many children are happy to be here. They are curious and enterprising, they want to explore and know the world, and they seem to feel at home right where they are. Sometimes, when we look at them, we want to identify ourselves with them, we want to understand what it must feel like to be in a world that is entirely new. I am convinced that this is an aesthetic experience for them. After all, in all our experiences of beauty, even the most sophisticated ones, there is at least a touch of childlike innocence, of the ability to perceive the world as if for the first time, with freshness and amazement.

According to anthropologist Ashley Montagu, children have capacities that we adults have partly, perhaps almost completely, lost: curiosity, the sense of wonder, contact with emotions, the desire to play and experiment, the faculty of relating with others in an immediate and honest way, spontaneity, the talent of effortless learning. Slowly, as we grow, these traits tend to weaken. Montagu believed that, because our childhood is so much longer than that of other mammals, we can express these capacities for a longer time and that is what has enabled us to evolve more than other species. We are more evolved because our childhood lasts longer. This trait of ours is called *neoteny*.

The faculties Montagu is talking about are adaptive ones; that is, they facilitate our survival. For instance, curiosity multiplies our opportunities. Play makes us more skillful. Fluent learning stimulates intelligence. The ease in relationship strengthens social bonding, and so on. In this list of qualities I would include the aesthetic sensibility, which belongs to the same family as contact with emotions and the sense of awe.

And why would the sense of beauty help us survive? The world is difficult, complex, hostile. To find something interesting and beautiful helps us feel more at home, cope more easily, and function more competently. To appreciate a human face, or the shape of trees, the color of flowers, the taste of food, the sound of the human voice, to feel life is worth living, puts us more in touch with our surroundings, helps us manage the tough problems that inevitably come our way, encourages us to meet our challenges. This is what makes the perception of beauty adaptive.

### Estrangement

Now we are ready to go back to our starting point: The feeling of strangeness and not belonging. At times, like happy children, we feel at home in our life. But at other times it is as if we were on another planet, like the man who fell to Earth. This state is about our attitude to the world we live in. What is our relationship with the people around us, the environment, the objects and circumstances of our life?

Sometimes, in my work as psychotherapist, I ask clients if they really want to be here. The answers are surprising. Many say they have an ambivalent relationship with the world: They are here, but do not want to be. They exist, but they are not really here. Underneath, they feel like strangers in a strange land—a hard and irksome world, its matter heavy and opaque, a life made up of clashes and frustrations, sometimes of unspeakable suffering, a situation where they do not know what to expect and why things happen. No one, they feel, has given them an instruction manual. The world seems slippery, dirty, chaotic. Its ugliness upsets us, its disharmony disturbs them.

At times this sense of strangeness leads to full blown pathology: Depression, for example, when it seems to us that we have been rejected from our real home, have lost everything that really mattered, and wander like exiles in a land blind and deaf to our values.

Or depersonalization—a feeling that we do not know where we are and who we are, a terrifying sensation of irreparably having gone astray.

Or alienation—an existential boredom in which every desire is switched off, nothing interests or satisfies us.

Or a divorce from feelings and from the flow of life, the suspicion of anything unpredictable, the numbing of the emotions, as in the schizoid personality disorder.

This estrangement does not involve only the external world. We can feel uneasy also—maybe above all—with ourselves, with the immense inner dimension. Sometimes our inner world seems to us boring and impoverished, at other times it is fragmented and disharmonious. Still other times, it weighs on us, heavy and painful. In all cases we are not at ease, not at home in ourselves.

These are often passing sensations. But in each case the source of unease is our relation with life at large. Ideally, this relation would be full and good: We would be 100 percent present, we would have chosen to be here, and despite the thousand horrors of this Earth, we would remain happy to be here.

But this does not always happen. Do I want to be here, or not? This is the deepest question we can ask ourselves. It is the crucial issue that conditions every detail of our existence—our relationships with others and with our work, our health and our daily life, the way we eat, sleep, and take our kids to school. Is it worth being here? Our reply colors all our acts and emotions.

Sometimes in my workshops on beauty, I use a technique first devised by my friend and colleague Diana Whitmore: I ask the participants to visualize a line on the floor. They have to imagine a time before they were born. Beyond that line is the world with all its marvels and its horrors. All they have to do is take one step, and they enter life. One single step . . . and yet many hesitate, draw back, postpone, or say an outright, No, I do not want to go there. Together we then examine the meaning of all this drama. Many people have never really made the decision to be here, to incarnate in this life and this body. They live, but they are not really here.

### Being Here

Beauty plays a central role in our decision to *be here*. The more we can perceive beauty in our surroundings, and also inside us, the more we will feel at home and glad to exist. Some perceive beauty in the sound of rain and shape of clouds, in people's faces and voices, in birdsong and the rustling of leaves. Some see it in modern design or ancient embroidered silk, in a cathedral's stained glass or an advertising poster, in the flowering of intelligence or in altruism, in musical phrasing or the melodic rhythm of poetry, in the dynamism of a statue or the lightness of a dance. For such people the world is a place of great interest, of continuing amazement. Their relation with life is erotic: They are in love with life.

Others feel uprooted—they are here, but do not want to be; yet they are obliged to live this life, here, among us. So a conflict arises between being here and not wanting to be here. Everything becomes more difficult and exhausting: I relate to others, and at the same time I do not want to be here. I work, and I don't want to be here. I carry on with everyday matters, and I don't want to be here. I go on a holiday, but I don't want to be here. My not-wanting-to-be-here accompanies me everywhere—at all times, like background music—subtracting energy, meaning, and pleasure from all I do.

Those who *do* wish to be here, because they see beauty all around them, are full of happy expectations and are more capable of living life to the full. To be sure, we must come to terms with this world—with its imperfection, density, and roughness. In Wim Wenders's film *Wings of Desire* (*Der Himmel über Berlin*), an angel is doing his job. He is invisible, moving as he wishes, secretly helping those in difficulty, reading people's intimate thoughts, noting the poetic moments of his day. In the film you see other angels who are doing more or less the same things. At one point the angel confesses to another that he would like to become human. He is tired of being an angel. He wants to get his hands black while reading the newspaper, return home tired, drink coffee. It won't be easy, since he must surrender his privileges as an angel. And so he falls into matter, becomes visible to humans, gets out of breath when he runs, bleeds when he cuts himself, loves a woman. After all, to be here, in this incomplete and imperfect world, is just what he wanted. It is only in this reality of ours—so harsh, untidy, tiring, and imperfect, but also wonderful—that he can be truly happy.

### A Sense of Belonging

In my interviews on the effects of beauty, a frequent response has been: Beauty gives me a sense of belonging. At first this reply surprised me. What has the sense of belonging to do with the aesthetic dimension? It is a social category rather than a subjective fact. Belonging to what? I asked them. The answers were invariably vague: "To a greater whole"; "I feel like a cell of a living organism"; "like an atom of the universe." Meaningful but generic metaphors.

Then I understood. The sense of belonging here is not just belonging to a group, a religion, a family, but *to life itself*. It is an answer to the question we continually, maybe unknowingly, ask ourselves: Do I belong here? To say no means that I feel estranged, painfully separate and different in a world I do not know and which could well do without me. It is the sensation that something in me is not right, makes me different and cut off from others and the rest of the world. To say yes means that I feel accepted, that my existence is legitimate, and I am part of all there is.

Immigration to a foreign country is an apt metaphor to describe the theme of this chapter. Consider this example: Dorothea comes from Brazil: "I left a marvelous country, a beautiful family, a job, the university, many friends, my city, and the wide open spaces of nature." Adapting to a foreign country: What an ardous enterprise that is. Having left all that was dear and familiar, you have to reckon with a new and possibly difficult situation, learn new tricks and new rhythms, read novel situations, start everything from scratch. Immigrants, more than others, find they must answer the basic question: How do I feel here? Dorothea wanted to bring a bit of Brazil to Italy. She learned to play Brazilian percussion, and then one day, at last, on the stage of a leading theater in town, she was able to express through music what she had kept inside for twenty-three years—the joy and vitality of her country's rhythms. In this way, the beauty of her music helped her want to be here. It was the decisive factor that created a connection.

Seen from this perspective, beauty is a potent aid to living. If we really want to be here, we are ready to fight for what we want, so it will be easy for us to parry the blows, spot the traps, work to full capacity without too much resistance and hesitation. The flow of information and energy between us and the world around us is more abundant, because the world is fascinating. As nothing stops this flow, the exchange is continual.

### Benefits for Health

You can see the results. From a Swedish study of twelve thousand people, we learn that those who go more often to the theater, movies, to concerts and exhibitions, have a greater chance of longevity. Their risk of dying is 60 percent lower. Another Swedish study of nearly four thousand subjects over eight years showed how even the perception of one's own health improves with attendance at concerts, theater, exhibitions, and cinema. In other words, enjoying beauty increased the will to live.

The explanations given by these researchers are psychoanalytical and biological. According to the psychoanalytical explanation, through sound, color, movement, and words, art can fulfill, in a socially acceptable way, our unsatisfied desires. According to the biological one, the perception of beauty stimulates the immune system, and moreover, by increasing the number of glucocorticoid receptors in the hippocampus, protects us from depression. In any case, this study shows that exposing ourselves to the beneficent effect of beauty makes us happy to be alive.

Beauty, however, does not exist only in museums and exhibitions. As we have already seen, and will see again and again, it turns up in the most unlikely situations—even dramatic ones. Amazingly, even at the deathbed. Daniel, about sixty, speaking of his aesthetic experiences, remembers his work helping terminal patients. There he discovered "the importance of life." With great emotion he recalls the moment at which a patient stopped breathing: "In that moment I held my breath, too, waiting for him to start breathing again. But the patient had drawn his last breath. And when I took my next breath, I saw that it was the continuation of life. I understood the value of living, I saw that I had not really lived before. It was an incredible gift."

# Fundamental OK

There was no way around it: The baby was ugly. He was about five months, his head and face were as asymmetric as could be. He looked like an old person who, by some uncanny error of nature or twist of destiny, had stayed an infant. Yet his parents and relatives adored him. They moved about him as in a dance, held him in their arms, handed him to one another, cuddled him. And he responded with his look and his smile. You could see he had a vast range of expressions and feelings. The baby was unsightly: No one would ever have chosen him for a baby formula ad. But, perhaps because I saw him through the eyes of his parents, I found him perfect. He could not be otherwise, it was right that he be like that. No doubt: He was ugly. And yes, he was supremely beautiful.

## Perfection

In the aesthetic experience anything can happen. We see perfection, for example, in a sonnet or a sonata. And someone might explain to us why we do see perfection: An ingenious network of contrasts, the echoes, the rhythm, give us a feeling of balance and completeness. At other times, however, no formal perfection exists in what we regard beautiful, as in the case of the baby, who was perfect in his imperfection. Many studies have shown that people have a general preference for symmetrical faces. Yet if a computer produces artificially perfect faces, simply by duplicating the right or left side so as to obtain perfect symmetry, the majority of people will find these faces *less* attractive. Perfection may become boring, imperfection attractive.

Which leads us to this question: To what extent is perfection inherent in what we see and hear, and how much is it, instead, our own inner state? We could argue forever on that point. Perfection may belong to reality, be out there. Or it may be in our own private state of consciousness. One fact is sure, and it is of most interest to us: The experience of beauty is often accompanied by a sense of integrity and perfection. We are certain that what we perceive should not be in any way different from the way it is.

When that happens, we are at peace with reality. That is no usual state of mind for most of us. Facing what our existence brings us, so often we disapprove, grumble, rebel, avoid. We wish life would flow the way we have in mind. We struggle and protest. We dream of a substitute world. But on those rare occasions when we experience perfection, we acquiesce. The sense of lack or dissatisfaction vanishes. The bug of anxiety disappears. We feel a fullness and a gratitude for the moment we are experiencing.

### *"Peak" and "Flow"*

The state of grace has been masterfully described by Abraham Maslow in his writings about *peak experiences*: Moments in which

we feel well-being, happiness, gratitude just for being alive, recon-
ciliation of contrasts and conflicts, intuition about the meaning of
our life, ecstasy. Similarly, Mihaly Csikszentmihalyi described *flow*:
a state of unity and identification with what we are doing, of intense concentration and forgetting of time, a sense of deep fullness
and effortlessness, as though everything happened by itself. Experiences of beauty, especially the most intense ones, fall into these
two descriptions or are closely related to them.

The aesthetic experience usually arises from some content: I see
these colored brushstrokes painting the flight of crows over a wheat-
field, or I hear a dialogue between a flute and a harp in an adagio, or
I see the reflections of pine trees in a mountain lake, and it all seems
beautiful to me. Something is at the center of my experience.

But the experience can be without any content, in a basic attitude, which allows me to feel that, whatever happens, I am alive in
a universe that is fundamentally all right.

In my interviews, I have found both types of experience, which
I would call "I am happy to be here" and "I am happy to be." Some
said that being here in this moment, in this place, was the best they
could want, that they could not desire any other condition more
than the present one, exactly because of what they were seeing and
hearing: "I was in Cappadocia, I saw the mountains at sunset tinged
pink. I felt I was in the right place at the right moment. I did not
want to be anywhere else."

Others, more rarely, talked about the beauty of just *being*, irrespective of where and when: "Whether I wake up, breathe, get up,
walk, whatever I do, I feel happy to *be*." In the latter case, beauty is
no longer linked to context. It is an inner state. It is as if events were
interchangeable: Whatever happens is okay. The basic rightness of
the universe is not tied to a single event: not to triumph nor defeat,

not to pleasure nor displeasure. It is not tied to the concrete context in which it occurs, but is an intrinsic feature of reality.

## Fullness

The expression "OK" possibly derives from Greek sailors who used to say: *Ola Kala,* everything is beautiful, to communicate that all was well. In the aesthetic experience, the beauty of one item at times expands to comprise everything: *Ola Kala.* We can reach this state in the experience of beauty, but also in other experiences— interpersonal, religious, or meditative, for instance. People who have had a near-death experience have also spoken about it. To feel, and to know, that everything is okay. Those who believe in the long-reaching influence of infancy, will say that this feeling derives from the sensation of perfect security and happiness the baby feels in its mother's arms. It is a sensation of surrender, trust, perfect symbiosis, a knowledge that someone is caring for us, that we are loved and protected. This warm, basic security is transferred then in adulthood in the form of a basic optimism. Surely it is so, but it is not the whole story. Some individuals, despite a childhood full of abuse and betrayal, may still be able to have this experience. In either case, this is a revealing moment, which remains in our life as a milestone.

Marcello is a thirty-year-old builder. One Christmas Eve he worked all night building a reinforced cement beam as it snowed through the night. The next morning he went outside. Everything was white and silent. The satisfaction in his work slowly transformed into a deep sense of fulfillment: "a feeling that it made no difference whether I was writing a book, working as a builder, a prostitute, or university professor, and that beyond all these roles, beyond everything, was this sense of life's fullness and beauty. With my feet in the snow, in the silence, the whiteness, I was overcome by this profound awareness that no matter what might happen in my life, to live was beautiful in itself."

## Love

Sometimes this feeling of perfection is linked with love, in the sense that love in its most intense aspects opens us to the experience. It is as if love helped us see the world in its timeless perfection. The usual world, so imperfect and incomplete, suddenly seems an ideal world. Every form, every aspect of our surroundings, has value— even a face, out of proportion according to conventional canons of beauty, is beautiful; even a cantankerous person, a garish dress, or offensive music is part of an underlying harmony.

A young man no more than twenty is driven to the airport by his girlfriend on a glorious sunny day. He is in love. Later their relationship will deteriorate, but he does not know it yet: "The air is extraordinarily clear, the contours of everything I see are razor-sharp, the colors unusually intense. I watch the usual urban land-scape go by, large and small vehicles, factories and apartment blocks, billboards, fields, kids playing football . . . Everything looks different to me, transfigured. It all seems out of time. Everything is perfect just as it is, inundated with the light of a summer's after-noon. I would not change anything." A woman remembers a time from her son's childhood: "It was the magical moment of sunset. The light was very beautiful. My eight-year-old son was playing and running in the fields with a friend. Both were bubbling with joy. I was watching them from afar, together with the other boy's mother. We could not have wished more for our children. There was no need to talk. Without saying anything, we both knew we were feeling the same immense happiness."

## Death

Still other times, this same state of okay is linked with death. When we have come face-to-face with beauty, we feel ready to die, as though we have now seen and felt all that is worth seeing and feeling. We perceive beauty because we are free from worry, regret, or discontent. Just for a while the same old mental reactions are gone. It is as if our fears and expectations had loosened their grip. We feel so complete and fulfilled, happy almost beyond capacity, we could die at that moment. Surprisingly, many people expressed this state in my interviews. It is by no means a depressing sensation. On the contrary, it springs from an intense love of life and a state of total surrender, which, by one of the strange paradoxes of beauty, allow us, as we say in Italy, to exclaim: *"Bello da morire."* Beautiful to die for.

TWO

###### THE UNIQUENESS OF
###### EACH MOMENT

# Taste

Imagine you are face-to-face with art or nature at its best—as general opinion has decreed: a statue, a sonata, a sunset. It is compulsory to agree. Michelangelo's sculptures are beautiful: No doubt about it. Beethoven's music is beautiful, everyone knows that. Dramatic, multicolored sunsets are a magnificent sight. That is the dogma.

But that statue, that music, that sunset, happen to leave you cold.

## Aesthetic Dissonance

Here you have a choice. Option one is, you frankly say so and risk unpopularity, maybe hostility. Option two is that, although you are not moved, out of politeness, fear, or convenience, you *pretend*: "What a masterpiece!" "Glorious!" "I feel so touched!" But behind the social pressure, behind the mask, in the inner world where you are secretly allowed to feel what you feel and be what you are, you disagree. And, as a result of this contradiction, you feel bored, tense, unreal.

"I was in America visiting my girlfriend's family," Oliviero, a thirty-year-old psychologist, tells me. "We went to see one of Fellini's films. Fellini is Italian. Fellini is extraordinary. I had to sound in unison with everybody: Ahhhh, Fellini! I could not afford to disagree. But I don't like Fellini. I find his films slow, boring, and heavy. I felt I was being false."

The problem is more serious if, under the pressure of conformism, we end up believing that we *like* what, deep down, we actually do not find beautiful. Thus we make ourselves fancy that which, in the truth of our inner being, we dislike. And we swim along, with the stream of general consensus.

But if we are not in touch with authentic beauty, and we follow canons which are not our own, we feel lost. We are not ourselves anymore. We are on remote control. I will explain by an example. A friend of mine once bought a high-tech barometer. He was very proud of it. The slick instrument read not only air pressure, humidity, time, phases of the moon, and so on, but also gave radio-controlled weather forecasts—its specialty. The problem was that my friend lives, as I do, in central Italy, while the barometer was connected to a weather station in northern Italy. So it gave weather data of an entirely different place, but you did not realize that if you just looked at it. My friend thus knew with great accuracy the weather forecast in northern Italy, say, snow and icy cold, but did not know that in central Italy it would perhaps be fine and warm because of a wind from Africa. Those who do not trust their own aesthetic sensitivity, and who *delegate* their taste to others, are a bit like that barometer: They make statements that are not their own, but pretend they are—and end up believing they are. They live and feel with other people's taste, and pass it off as their own.

This kind of aesthetic betrayal causes an inner dissonance, a disparity between what we feel obliged to feel and what we really feel. We are divorced from our own experience. How can we truly be ourselves if we do not know what is beautiful to us?

## Autonomy

Luckily, we can rebel. Remember the tale of the emperor's new clothes? Nobody has the courage to voice the obvious until a child steps up and says, loud and clear, that the king is naked. We can be like that child.

A fifty-year-old man talks about his path to honesty: "I *wanted* to like the *Man Without Qualities* by Robert Musil. I thought I liked it. Cultured people love it. It spouts intelligence and good taste. The critics regard it as a literary masterpiece. If I liked it, I felt intelligent and refined. Or at least that is what I told myself. But I just couldn't finish the book. And one day I listened to a voice inside: I couldn't care less about the *Man Without Qualities*. Straightaway I felt relieved of a burden."

A thirty-year-old man says: "If I decide what I find beautiful, I feel strong and independent. I am in possession of my subjective space." Many others speak like this. In one interview, a young man told me: "I am sorry to disappoint you, but the classics bore me. I do not go to concerts or exhibitions, and school turned me off poetry. My taste is completely different. I love horror movies (though not all), and I think some comic strips have great drawing. I go to markets looking for kitsch objects that everyone overlooks. As for nature, I only appreciate the snow, when I go skiing. But that I really love."

No disappointment at all. On the contrary, my congratulations. This man knows exactly what he loves. He is in contact with his taste and has the courage to express his convictions. His aesthetic criterion is precise and original. He is much more authentic than those who, out of duty and without real conviction, praise a noble beauty everyone bows to.

### Social Pressure

I suspect that aesthetic dissonance is widespread. And why? Emotions in their raw state, like aesthetic emotions, are scary. They are intense, unpredictable, anarchical. We are all a little afraid of them—or even very afraid. We can understand how dangerous raw emotions are if we take a look at totalitarian states, because they are extreme cases of social control. Dictatorial power tries to direct or suppress emotion in response to beauty just because it is so free and spontaneous.

Nazism condemned *Entartete Kunst*, degenerate art, meaning art that departed from emotional safety and expressed uncertainty, desperation, difference, and horror. This is why jazz and expressionism were seen with suspicion, and only Greek and Roman art were praised. In the USSR the communist dictatorship promoted socialist realism, art which was supposed to function also as propaganda for the regime: It showed idealized, happy workers and inspired leaders, like Lenin or Stalin. Anyone who moved in original, independent territory was sabotaged and persecuted. Fascism, too, tried to control aesthetic expression. In Bologna in 1936 the local authorities asked Toscanini to perform the fascist hymn before a concert. Toscanini refused and put down his baton. Never again was he to work under that regime. It was not just a question of political incompatibility, but also of taste. You just cannot impose beauty.

But even in the freest societies social pressure is strong, submission to its power widespread. The reason for our compliance lies in our distant roots. We have survived in the course of our evolution because we have always lived in groups: This has been a most use-ful strategy for facing the hardships of life, our own fragility, the threat of scarcity, and the adversities of nature. Those who did not belong to a group did not make it. This predicament led to a cate-gorical imperative: Belong or perish. Our condition has of course greatly changed since, but deep down we are still frightened by the specter of exclusion. The need for belonging to the pack is stron-gest in adolescence but is active throughout our life.

It has been well known for decades that social pressure can make us change our minds, even deny evidence. In Solomon Asch's fa-mous experiments, more than 30 percent of the subjects agreed that a line was longer than the other, though clearly it was not, simply because others in the group, secretly instructed by the experiment-ers, said so. And those who did not go along with the group's opin-ion had a hard time. In another classic experiment, the subjects were seated in the dark, with no visual frame of reference, and watched a point of light. They had to describe its movements. Soon they responded in unison: Now it is moving a little to the right, now it is moving up, now it is going downward fast . . . But the point was constantly still. The group had created a consensus. In other words, the group decides how we see and interpret the world. These stud-ies are the benchmarks of social psychology.

We know that social pressure is responsible for serious psycho-logical disorders, such as anorexia, where someone, often a young woman, tries desperately to conform to an unattainable standard of physical beauty imposed by the media: a very thin and ethereal model figure. And how about smoking and alcohol, which initially become addictive because of group pressure? I do not like it at all, in fact, I know it harms me, but I drink whiskey or smoke Camels to show that I belong.

We have all felt this kind of social pressure and perhaps also perpetrated it. It occurs in groups, but it is also common in twosomes. We intensely hope that a partner, child, or friend will like what we like. It would make us feel they were closer to us, belonged more to us.

But if aesthetic imposition succeeds, relationships become fake. For example, in a couple, she likes thrillers with breathtaking chases, spectacular shootings, and a fast rhythm, while he likes romantic, introspective, slow films. They go to see a thriller together. He pretends to like it, but actually cannot stand it.

If, on the other hand, each goes his own way but criticizes or derides the other, the relationship weakens as well. She goes to see the thriller, he the sentimental film, after arguing and putting down each other's choice.

A third possibility is aesthetic tolerance. These two people give each other carte blanche about taste, without mocking or belittling the other's aesthetic preferences. Their relationship has a much greater chance of being strong and true. Each goes to see the film he or she wants, which is fine, because there is no accounting for taste.

I know of no specific study about social pressure on aesthetic preference, but there is no doubt about it: It exists and it makes an impact. How much is our taste conditioned by what other people decide? From what I have learned in my research, psychotherapeutic work, and just plain observation, I must say a great deal.

When we bow to outer pressure, we unconsciously convince ourselves that we like what really leaves us cold. This inner dissonance has a price. In the secret recesses of our being we feel discomfort. We feel we have betrayed our sensibility. And in going along with the general view, in listening to the experts, in conform-

ing to current fashion, we have lost touch with ourselves. We have
lost, or never found, our own taste.

### Intimacy and Beauty

You may find puzzling that we use the metaphor of taste in connection with beauty. But we should not be surprised. After all, each
one of the senses corresponds to a metaphor. To see, for instance,
is to understand. You can listen to your inner voice. An intuitive
person has a good nose. Tact means common sense and courtesy.
And taste conveys the beautiful. In many societies, as the French
anthropologist David Le Breton tells us, taste has to do with aesthetic appreciation, with savoring what we like, enjoying what life
offers us. Even more than touch, it is the most intimate of the
senses. If you think of it, sight, hearing, smell, are more public. But
for us to taste, food must *enter* our organism. No one else really
knows what we are tasting. It is the most secret of the senses.

Thus the experience of the beauty we taste is also intimate
and secret. Society tries to control it. Its influence, to the extreme
of emotional blackmail, is powerful. We are afraid of being criti-
cized or ridiculed: "What bad taste!" "Do you really like that
stuff?" "How old-fashioned!" The judgment may be more or less
implicit—a tone of voice, a look of disgust, a telling silence—but
strong enough to evoke in us feelings of doubt, insecurity, and
shame. Strong enough fo us to succumb.

And yet the experience of beauty can be immediate and overwhelming: Like love at first sight. No need to worry about what we
*should* like or dislike. Just as in tasting what we eat we know straightaway whether we like it or not, so it can be with aesthetic taste. It
makes no sense that someone, drawing on his greater knowledge,
wants to impose his own taste. I would go so far as to say that such

manipulation is unethical, because it tries to invalidate an expression of our very identity.

### Independent Evaluation

On the other hand, like taste in food, aesthetic taste can also be refined and developed. I was once in a shop that specialized in balsamic vinegar—that was all it sold. Some bottles were fairly cheap, though definitely more expensive than the ones you find in supermarkets. And then, neatly lined up on the shelves, you could see smaller bottles, gradually increasing in cost, finally up to twenty or thirty times the price of the cheaper ones. That vinegar came from selected wines aged in seasoned wood, following traditional techniques. The woman who ran the shop advised me, kindly and against her interests, to start with the less expensive types. Not that I had any intention of buying the dear ones, but I was curious and fascinated by the bottles containing the holy grail of balsamic vinegar. She explained that you have to acquire the taste. Had I tried a few drops of the sublime best, I would not have tasted its excellence, because I was a beginner. I had to start low down and slowly move up the ladder of refinement. It is the same with aesthetic taste—you gradually deepen and refine it. If you have no experience of classical music, for example, you would find it hard to distinguish between a mediocre player and a great violinist playing the same piece. If you are not very familiar with poetry, you might be unmoved by a great poet's verses and appreciate more the sugary poem of an amateur.

Instant love or gradual discovery: It can happen both ways. But in either case, we may want to refine our sensibility. That by no means goes to say that in order to enjoy beauty we are obliged to be cultured and informed. Of course, reading books, listening to other

people, comparing views, and so on, might be helpful. But the starting point is taking into account what we feel and *trusting* it.

For the experience of beauty to be strong and true, we need
to be, first of all, free in our judgment. And by deepening our familiarity with beauty, we are coming in contact precisely with
ourselves. We are becoming more authentic, stronger, and more
secure. To trust our own aesthetic judgment means to have self-
esteem: We learn to be at ease with ourselves, in touch with our
emotions and sensations, courageous enough to say what we feel
and think.

At this point we can tackle the concept of an aesthetic in the
sense of a shared mode of perceiving and creating beauty. An aesthetic is like a personal taste, but more seasoned, so to speak, more
organized and more solid. Rather than to an individual, it belongs
to an entire society or era. For example, the Japanese aesthetic of
*wabi sabi* sees beauty in what is old and worn, recalling poverty and
impermanence. It has to do with silence and tranquillity: An old hut
by a bamboo grove, for instance. The Pop Art aesthetic lends a sly,
ironic twist to certain aspects of mass society and places them in a
different context: Thus an enlarged comic strip, or a photo of a
diva, or an everyday tin of tomato soup, is beautiful, or at least
strikes or tickles us. For the aesthetic of Gothic cathedrals, what
draws us close to God, or to a multicolored visionary world, is
beautiful, and it distances us from the imperfect world of matter
and time. For the aesthetic of nature, beauty is found in the contours of a shell or the grain of wood, where nature in her spontaneity and infinite wisdom has created timeless harmony.

A particular aesthetic can be an aid to appreciating beauty, because it emphasizes certain aspects and aids the sharing of emotions. It can indirectly teach and enlighten us, yet, if taken as the

absolute rule, it can also become a prison. It may be useful to seek aesthetics other than our own—indeed it has never been easier than now, in our global village. And it can be useful to meet people with different tastes. It is good practice for becoming more flexible and widening our aesthetic sensibility.

### Bad Taste

And what about bad taste? Try this experiment. Think of two or three examples of what you consider bad taste (naturally, everyone has her own idea of what bad taste is): a whiney song at a restaurant, a TV show which is an insult to intelligence, a film with bad actors, undignified advertising, a garish villa for nouveau riches. And now think of the effect these examples of bad taste had on you when you were subjected to them. It was very likely depressing, irritating, tiring, or just disgusting.

Unfortunately bad taste, like a rising tide, is moving forward. We are often its victims and do not even notice how used to it we have become. In my opinion we ought to have zero tolerance. Is the film unbearable? Get up and leave—even after only two minutes. Is the TV program painfully vulgar? Change the channel. Is the ad degrading? Buy another product. Forced to hear sickly music over and over while waiting on the telephone? Hang up (when possible). Bad taste is a social danger because by changing us into passive subjects it blunts our sensibility, causes malaise, and dulls our thinking. We can defend ourselves if we want.

### Regimentation

The road to discovering and developing our personal taste, however, is replete with obstacles. Over and over again, we see that taste is governed and steered for practical and economic reasons. As I live in Florence, I often see hoards of tourists who have come a long way to appreciate the beauty of art in this city. On the one hand I admire such people for making the effort. And I believe I understand their motivation. After all, I have been in the same position at other times, in other cities. But I cannot help noticing that they often go to visit the places that tourist guides dictate, in the reassuring spirit of "been there, done that": This is the Duomo, so it must be Thursday; this is Botticelli's Venus, now I can send the postcard. I get the feeling that the only works regarded as masterpieces are those near the coach stations, the tourist routes, and the souvenir shops. Yet there are a thousand beautiful buildings, churches, frescoes, paintings, squares, alleys, arches, ruins, landscapes, vases, jewelry, dresses, which, because farther and inaccessible, have been forgotten. Also, what is the quality of attention? We know the average museum visitor stops two seconds in front of each painting. How much beauty can you absorb during that time?

## The Development of Identity

If we want to appreciate beauty, we have to be vulnerable and willing to lose our certainty. A rigid, steely person, sure of what is beautiful and what is not, is unlikely to be in awe, to feel the wonder beauty brings us, because he sees it where it is already known and approved. His arrogance hides the insecurity of one who must conform to the tyranny of the majority.

To be honest with oneself is an invaluable form of inner training, and the aesthetic dimension is the ideal laboratory for practicing this sincerity. It is the way to acquire, bit by bit, a personal taste. When they feel too insecure, many individuals do not have their own taste. They think their opinion does not count. Or else they believe they cannot make a judgment. Developing our own taste is a way to build a base, without which inner security could not exist. This is the perfect road to being authentic: Being in touch with ourselves, and thus knowing what we hate and what we love.

The evolution of personal taste coincides with the development of our individuality. They go hand in hand. Susanna, a woman of forty, is a highly talented fashion designer with sure tastes and a well-developed aesthetic intelligence. She likes, for example, Japanese teapots: their essential lines, the harmony of the materials— finely worked with ancient techniques, attained through many reworkings and great manual skill. She likes the streets and churches of Paris, which seem to her familiar, as if they were places where she once lived. She adores heavily worked materials like brocade, special shades of color, embroidery at its best. When she sees spun yarn set out in all the gradations of color, she literally hears music. She loves contact with nature, where her love of beauty started when she was a child at the seaside.

Susanna came to her aesthetic and creative ability little by little. At first her mother, a seamstress, directed her and awakened in her the taste for beauty, letting her play with materials when she was little. But in adolescence Susanna had to free herself from her parents' taste. Only thus did she find her own voice. "To express my personal taste, I had to let go of my family." She went to live in another city, won her emotional independence, overcame the bourgeois preferences of her family. She began to draw strange clothes, to rebel and experiment. Later, after the birth of her child, her aesthetic sensitivity and her creativity grew further.

We do well to find out, each day, gradually, what we love; to put in brackets all the prejudices, pressures, opinions, authorities; to let the experience of beauty come to us; and to receive it in all its intensity and truth, without anyone having to tell us what we must like or not; to have the courage to say what touches us—if not to others, at least to ourselves.

Here is where our story begins: from a space of freedom. And in this space we start with the emotion we feel right now. Doubtless, we are not in a void. The social atmosphere in which we live counts, as well as our conditioning and personal history. But the more we manage to free ourselves from pressures and taboos, and the more we listen to our feelings and sensations, the more we will develop our taste and venture into the world of beauty.

In conclusion, we all need a reference point—call it what you will, a philosophy, a moral code, a rule of conduct, a worldview, a faith. A lighthouse in the storm. But how can we find a point of reference in the contemporary world, where no one has the power to reassure us, the stimuli we receive are overwhelming and contradictory, institutions are crumbling, and the authorities are puffing and panting to keep up with the times? The answer is that we have to find the guide inside ourselves—not outside. One of my clients, who suffered from panic attacks, often told me: I need an *ubi consistam*. Translation from the Latin: I need a stable point to steady me and give me security. This point, this guide, can be beauty (as it has been for my client). If we develop an original, honest, courageous capacity for perceiving beauty, we will have found a value we can always trust. In a night full of snares and demons, we will rely on a friendly light to comfort us and show us the way.

# Spontaneity

From the day the Romans conquered ancient Greece, they fell in love with her. *Graecia capta ferum victorem cepit* is Horace's beautiful verse: The Greece that was conquered by the Romans, in turn conquered her fierce victor. But her conquest was of a very different order: It was through the beauty of her art. The rich plundered the most beautiful masterpieces from Greece and had them brought to Rome.

The booty arrived by sea. Greek art was given new life under the Roman sun. Countless vases, statues, and other handiworks adorned the houses of those who could afford them. Not all went smoothly, however. At times the gods took revenge, and some of the ships that were bringing the stolen art to Italy came into terrible storms and sank. The loot went down to the bottom of the sea forever.

Well, almost forever, and not just to the bottom. At least not in one important case: In 1972, roughly two thousand years after the shipwreck, a young diver found, on a seabed of sand eight meters deep and a short distance from the coast of Calabria, two statues from classical Greece. The two masterpieces were restored in Florence, by highly skilled hands at the Opificio delle Pietre Dure, and they took the name of "I Bronzi di Riace," the Bronze Statues of Riace, or the Riace Warriors. Before ending up permanently in the Museum of Reggio Calabria, they were exhibited in Rome in 1980. People queued for five or six hours in the sun just to see them.

People's intuition, it turned out, was right: The statues were magnificent. After Rome, they were exhibited in Florence. A friend of mine went to see them before I did. He told me they were an amazing sight. They were on show at the Archaeological Museum in Piazza Santissima Annunziata, one of the most beautiful squares in the world. But my friend said that when he went outside again after seeing the bronzes, he felt a sort of aesthetic short circuit. Suddenly Piazza Santissima Annunciata, which he had always admired, looked decadent to him, "like Art Deco." It had lost nearly all its beauty.

I had to laugh: How could such a jewel lose its beauty—a piazza that feels like a living room, with those archways in pure Renaissance style and Andrea della Robbia's blue and white decorations? Not to mention its great humanitarian tradition: Unmarried girls unable to take care of their newborn babies could surrender them to the Istituto degli Innocenti (Institute of the Innocents) at a revolving door. The babies would be transported inside the institute, no questions asked, and the young women remained anonymous. Here was Christian charity married to architectural beauty. It was the home of the Florentine Renaissance at its greatest splendor. I was skeptical about my friend's reaction: If something has beauty, how can it suddenly lose it?

## Mysterium Tremendum

Anyway, in I went . . . And I was dazzled. From those statues emanated an energy that struck not just me, but all who were present, with huge power. They are two athletes, or perhaps two warriors, one calmer, the other more aggressive-looking. I was transported into another world, to a plane belonging to all men and women, all times and all cultures. This was not simply ancient Greek art. The German philosopher Rudolf Otto referred to this very quality when he spoke of the *numinous*: The force that sometimes emanates from nature and certain works of art (he mentioned the *Et Incarnatus* of Bach's Mass and some Chinese landscapes) and that leaves us in awe before the *mysterium tremendum et fascinans* ("the awe-inspiring, mesmerizing mystery"). I felt as though lots of superfluous pieces had fallen off me: anticipation, cultural prejudices, past experiences, ideas about what is beautiful and what isn't. Instantly I felt purified and taken to the essence.

When I went out after a while, I was in an altered state of consciousness. Finding myself again in Piazza Santissima Annunziata, I noticed, to my great surprise, that this square now seemed old and decadent to me, too. This had been an amazing shift in perception. What had seemed beautiful to me, now looked banal.

## The Ephemeral

So I understood that the experience of beauty is not a given. It is precarious, subjective, and fragile. Precarious because there is nothing sure and predictable in this experience. It may or may not happen, like spiritual enlightenment or the state of grace. Subjective because what is beautiful for one person is not for another, even though some of the universal masterpieces, like the Bronze Statues of Riace, or

Beethoven's *Ode to Joy*, or Shakespeare's *Macbeth*, are beautiful for a great number of people. Fragile because nothing is more easily destroyed than an aesthetic experience. It is easily repressed or forgotten. It can suffer from juxtaposition with other experiences, from social pressure, mood changes, indoctrination, prejudice, the interference of memory, and the context in which it happens.

Piazza Santissima Annunziata had become for me, as for my friend, decadent and graceless. However, when I returned to the scene of the crime a few days later, I was able to marvel again at this square, and I have appreciated it many times since. And should I go to see those bronzes again, I might even be disappointed. To tell the truth, when I saw them reduced on a postcard, they did not make much of an impression on me. Yes, that is how it is: With beauty, there are no guarantees.

### Beauty Is Imponderable

We venture in areas beyond our systems of control. The experience of beauty is impalpable and imponderable, and thus hard to pinpoint. It is a little like paranormal phenomena, which, not being repeatable at will, cannot be studied by science—at least not in the traditional ways. Experimenters can show photos of human faces or geometric figures to a thousand subjects and ask them which ones they do and do not find beautiful. Meanwhile, they do a brain scan and are able to see which areas of the brain are active in that moment. But nobody so far has been able to subject me to this procedure, when, for example, on a lovely autumn morning, taking my usual road, while the sky is opening after a heavy rain, I unexpectedly see the silvery olive trees blowing in the wind, contrasting with the vivid yellow of the chestnut trees, in the clear November air, and I feel my heart leap. I was not expecting this experience, and if tomorrow I take the same road at the same time, it will all be different. How can we build an experiment on *that*?

We are dealing with phenomena that are strong and intense and at the same time subtle, perhaps inexplicable. Take piano playing. The laws of physics tell us that we can measure only two variables in piano music: beat, that is, the rhythm, and intensity, that is, the pressure applied to the keys—giving a range from soft to loud. But in reality we know it is not so: The sounds can be bright, mellow, shadowy, happy, defiant, authoritative, uncertain, creamy, and can have a thousand other connotations that we have no way of measuring—and yet we feel them.

This is the mysterious realm where beauty thrives. One day I happened to sit in on a master class of an extraordinary piano teacher. His students, one by one, took their place at the piano on the stage, to rehearse for a coming concert. The maestro would listen, and then say something like: "Make that D brighter!" Brighter? What does that mean? How do you strike a key brightly? And yet when you listened, the note really did shine. The maestro would tell his pupils not to try—just to let the image he offered them act spontaneously. "Can you play this phrase like soap bubbles, floating in the air, with no force of gravity?" "This bar is a gust of wind," "Sound this A as if you were slowly pulling it with a rope like a heavy weight," "Don't play the refrain in the same way you did the original: It is the same motif, but played like the memory of the first time." "This piece has the enchantment of a fairy tale." "Play these notes with the relentless precision of the mechanized world!" "This is like puppetry." "You are not playing the piano—the piano is playing you." "Don't *try*, let it happen!" And gradually the music, though already played impeccably, gained a stronger and more beautiful shape. Each piece was transformed by a kind of magic that transcended explanation. Those notes really were like soap bubbles, or a gust of wind, or a distant memory, or puppets. Once more I understood how music (but it could have been a landscape or a film or a person) expresses the soul—an intangible, mysterious dimension that no one can define, measure, or possess.

### Unpredictability

Yes, beauty is often shy and tricky. It shows itself when it will, only to disappear as quickly as it came. If you seek or court it, you may be disappointed. Then without warning, it appears again, catching you off guard. You think you have caught it, and a moment later you find yourself empty-handed.

It can be like a game of hide-and-seek. One December evening I was walking in the center of Florence. The air was terse and crisp: It was one of those especially beautiful, sharp winter evenings. I went to Piazza della Signoria, where Palazzo Vecchio, recently restored, looked like an otherworldly vision. The restoration had been a success and revealed the architecture in all its sober elegance. But what struck me most was a little nearby church I had never noticed before. I walked by, saw its door was open, and inside glimpsed a painting that looked like one of Giotto's, though I knew none of his paintings were in that church. For a moment I sensed an atmosphere of magic and intimacy. But I was in too much of a hurry to stop and have a look. I had more urgent things to do.

During the next days I kept remembering the scene. It was a fine treasure that I had glimpsed for a second. Now I knew it was there and could go back to see it when I was less in a hurry. If I had such a strong reaction seeing it so briefly, who knows what could happen if I were to stop for a longer time and look inside the church at my leisure? Entering the center of Florence is a feat nowadays, because of traffic and parking, so I had to postpone my visit. A month went by, and the scene kept coming to mind. Instead of weakening, its power grew. The magic of that painting illuminated in the night, the golden image of the church's intimate interior, went on nourishing me. I just had to go back.

So I did. I was home from a long trip and back in the center of town. I headed straight for the church, my hopes high. But when I got there, I was disappointed. It was daytime, and the church was lit by a neon light, full of devotees singing out of tune. The painting was not nearly as beautiful as it had seemed. Perhaps I had invented the entire beauty on my own. Or, more precisely, the experience was born of an unrepeatable combination of the church, the golden painting, my state of mind at the time, my lack of expectations, the clear air of that evening, my imagination, and possibly many other factors. The true aesthetic experience is spontaneous and unrepeatable.

Indeed the same thing had happened to me at other times. Such as many years ago, during my compulsory military service: I was at the barracks in the dormitory one day, together with another thirty young men my age. You can imagine the din and disorder. One recruit had a radio with poor reception and was channel-hopping. Suddenly I heard Bach's music. Right then, in the chaos, my ears caught the sound of Bach, albeit rough and distorted, coming from that cheap radio. It was a miraculous visitation. It took me away—as if the radio were tuned in to Heaven. But my fellow recruit was not interested and soon tuned to another channel. He preferred pop songs.

Sometime later I listened to the same piece at home, comfortably, on a much better sound system and without interference. Bach is Bach, and yet I did not have such a strong reaction. The aesthetic experience is spontaneous, it comes without being announced and without planning. Like any inspiration, it cannot be forced or willed. We cannot simply say: " I will experience beauty this evening at 6 p.m." It takes us by surprise when we have lowered our guard. This is a well-known phenomenon, as when, for example, we get our best ideas. They come when we are in the shower or driving, at any rate, when we are not making an effort to have a brilliant idea.

It is as though beauty were in the hands of a capricious and unpredictable god, and if we are ready when it arrives, all the better; otherwise, tough luck. Who knows when it will come again? In a Sufi story, you stand before a door. When the door opens, you can glimpse heaven, but you do not know when the door will open again. Maybe it will take a thousand years, maybe a few seconds. Are you ready?

### Surprise

All this means that a crucial aspect of the aesthetic experience is to let ourselves be surprised. It means to be vulnerable, to expect nothing, to hold no preconceived idea about what is beautiful and what is not. The spontaneity of beauty teaches us to be in a free-floating, open state, because beauty cannot be forced into our pre-existing mental categories. For it to happen, it must be ever new, even when it is old, even when ancient—when it is music we have heard a thousand times, a view we have seen over and over again. Yet in that moment the music, or the view, is like a breath of fresh air. It carries all the power and vitality of the new.

This is why beauty teaches us to be true: Because if we look for it, following our ideas about what is beautiful, most likely we will not find it. Beauty teaches us to seize the moment. We cannot fabricate, and we cannot force experience. We can only accept what *is*. And if we do that, we will not pretend anymore, with ourselves or with others, consciously or unconsciously. We will be getting closer to the truth.

This is a hugely important lesson, since it is the opposite of living by force of habit, each day like every other, each experience a photocopy of the known, each moment a déjà vu. In that perspective, beauty may be secure, but it is far paler. It is quite another story to live by seizing each moment, knowing that nothing is repeatable and today's beauty will be gone tomorrow.

We never know when beauty will appear. We can learn where to find it in life's secret hiding places, in the least likely moments, and in apparently incompatible situations. In this view, knowing how to find a treasure we can keep for but a few seconds, will make us more aware and perhaps more grateful.

Beauty, then, brings us back to the here and now. In the presence of beauty it is harder to be distracted. To follow the way of beauty means to live in a state of mindfulness that does not admit distraction or escape. We are here with our whole being. This is our *kairos*, as it was called in ancient Greece: the moment of opportunity, the timeless instant when revelation comes.

All this is of course good. But we have a problem here. The present lasts a fraction of a second. To be more precise, it is infinitely short. We cannot catch it, we cannot freeze it. This situation could become a torture: Beauty is offered to us with extraordinary richness and leaves us in awe. But in an instant it is all gone. What remains is the memory—but it is not enough for us. "The word that comes to mind is 'longing,'" said one of the people I interviewed. "The stronger the experience of beauty is for me, the more intense the pain that goes with it, because I know it will soon end."

And instead we want to freeze the moment and *own* that beauty. We would like it to stay as part of our lives forever. Yet we know it vanishes. This may cause us pain.

### The Unexpected

In another way, too, the aesthetic experience, if felt in all its depth and intensity, can give rise to disquiet or uneasiness. It confronts us with spontaneity. Some of us are more at ease with spontaneity, with all that is unpredictable and out of our control. Children are the champions. They are much more spontaneous than we are, because they trust what happens. To us as adults, the unexpected can be scary. I once did a search on the Internet about "reactions to the unexpected." The vast majority of responses spoke of the unexpected as an irresistibly negative event—a terrorist attack or a natural catastrophe—explaining how to defend oneself against it. This is quite legitimate, but it also shows how much we fear the unexpected, which is why we have timetables, schedules, appointments, and deadlines; why we watch weather forecasts and read horoscopes; why we need rules and order. Anguish in the face of the unknown somehow has to be lessened.

And yet our inner growth is spontaneous. We could even say it is *fed* by spontaneity. Think of the memorable episodes in your life: A chance encounter, falling in love, the birth of an idea, a sudden moment of happiness, a creative inspiration. Almost all the decisive moments of our life come unexpectedly. We may prepare the ground, but the experiences themselves are not within our control. They are surprises.

To be predictable, to follow always the same schemes, to seek haven in reassuring structures, is often the opposite of growth. To find our spontaneity, instead, means to find our naturalness. Since it is not prepared or fabricated, it shows us the truest part of who we are. Taoism speaks of *ziran*, "to be what we are," usually translated as "spontaneity." It means to be in harmony with nature, to be without pretenses, without dishonesty or effort. To find our spontaneity means to free ourselves from what others impose on us, from what we impose on ourselves. Our true self is by definition spontaneous.

One of the most spontaneous products of our psyche is dreaming. Perhaps because they are out of our conscious control, dreams fascinate us. To be sure, many dreams are banal and repetitive: Having to sit yet another exam, losing the house keys, being late, are very common themes and do no more than reflect our anxieties. But we also dream beautiful dreams. We might dream of meetings with charismatic people, being in extraordinary places, receiving splendid gifts, flying, nature in her most wonderful aspects, states of well-being and euphoria. It is no coincidence that we say of something beautiful: "It is a dream."

For instance, a forty-year-old woman needs to make an important decision: Whether to buy a house or not. Confiding in a friend, she tells her that if she were to follow her brain, she would not buy it. But if she were to obey her heart, she would. That night she dreams: "There was a red-gold space, which could have been a marvelous sunset, but there was also gold, and in this space a figure slowly appeared; it offered me a heart of amethyst and said, as for that problem of yours, listen to the reasons of the heart. In that moment, I felt very well. And then I decided with my heart."

## Letting Go

So, in reality and in dreams beauty comes unexpected. Certainly there are places, like art galleries, concert halls, flower gardens, or natural parks, which make an encounter with beauty more likely. But beauty rebels against any set of rules. If we try to grab hold of it, we find it slips through our fingers. If, in the moment we enjoy it, we are distressed at the thought of its disappearance, we make our lives impossible. If we try to bring it about through force, to define it, to create unarguable canons, we are left frustrated.

So the only alternative is surrender, to let ourselves go. To accept that beauty will vanish. To welcome it when it comes, let it go when it leaves. It is not easy for us to let go of our attachment to all that we want to keep forever. Beauty may help us surrender, and that is one of its most powerful lessons.

In my research on the aesthetic experience in people's everyday reality, I have noticed that those who were most successful in experiencing beauty were the ones who were easy and relaxed about it, who were not making a big effort, even though they fully realized its importance. I am persuaded that if we want to encounter the beautiful, we learn to do less and less. We do not try to embalm beauty, nor to obstruct or inhibit emotions that accompany it, nor to contaminate it with explanations, nor to imprison it in predefined canons, nor to impose it on others. All we need to do is stand before it without adding or subtracting anything, to let beauty enter our inner space cleanly and freely. And in this way, instead of trying to possess beauty, we let ourselves be possessed by it.

# The Reality of Reality

I was in Germany, teaching. One of the students had a birthday that very day. As a surprise, before the group started, the other participants began singing the German equivalent of Happy Birthday, wishing happiness, health, and much success. While they were singing, Kristina, a participant, stood up, and with an elegant gesture divided the group into two halves; both continued singing in perfect tune, but now in rounds—a two-voice canon. It was Kristina's spontaneous idea, which the group followed without difficulty. What struck me most about this episode, other than the immediate musicality of the group, was the atmosphere—full of warmth and cheer. The singing participants were smiling. The words were pleasant. The birthday person was moved. This was no routine. It was a heartfelt homage.

In that moment, I thought of how idiotic stereotypes are. How often have I heard or seen Germans depicted as hard, cold, and militaristic. But I have never met that German. My experience in Germany has mostly been the opposite. I have always been warmly and affectionately welcomed. How false is this stereotype. And—

like all stereotypes in the world—how harmful. Stereotypes harm their victims, who are forced into boxes that hide who they truly are. But they also harm their perpetrators, because their outlook, and thus their living experience, becomes impoverished and dismal.

## The Illusion of Knowledge

Stereotypes are an abridgment of reality, a shorthand of the mind used for quick reference. We generate stereotypes of Jews, Africans, women, the elderly, the obese, homosexuals, musicians, lawyers, nuns, and only children. At the very mention of these words, ready-made concepts and associations spring to mind and give us the illusion of knowledge. If I ask you to think of an Englishman, or an immigrant, or a cabaret actor, what image forms in your mind? Perhaps you feel you already know him or her. You do not need to find out anything about what this mysterious and multifaceted human being may be like. You do not need to ask any more questions, look him in the eye, see how he is dressed, what his gestures are, what the sound of his voice is like. You do not need to explore his world, confront him, or just be puzzled. Before you begin, the work of knowing has already been done for you. But has it?

The advantage of thinking in stereotypes is comfort and speed. Without much delay, you can fit any item into a category. It is an ancient heritage and a capacity without which we would never have survived. Something moves in the undergrowth—is it threat or prey? I see red berries—are they food or poison? A human being is approaching—is it friend or foe? The ability to use categories quickly is vitally useful.

But this very ability can become an impediment to knowledge, a risk to human relations, and an obstacle to enjoyment. Every category, every stereotype, is an abstraction. If we move only among stereotypes, we live in a world that is perhaps reassuring and predictable, but incomplete and impersonal. What is more, we think we know, but, in fact, do not know at all—because every flower is different, every cloud, every person, every starry night.

Alfred Korzybski, the founder of General Semantics, used to say that most of our problems come from words. "The map is not the territory"; that is, the name of an object is not what it denotes. The word "tree" is not a tree. This statement is so obvious as to appear ridiculous. But if you think about it, you see that its consequences are revolutionary. The word "tree" is a simplification— just a sound. Then there is the real tree, a far more complex entity or, rather, process. You touch its bark, for instance. Or you look at the design of its branches. There are apples, you eat one; it has a slightly tart taste. The tree emits a scent of earth and damp; you hear the rustle of its foliage in the wind. This is the tree you used to climb as a child: All kinds of memories are associated with it. And it is so different according to the seasons—fresh blossoms, or yellow and red leaves, or naked, snow covered black branches? By comparison, the word "tree" has so little to do with the real thing, it is so painfully general and empty.

### The Dangers of Clichés

It is the same for everyone and everything. I think of an Italian, a Moroccan, a Japanese. But which Italian, Moroccan, Japanese? A stereotype, or this person right here—unique, multiple, and unpredictable? Those who live in the world of concrete reality find themselves in a world that surprises, enriches, perhaps challenges them. Those who live in a world of clichés live in a world of empty boxes. Stereotypes are the sleeping pills of the mind.

And sometimes the mind asleep generates nightmares. Behind the biggest crimes in history you find stereotypes. Millions of people have been killed or discriminated against because they were classified into "races." When a stereotype is loaded with hate and taken to its extreme consequences, it becomes a vehicle for explicit violence.

More often stereotypes are a means of social discrimination and an obstacle to the full expression of our abilities—even those we apply to ourselves, because they influence our self-image. For example, in an experiment at the University of Texas, researchers ostensibly measured the ability to mentally rotate an image of a geometric solid, a task in which men usually do better than women. In this experiment three groups of female students first had to answer a questionnaire that, without their knowing, was aimed at sparking specific reactions. In one group the questions evoked in the students the feeling of being a woman, and specifically the feminine stereotype, which includes a lower spatial intelligence—a fake weakness. In another group, the questionnaire, through leading questions, stimulated in the students the awareness of coming from an elite school—a true strength. The third was a control group, which had to answer neutral questions. Result: The girls who had been reminded they were from a good school did much better in the test than those whose female stereotype, and thus inherent insecurity, had been stirred.

Usually we do not like to have stereotypes applied to us, even though we may liberally apply them to others. I remember one time, during a session, a woman talking to me about her emotional ups and downs: One day she was happy; the next, depressed. "*La donna è mobile qual piuma al vento*" (Woman is fickle like a feather in the wind), I heard myself saying. I was trying to lighten the situation. But this person was not amused. She told me she felt diminished by the cliché of the voluble and emotional woman. I did not see who she really was. And she was absolutely right.

Gianluca has always liked women, but not all—only young, attractive ones. At fifty-six he suddenly has a profound transformation, and finds that *all* women are beautiful, not just the models: "It is like having developed a sixth sense, a different way of perceiving. It is wonderful and it gives me a sense of freedom, as if the energy that was imprisoned in an idea of beauty linked to ownership and desire were freed. It is about feeling the beauty of somebody or something *just as it is*. The sense of perfection of what is. I am freed of all weights, and feel very moved. Beauty is no longer tied to an aesthetic criterion, a canon . . . I see a face, with all its years, wrinkles, a special look in the eyes, I see the hand that moves as though it were making music. All this has brought me to a feeling of uniqueness—the opposite of standardization. I feel outside the bounds of all categorization."

Sometimes, rather than placing a person we know in a predefined box, we create, without knowing, a special category. This category is "everything I expect from you." If you once arrived late, you will always be late. If you were rude to me two years ago, you are nasty by definition. If you were kind and lovely one evening, you must keep being that way—and never disappoint me.

If we place someone in a category, we load that person with expectations, and our relationship grows difficult or sterile. We shall see in a later chapter how it is possible to discover someone's beauty—not just exterior beauty, but also her subtler and more elusive inner beauty. For now we will simply look at one example. If we look beyond our mental categories, we discover the unfathomable abundance of the senses. A mother says: "People are a stimulus for beauty. This my father taught me. When I was small, and even now when we greet each other, we kiss and then he sniffs my head. I do the same with my daughter. This scent is her very own, yet also mine. To sense someone with your nose. Smelling can somehow give us the depth and beauty of feeling. When my daughter was born, I smelt very strong aromas of flowers and fruit. Yet she had just come out of my belly. In that moment she was a flowering garden. And I still smell on her that same perfume every now and then. It is a wondrously beautiful and strange sensation that comes all of a sudden."

### Abstract and Concrete

The experience of beauty is not possible when a stereotype is active. By definition, the experience of beauty carries with it a new emotion, a new way of seeing and feeling, whereas stereotypes are a mental habit. For example, what color do I like? Now there's an abstract question. I look at the red of the poppies next to the purple of the mallow plant on a late-spring morning and I feel those colors generating an explosive emotion in me. Or on an autumn day I look at the yellows and reds of the vineyards: A miracle! Or I look at all the subtle shades of gray in a cloudy sky. Such variety, such richness and form. But show me exactly the same colors on a color chart, and I could not care less. It is as though the colors were embalmed.

There have been studies on our reactions to colors. The reaction to red, for example. But which red: a setting sun, a ripe orange, a spurt of blood, or 531 in the color catalogue? It makes quite a difference. Many such studies are valuable, yet they do not capture the importance of context as well as the full subtlety and variety of our experiences.

Nowadays, clichés are on the rise. Our brave new world, frenetic and distracted as it is, favors stereotypes. Information expands unrestrainedly, but greatly diminishes in depth and specificity. Computer and television, by their very nature, encourage ready-made categories. Virtual reality is simpler and easier to understand in two dimensions. An e-mail is less articulate than a letter. Television dramas and movies often tell predictable stories over and over again. The same gestures, expressions, words, plots, settings recur as in an assembly line. To be sure, you may still meet beauty after all. But stereotypes are lying in ambush at every turn.

### Standardization

Mass production is based on universal standardization, which kills uniqueness and originality. This is why it is worth rediscovering artisan traditions of all products that are made locally and in small quantities. Starting with food. An example: I am with my family in Sardinia, in the Ogliastra region. In this part of the island, and only here, you find the tradition of the *culurgiones*, a pasta filled with potato and mint. We know a woman who makes them by hand and sells them. She is a sweet lady whose face expresses a natural frankness and wisdom. Her *culurgiones*, as well as other specialities, are displayed in tidy rows in a glass cabinet. They are works of art, a beauty to look at and not just to eat, and the lady, without boasting, is proud of them.

But one Monday we find the shop closed—it is their day off. We go to the supermarket, and there, sure enough, we find *culurgiones*, too. They are machine made, packed onto a tray of polystyrene with a clear plastic wrap over it. They look like six little corpses under the neon light. But we are hungry, so we buy them anyway, and eat them: It is an entirely different experience. The machine-made *culurgiones* are the stereotype of the handmade ones. They are a simplified version, in which all the characteristics seem to be preserved, but the essential aspect is missing. The freshness.

The examples are many. Every beautiful form can have its impoverished version or caricature, unable to evoke the sense of beauty. Botticelli's *Venus* becomes the trademark for a soap. The Leaning Tower of Pisa turns into a plastic souvenir. The opening bars of a Chopin nocturne can be the tune for an answering service. And just think of the famous theme in Mozart's Fortieth Symphony: You have probably heard it coming from some cell phone. But where are the richness of the instruments' timbre, the amazing sonority of the orchestra, the rhythms and accents of a particular interpretation, and, in a live concert, the presence of the musicians, the rapture of the audience? All are reduced to a few, anonymous, cold electronic vibrations. Or think of a mountain landscape—the mountains' profile, the murmur of a stream, the perfume of the firs, the pure, pungent air, the sense of space and mystery. Then put the mountains on a postcard. And there is the cliché—nothing is lost except what counts.

Take the case of cartoons. Some educators rightly worry that these images may alienate children from the real world of nature. Let us say the main character is a cat. A few lines of drawing on the screen, and there it is. Then think of a real cat in flesh and bone, a cat that purrs and rubs against you, looks at you with its enigmatic stare, jumps onto your lap and lets you stroke it, plays with a paper ball, and so on. The danger is that children learn to live in a world of ducks and zebras, elephants and penguins, mice and giraffes that

are all stereotyped simplifications of animals, far from the true
world of nature.

### Awakening

For many people the experience of beauty is an awakening: Seeing the world through new eyes, leaving behind their own concep-
tual habits and narrow-mindedness. It can also be a shock, a shake-up
that makes them see life anew. "The contact with African music
threw me into crisis—a positive crisis." "Diving deep in the sea or
going up a high mountain renews me and removes me from my
comfortable, predictable world." "Reading Proust has shown me the
depths of memory." "Entering a cathedral changes my perception
of space." Other times there is no shock, but still a transition to a
richer way of seeing things, a goodbye to the shriveled, arid world
of stereotypes.

Much contemporary art uses this very means of renewed perception to shake us out of our clichés and preconceived ideas. Let us go
and hear John Cage's *4'33"*: The pianist enters, sits at the piano, and
once in a while turns the page of his music, but never plays. What
an offense! What a provocation! They make us pay for silence! Actually this piece of music (Cage's favorite), is anything but silent,
because it forces us to listen together to the little noises that fill the
hall: tiny movements, breaths and sighs, squeaking of seats, the
turning of pages, maybe the distant hum of outside traffic.

Christo and Jeanne-Claude wrap in polypropylene and other
synthetic materials (later recycled) famous buildings like the Reich-
stag in Berlin or the Pont Neuf in Paris, or natural sites like the
coast at Little Bay in Sydney, or trees, or a piece of the Rocky
Mountains in Colorado, as if to remind us how precious and vulnerable these places and monuments are; by wrapping them they

make us see them in a different way. Lucio Fontana makes deep cuts in the canvas and suddenly you have a masterpiece: a diverse configuration of space! Tactile metaphysics! A window onto nothingness! Maurizio Cattelan sculpts Pope John Paul II struck by a meteorite—certainly a new way of seeing the pope (this statue was sold for three million dollars). All these and many others are provocations that shake our mental and perceptual habits. But maybe this is all that is left of beauty—the shock, the surprise—while the harmony and the joy are gone. The beautiful, one way or another, always shakes us. But not all that shakes us is beautiful.

Luckily we can always go back to nature. The experience of natural beauty almost forces us to leave behind the empty boxes of our clichés and to perceive the world around us in all its complexity and richness. Through concrete contact we discover the immense intelligence and incomparable originality of nature. Just a few moments' attention is all that is needed sometimes. Here is an example. I am in the open countryside with my nine-year-old son Jonathan, who loves the natural world and always has something interesting to show me. This time it is a multiform icicle covering several plants. It has rained a lot, the rain has collected in one spot, frozen, and covered some leaves with a transparent layer. In particular there is a small ivy leaf caught inside the ice, like a jewel mounted under clear glass, highlighting its perfect shape and its pale green veins on a darker background. The ice, by a lenslike effect, enlarges the magnificent details. It is a gift of winter.

I look at this ivy leaf set in ice as a jewel, yet I know the ice is melting, the sun is getting warmer, soon the jewel will not be the same. If I think of ivy in general, I can take it or leave it; if I think of ice, I find it banal; if I think of winter, I shiver. But the little leaf set in ice inspires and enchants me.

Often our ideas encase us. We end up stating the same old opinions, believing the same clichés. It is a bit like living in a museum, moving among the same exhibits we have seen time and time again. Beauty brings a fresh wind to our minds. It makes us feel and think differently. It does not attack with logic the stronghold of our beliefs, rather it introduces a new dimension that amazingly changes our viewpoint. Perhaps it throws us into crisis, but that is better than living our whole life among mummies.

So beauty leads us by the hand to the pulsing reality of the world—that reality which we, perhaps for fear or convenience, have forgotten so as to take refuge in the reassuring haven of our abstractions. A woman tells me: "A friend of mine was complaining that it was raining and gray. For me, gray and rain are also beautiful. A softened day. There is beauty in all seasons and weather.

"Last autumn, I was walking along a tree-lined avenue; the wind sent down a shower of leaves. It was so exciting! I have realized how little we notice what is happening. When I collected the leaves, I found many kinds, I saw that there, a place I pass through often, is a carob tree. I saw different yellow leaves of many shapes and nuances, and also dried flowers, various berries of many forms, all in a fairly short tract of road.

"When I see this beauty, I feel a vibration in my heart. It is like the feeling of being in love."

Beauty takes us out of a ghost world, opens us to an immeasurable, unpredictable abundance of sounds, perfumes, lines, textures, colors that amaze and renew us. If, on the other hand, we forget beauty, we risk losing touch with the concreteness of life. In a story by Kafka, the god Poseidon (Neptune) is still the god of the seas, but he has become a bureaucrat. What a nuisance! The administration of the seas is a lot of work, so he has to stay at his desk all day. Being conscientious, he delegates his job to no one. Thus he never manages to do what he most would like to do: Take a long trip around all the oceans to see what they are like and have a good swim. We risk the same as Poseidon—living in the bureaucracy of reality, instead of in reality.

THREE

HEALING

# How Beauty Cures Us

Near my home stood a huge tree that was abode to many birds. They would sing most cheerfully at sunset, but, depending on the season, also in the mornings and at other times of day. Their song was pure joy. They would hold great speeches, sing both in chorus and in solo, tell one another tales, and enjoy improvising variations. I could have listened to them for hours.

Several musicians have noticed a simple fact: birdsong is wonderful music that soothes and cheers. Thus Vivaldi composed *Il Cardellino* (entirely dedicated to the goldfinch's song, interpreted by the flute), Beethoven wrote the Pastoral Symphony (representing the beauty of nature, including birdsong). Rossini's *La Gazza Ladra*, Respighi's *Gli Uccelli*, Dvořák's String Quartet No. 12—which was inspired by a bird's singing during Dvořák's trip to the United States—are other examples. Paganini used to entertain people with his violin, imitating the singing of several different birds.

As a psychotherapist, I know one thing for sure: Birdsong has magnificent healing powers. Several of my clients have mentioned receiving great benefit from listening to it. One in particular told me about when he was ill in the hospital. He had completely lost his strength and joie de vivre. Then he heard, from the branches of a tree outside, the singing of birds: There and then he decided his life was worth living. Birdsong had healed him better than any medicine.

Back to the grand tree near my home. Birds on that tree sang a wonderful concert. But one day a violent storm broke one of its largest branches, leaving it dangling in a way dangerous to anyone passing underneath. An emergency team came, and, not content with cutting the threatening branch, chopped down the whole tree. For me and my family it was a day of mourning. No more rustling of the leaves in the wind, no more birdsong. Beauty is precarious—it comes as an unexpected gift, disappears suddenly, and we are powerless to do anything about it.

Yet despite its precariousness, all of us can recall moments when beauty has come at a difficult time and healed our malaise.

### Therapeutic Effects

Earlier we saw how beauty can give us back the love of life. Here we will see how it can cure us. How it heals our emotional wounds, lightens the weight of our worries, guides us in our confusion—and, to some extent, how it can also heal, or at least soothe, our physical suffering. Luckily, beauty shows up in all kinds of places, and, thanks to our stunning and ever-improving gadgets, it can be reproduced and multiplied indefinitely.

The good news is that more and more people are studying the healing power of beauty. Take architecture. Our habitat can help or obstruct our healing and well-being. It can be a great support or a great obstacle. What is your home or office like? Are there paintings or photographs on the wall? And what effect do they have on you? Are they oppressive relatives or calming landscapes? How is your space organized? Is the light aggressive and cold or warm and supportive? And what about the colors? We cannot always live and work in the ideal place. But we can do a lot, at little expense and in a short time, to make our immediate environment more pleasant and friendly.

In recent years several studies have examined the effect of the hospital milieu on the course of sickness. Naturally this topic has been relevant since the days of Nicola Pisano, the Italian Renaissance sculptor who created statues for hospitals, to comfort the ill. Now research is trying to answer the question: Can beauty in hospitals help? An English study seized a unique opportunity: A hospital was closing and all the patients, nurses, and doctors were moved to a new hospital, built according to all the criteria of sound architecture: maximization of space, ventilation and light, furniture design, colors, protection from unpleasant noise. All factors had been carefully studied. Furthermore, the rooms were disposed in such a way as to let patients choose between privacy and communication with others. Everything was done to make the environment not merely functional, but also beautiful. The results were noteworthy: 21 percent shorter recovery time, drastic reduction in painkillers, greater satisfaction of patients.

Another example: In a study by Professor Roger Ulrich, published in *Science*, we find the description of postoperative progress in two groups of patients following a cholecystectomy. The patients in the first group were in rooms with windows looking out onto trees, whereas the second group had windows facing a brick wall. The first group had a shorter stay in the hospital, registered fewer negative comments by the nurses (such as: "Patient is anxious and cries," "Patient needs to be comforted," etc.), and had less need for painkillers.

Another of Ulrich's studies, conducted with Swedish and American researchers, looked at patients in a cardiac ward. These patients were in various rooms, some of which had photographs of natural landscapes, some had abstract paintings with curved or straight lines, and others had nothing at all. The pictures were at the foot of the beds in front of patients' eyes—they were the first thing they saw upon waking after their operation. To the researchers' surprise, the abstract paintings seemed to increase patients' suffering and lengthen their stay in the hospital. For ethical reasons this part of the experiment had to be suspended. But here comes the most important finding: Patients who were exposed to images of natural scenery improved sooner than the others. All their stress indicators were positive: They had lower blood pressure, slower heart rate, less need of anesthetics and painkillers, and had a shorter hospital stay.

Perhaps even more than the figurative arts, music can heal. Several studies show its efficacy both during and after surgical operations. Postoperative stay in a hospital is shorter, the need for painkillers reduced. Someone objected to these findings, asking whether music's effectiveness was possibly due to just blocking out the metal sounds in the operating theater—a big source of anxiety for the patient. So in another study some patients heard their favorite music through headphones during surgery; others heard only white noise—a neutral sound specifically used for blocking external sounds; and a control group heard nothing. Result: the only ones to enjoy any benefit were those who listened to music.

Music seems to be helpful also in some cases of recovery from stroke. German neurophysiologist Eckart Altenmüller, director of the Institute of Music Physiology and Musicians' Medicine in Hannover, and himself a musician, teaches patients to play the piano. After just fifteen sessions during three weeks, patients improve in precision, regularity, and speed of execution. Because of the connection between hearing and motor areas in the brain, he succeeds in helping patients recover lost motor abilities where other traditional methods fail.

Books can heal. More and more studies show that bibliotherapy has tremendous value. We all know that a beautiful book can change our life. Lately there has been a flowering of initiatives for putting to good use the power of the written word. I will mention only one example: In the UK, Jane Davis organized Prose Not Prozac, an initiative that sponsors reading groups in community centers, resting homes, day hospitals, libraries, and so on. A number of people meet and read together. They assemble once a week and read a book aloud. The participants belong to all kinds of categories: senior citizens, homeless, single mothers, people with drug problems, psychiatric patients, and several others. The results are very encouraging. Participants feel less lonely, forget their cares and pain, improve their social skills, feel more at ease.

### The Process of Healing

In the example of reading we can see that healing is not just a physical fact. It is, perhaps above all, a psychological and spiritual event. Human discomfort, before it is physical, is an emotional state—it is anxiety, loneliness, rage, anguish, sorrow, self-destrucion, desperation. In thinking about my work with clients, I have wondered time and time again: In what does healing consist? It is not just getting rid of symptoms and suffering. It is not just *fixing*. It is, instead, an organic process in our entire being. An external agent, like medicine or the landscape seen from the window, does not produce it. This is an inner process which is perhaps protected or stimulated by an external agent. But our inner physical and psychological resources originate it. If I cut my finger, the disinfectant and the bandage protect me, but the healing is brought forth by the forces quietly operating within *my* organism. If I feel confused or torn, a friend's warm presence may activate *my* potentialities for self-regeneration. And so on.

The process of healing arises inside us. If I have indigestion, if I have been insulted and offended, if I have sprained my ankle, or if I have lost a dear one, my bodymind has suffered a blow, big or small. It tries to regain its original wholeness. We need to help this process, without interfering, without overdoing it. My barber once told me this story: He had the flu, and the doctor came. He wanted a lot of medicines so he could feel he was getting rid of the sickness as fast as possible: aspirin, antibiotics, cortisone. The doctor, an old-fashioned pro, did not agree: He told him to do the seven bean cure. And what is the seven bean cure? Simple, said the doctor. You put seven beans in your pocket. Each day you take one out. When you have none left in your pocket, you are cured. A good lesson in our organism's powers to heal itself.

But healing, whether physical or psychological, needs to be eased and supported. Often, instead, we obstruct it with hurry or stress or negative thoughts. On the other hand, rest, silence, space for just *being*, help us recover. Other factors also promote healing. Everyone has his favorites: music, reading, a walk in the park. Certain people seem to have a calming, regenerating influence. It is helpful to have them nearby. On a more superficial level, even watching television or eating chocolate may help.

We may experience healing as momentary relief. But full healing is a deep regeneration, a radical change that fills us with vitality, well-being, and joy, that opens new possibilities in our life and transforms our worldview. This spontaneous process amazes me every time I see it. We cannot control it, since it happens by itself, but we can evoke and facilitate it. To be aware of this potentiality, to know how to stimulate it: These are skills that all of us would find useful to develop and that should be taught from primary school.

## Facing Pain

First of all, however, we need to face our suffering. Instead of avoiding it, we courageously go *into* it. In an Inuit story from Alaska, the crow created the world and decided to stay because he was curious to know all animals. One day he went to see the whale, then managed to get inside it and see what it was like. He found a beautiful girl dancing. The crow fell in love with her and wanted to marry her. But the girl could not leave the whale: She was its soul. The crow thoughtlessly ignored this bond. He shed his crow's form and became a man. The girl danced, and the whale swam, following her rhythm. The girl and the whale were one. The crow was in love: He decided to kidnap the girl. He took his crow form again, lifted her, and flew away, out of the whale. Then he saw that the whale, its soul stolen, struggled for a while, then died. Inert, it lay on the beach, hit by the waves. Meanwhile the girl grew smaller and smaller, till she disappeared altogether.

The crow was desperate. For days and days he cried, next to the whale's lifeless body. Then he began to dance, and he danced for several weeks. At last he started to sing, and he did so for a long time. He then felt healed, and finally understood that all living beings have a soul. In order to be healed, the crow had to immerse himself fully in the pain, cry it out, express it in any way he could. And so do we. We need to face suffering as we face beauty: with no defenses, no excuses.

### Symbols of Healing

Healing is a varied and mysterious process. It arises in the depths of our being, and has its own life. It is hard to say for sure where and when it starts, and how it happens. We cannot take it apart and then put it back together piece by piece. Perhaps we can best understand its characteristics through the symbols we normally and spontaneously use to describe this process. Here are the ones I have most commonly noted in my work.

First of all, *the wound that heals*. We have all been wounded by events in our life, sometimes by the people dearest to us. The symbol of the wound describes our feeling stabbed, the hurt and incapacity that result from that offense, our sense of being violated, and the ordeal of losing our integrity. The very capacity of the organism to heal its own tissues reminds us that emotional and spiritual wounds can also heal.

We often hear about *disharmony* of sounds or colors, or within a group of people all of whom hold different ideas, or in a family where everybody argues with everybody else. We feel out of phase, scattered, disorganized, in a mess. Healing in this case is *harmony*, as with the notes of a chord. Harmony gives joy and serenity.

Sometimes we feel *emptiness*—such as when we are empty of hope or plans, of stimulation or ideas. Emptiness is a modern category. We think of treeless suburbs, or an empty room which contains only solitude and alienation. We feel as if we have lost all that had value for us—like when we miss someone terribly, or are homesick for a place we love. We heal this emptiness only by filling the void with the richness of *meaning*.

*Conflict* is the result of disharmony. Our various parts are at war, and so we feel torn and tormented. Conflict often requires an enormous expenditure of energy to prevent serious damage. And what can be more desirable than *peace*? It is perhaps the highest form of healing we can hope for.

*Chaos* is confusion. Nothing is in place, we feel lost and disoriented, without a reference point, prey to anguish. We have lost sight of our direction in life. Often chaos goes hand in hand with darkness—they are both cases of not knowing. Order, the *cosmos*, is when each part of the whole is in place, free to be what it was destined to be.

*Knots* imprison us within and without. We feel entangled, powerless to free ourselves from the ties of our own complexity and contradictions. The more efforts we make to get out, and the harder we try, the greater the tangle, and the more anxious we become. To heal is to *unravel* and free the thread.

*Heaviness* is another way of describing discomfort. Everything within us and around us feels unwieldy. Inner and outer movement becomes difficult and exhausting. To lift a sheet of paper is like lifting a chest, taking a few steps is like (sometimes as in dreams) walking in a bog. Life is an immensely tiresome task. Healing of this state comes from *grace* and *lightness*—when, as in a miracle, the weight of gravity is lifted, and our actions become effortless.

Then we have *exile* and *the loss of self*—to feel far from home, in a strange land. Here we have lost ourselves in life's multiplicity, we have forgotten who we really are, have wandered far and lost our way home. Naturally healing means finding our way back to ourselves—from the inessential to the essential. It means to come back *home*.

Finally, *death* is the extreme consequence of discomfort. It is the state of no hope, the end of all possibility. Death is healed only by *rebirth*, a thorough renewal of life. Rebirth feels like a triumph, a miracle in the face of hopelessness. After sorrow and despair have ruled, enter vitality and joy.

### The Perfect Medicine

These are all metaphors to describe the miraculous process of healing. And they recur in the kind of healing that interests us here—the healing that beauty engenders. In my interviews with people, these metaphors have all turned up at one time or another. Beauty has the power to unravel the knots of our feelings, to show us the way back to ourselves, to heal our wounds.

Let us look at a few examples. Marilù is a teacher in an elementary school, and remembers, among her various experiences of beauty, one winter's morning when it started to snow: "I was anxious about a number of problems, especially economic and administrative ones. Suddenly it began to snow. From the window I saw the snow falling silently onto the fields, trees, countryside and hills in the distance. The sight of the snow took away all my anxiety. In that moment I felt nature as a companion. The silence and whiteness moved me. Within a few minutes everything had changed." Another woman, Giovanna, had been badly abused. At a difficult time in her life she was thinking about her past maltreatment. Though not religious, she walked into a church for a moment of quiet: "I was straightaway struck by the beauty of this simple Franciscan church. I saw a magnificently blue-colored glass, through which the sunlight was shining. That was all I needed to feel reborn. Suddenly I was sure: Someone or Something is taking care of me."

At times we have our rites. We return, like wounded soldiers after the battles of daily life, to a piece of music, a place, a book, because there we find the beauty that has the power to heal our wounds. Esther, a young woman beginning her career in medicine, returns to Van Gogh's paintings: "When I look at them something stays with me and transforms me. Van Gogh's paintings are often anguishing, yet seeing them relieves me of anguish. For instance, the Church of Auvers ( I have a reproduction hanging on my wall) lightens and cheers me. I could have painted it myself, in the sense that the feelings it expresses are mine and I recognize myself in them, and that's what makes me feel better."

Beauty is the perfect medicine. Rather than lowering our consciousness, as so many treatments do, it lifts us above our problems. Beauty has no side effects, its benefits last, the relief it brings does not dull or diminish us in any way, it creates no dependency, and it actually makes us feel clearer and stronger. No multinational company has yet succeeded in trademarking it. And to enjoy its benefits, we do not even need a prescription.

# Creativity

This was the finest statue he had ever made. It was a young woman, and she seemed to move and breathe. She seemed alive. He had always been suspicious of women, but now he had fallen in love with her, as with a real woman, in a way he had never before fallen in love. And it had all happened in such a short time. As he would to a live woman, he offered her seashells, flowers, love, and tears. He dressed her in expensive clothes, then undressed her because she was even more beautiful when she was naked. He talked to her, embraced her. But she did not move. After all, she was just a statue.

His name was Pygmalion. In Ovid's story, he was not only a king, but also an excellent sculptor. Yet despite his talent and power, he did not know what to do. He had created a beautiful statue of a woman, but this beauty did not respond to him. The silence, the immobility, the eyes perpetually staring into the void—it all drove him crazy. Finally Pygmalion decided to ask Venus, goddess of love, for some help. He went to her temple and lighted a fire on her altar. He saw that the flame quivered twice—a good sign: It was Venus's response.

When he returned home, he ran straight to his beloved. As always, the statue was there, faithfully waiting for him, but mute and immobile. Yet when he touched her immaculate skin, Pygmalion noticed a difference: The marble felt like flesh. The statue was no longer rigid: It was softening, like wax exposed to the sun. The man in love touched his dream. His creation started to move, looked around, spoke to him, asked questions. Not quite knowing who she was, she felt lost at first. But she was alive, and her name was Galatea. Now she was a real woman able to reciprocate his love.

### Eros

The myth of Pygmalion reminds us that the act of creation is pervaded by eros. It is never neutral. Never impersonal, but intimate. Never cold, but passionate. Whoever creates, falls in love. There may be a thousand interferences: the critical mind, a sense of inferiority, intellectualism, other people's expectations. But in its essence the act of creation is an act of love. Shelley likened it to incandescence: "The mind in creation is as a fading coal, which some invisible influence, like an inconstant wind, awakens to transitory brightness."

So creativity rekindles passion, makes us feel vital and alive. And if this creative act were not happening, the result would be sadness and disease. Abraham Maslow once wrote down a list of all the traits describing the healthy person: strength and self-confidence, expressiveness, capacity to feel at ease with the irrational, openness to beauty, spontaneity, lack of inhibitions and defenses. Ability to forget oneself. Innocence. And so forth. Then he made another list:

all the characteristics of the creative individual. Then he realized
that the two lists were identical.

### The Need to Express

We can understand that health and creativity are one and
the same if we accept this basic fact: Creativity is not a talent for
the few, but a central trait of everyone. Deep down, our self is alive
and craving to express itself, to improvise, and to play like a child.
Surely, various events in life may cause it to change and become
passive, inert, tired. We become rigid and shy of expressing ourselves, even of having new ideas, of inventing something new, because we might look silly and embarrass ourselves. Better keep a
low profile and be a conformist—that way we are less visible,
and therefore safer. The problem is we may end up becoming
zombies.

The eclipse of creativity does not happen overnight. In the lives
of us all there has been at least one individual who (perhaps with
the best intentions) has somehow or other discouraged us in our
expression: a family member, a friend, a teacher. We have then in-
corporated this person (or these people) as an inner voice that stops
us from fully expressing ourselves. I ask my clients to imagine a
figure who obstructs their expression. A strict, frowning judge usually appears, or else a snob for whom nothing is ever right, or a
mean critic who finds fault with all we do, or a coward who advises
against too much expression, or a petty bourgeois who chooses
to conform, or, finally, a scoffing pragmatist: "Poetry won't pay
the bills."

We have to come to terms with this figure, and free ourselves
from its dominance. If we truly manage to express ourselves, much
will change. Energy will circulate more freely. We will be more in

touch with our emotions and with what is really important to us. And we will discover that we, too, have something to say. It is not just a matter of painting a few colors on a sheet of paper or of writing a story. It is a case of reorganizing our whole personality.

In a longitudinal study a few years ago, nine women met once a week to express themselves through embroidery, knitting, crochet, weaving, and other such activities. The experimenters gave much importance to originality, surprise, and new creations. Before the beginning of the group, the women's personality characteristics were evaluated by family members and friends who knew nothing about the purpose of the study. At the end of the year, they were once again evaluated and the findings were impressive. The women had changed deeply: They showed less anxiety in novel situations, more playfulness, less caution, more capacity to make hard decisions, more independence and vitality, greater ability to show imaginativeness, more capacity to stick to a task and maintain a goal-directed attitude. Not bad, is it?

And now let us look at a particular case. Serena, forty years old, has persisted with her vocation in painting and drawing despite the criticism and constant opposition of her oppressive parents: "To draw and paint meant to get out of the suffering in the conflictual relationship with my parents. I had my own corner I would shut myself in, and to create art was a huge support to me. I drew the face of a woman and have hung it on the wall—it supports me even today. The vital step was to take possession of my capabilities. It is not the fact of drawing in itself, but of beauty. To see around me things that I can do, to observe others, to resume contact with works of art calms me, makes me feel alive."

There is no better therapy than creative expression. If we go digging beneath our calcified, institutionalized personality, plastered in its roles and habits, we find that our self wants to play and create, and we can help it to express and manifest itself. Many of our troubles come about because we do not bring out what we are and could become. Thus we condemn ourselves to an unfulfilled, frozen life.

What to express? What to create? The choice is ours, the possibilities are endless. We can express ourselves in theater or in writing, in cooking or wood carving, interior decoration or photography, collage or clay modeling. And this expression hinges on beauty. We want to express something that we and others will like, that gives satisfaction. Not a banal, chaotic expression. We want to say something new and say it well.

It is worth remembering that the creative impulse taps a deep source. When we express ourselves in an original way, we are not scraping the surface. We are reaching to our deepest roots, to an ancient need. Humankind has been creative since its distant dawn. The first flute, cut out of bone, dates back thirty thousand years. A decorated ivory statue with a lion's head, found in Hohlenstein-Stadel, Germany, is about the same age. The marvelous paintings in the caves of Lascaux in France are seventeen thousand years old, but others are much older. And the first findings of artistic expression go back earlier still—between sixty and thirty thousand years ago. These expressions, some of them splendid, were not created in easy and favorable circumstances. On the contrary, they were born during the peak of the last ice age, in situations of dire need and danger, in which the priority was, day after day, to fight for survival. According to Professor Steven Mithen's most recent theories of cognitive archaeology, artistic expression is the result of three abilities, present already at those times in the human brain: producing a mental image and wanting to represent it in concrete form; understanding the meaning of that image; and being eager to share it with others. When these three distinct types of intelligence combined, there was a huge leap in our evolution. To be creative means to be fully human.

### Genius vs. Everyman

At this point we run into a word dilemma. We speak of creativity in relation to geniuses. In their best moments, they created masterpieces that have illumined human history. Can we use the same word in describing such sublime episodes as the writing of Mozart's *Requiem*, Shakespeare's *Macbeth*, the painting of Raphael's *School of Athens*, as we do in speaking about our own inventive moments, when we improvise on the piano or shoot a few photos of our kids on the beach?

It seems sacrilegious to say so: Perhaps we should use different words. Here we have two contrasting points of view. The aristocratic one sees creativity as the gift of the few. The democratic one considers creativity an essential trait of everyone. The aristocratic view rightly honors the marvel of talent. But it does so at the cost of underrating everybody else. In this respect it is false and damaging, as it underestimates the potentiality of a great number of people.

The democratic view sees every creative expression as intrinsically valuable. It may not fully acknowledge the miracle of genius—so frighteningly different from everything else, so huge as to seem divine. And the danger here is acclaiming all with equal generosity. Everyone wants to publish a book, make a film, paint on walls, sing before an applauding audience. But what comes out may not exactly be beautiful. How many untalented performances have you attended? How many friends' poems have you had to praise? And how often have you been obliged to rave about painfully horrid paintings or sit through boring amateur concerts? Too benevolent an attitude risks submerging true talent in an ocean of expressive mediocrity. Would-be geniuses can get quite excited with their own material. Persist in this approach, and you will fill the world with tone-deaf singers, untalented poets, mediocre musicians, and writers of poor taste. And all will demand your attention and enthusiasm.

However, the democratic point of view has one enormous advantage: It underlines the creative potential of everyone, and thus it helps us better understand the essence of mental health. Of course not everyone can be creative at the same level. But that does not negate that creativity is an elementary process of our mind, and everyone's right, since it has to do with the expression of self. No doubt: Talent has an enormous gamut. Many like to play soccer, but you do not have to be Pelé or Diego Maradona to have fun. Thus some enjoy photography without being Cartier-Bresson, playing piano without being Rubinstein, writing poetry without being Keats. The benefits of creativeness are a gift for everyone.

### Beneficial Effects

Studying how creative expression changes people's lives, I cannot help but stress how it makes people happy and more confident. Francesco, a man in his fifties, is creative: He writes stories and plays and carves wood. For him it is essential to create, and if he does not, he feels unwell. Speaking about his preparation of a play, Francesco says: "At first there is a tension of the opposites. It is a problem of compatibility. To reach synthesis, you have to fight. It is like trying to find a recipe for putting together peppers and jam. Something is pressing from inside, and you have to give it shape.

From chaos a star is born, as the words on a T-shirt say (I think it is a quote from Nietzsche). The sensation of beauty comes first from feeling alive in the conflict, then from working to refine, balance, perfect. You have to find the inner balance, and hone. That is beauty."

Gianna prepares essential oils. She loves to work with flowers and their perfumes. I have no doubt that the same processes are at work here as in playing the piano or creating poetry: The pleasure of interacting with the material, plus the joy of generating an artifact that is both beautiful and beneficial. This, too, is a form of expression: "The other day I was bottling some oils. As I started, a beautiful perfume drifted in the air. It was a base of oil of rosehips. I felt a moment of pure well-being—an instant when I appreciated the perfume, the fact of being there. It was a moment when the sensation drew me in and gave me a feeling of lightness and inner space, as though the body were freed of tension. I felt as if I were on a different frequency than usual."

Sometimes creativity is a subterranean stream, but becomes a dominant theme throughout an individual's life. Estella works in the social-work field. She has founded a society for helping young people in difficulty: That is her masterpiece. She is having great success and public recognition: "For me it all began when I was a young girl. I was walking near my home. I heard a voice inside myself say: 'Something is not right here. There is no love here.' It was then I made a choice: From then on I would try to create love and beauty. Since then it has been the goal of my life."

### The Many Fields of Creativity
In her groundbreaking book *Art and Intimacy*, Ellen Dissanayake takes on the challenge of trying to understand the biological

and evolutionary significance of art. This American ethnologist explains how some of our age-old abilities are used in artistic expression. They include discipline and persistence in a task, manual dexterity and kinesthetic control, the ability to solve problems, to invent and tell stories, to create visual images. They are ways in which many human populations have, for thousands of years, affirmed their cultural identity, have allowed their community members to feel part of a greater whole, and faced and resolved their worst anxieties and fantasies. In our digital age, all these abilities risk being neglected in favor of verbal or mathematical skills.

Creative expression in its many forms is a deep human need, and if it is recognized and satisfied we feel healed and regenerated. It is as simple as that. This principle has been used to help people deal with various disturbances. If they write, dance, paint, photograph, act, tend a garden, and so on, they simply feel better afterward.

At the Georgetown University hospital, for example, in the Lombardi Comprehensive Cancer Center, patients are invited to dance, string pearls, make collage, or model clay. Afterward, the chemotherapy they have to go through is much more tolerable.

At the Medical Center's Health Arts Network, at Duke University, patients are asked to rate their degree of suffering by a number. They then do some artistic activity. Afterward they again rate their degree of pain. Often it has diminished without analgesics.

Jan Taal, founder of the School voor Imaginatie in Amsterdam, has done great work with cancer patients, inviting them to express their inner experience through painting. The result is a series of extraordinary images that describe the trauma and anguish, the feeling of a mutilated body, but also the freeing of emotions and the rediscovery of self, which at times accompany grave sickness. The patients redeem pain, and represent liberation, by painting them. Creative expression for cancer patients can achieve what conventional cures cannot. It can give comfort and help patients accept their feelings and once more find strength and faith.

Now we come to writing. James Pennebaker, who teaches at the University of Texas, has found beneficial effects in creative writing. The kind of writing in which we express our intimate feelings about events in our life improves the immune system and strengthens our bodies. After doing some creative writing, AIDS patients had a higher white blood cell count, asthma patients had better lung function, arthritis patients had less pain. In other patients, Pennebaker found improved liver function, and in all he found a reduction of stress. The psychological effects abound: Mood often worsens straight after writing (if a person writes about sad events), but improves in the following months; anxiety and depression diminish. With students, writing produces an improvement in grades, as well as an improvement in working memory—the capacity for handling complex problems.

Another beautiful study is about middle-aged men who had been fired from jobs in the high-tech field—clearly a situation of distress. Eight months after participating in a group for creative writing, 52 percent had found a new job, while in the control group of people who had not engaged in expressive writing, only 20 percent had found work. Those who had expressed themselves in writing had overcome the trauma of being fired and were therefore freer and more able to move on to new experiences.

These studies mostly look at the beneficial effect of writing for healing wounds. But we cannot always draw a clear line between creative expression and what would seem to be merely a venting of emotion. In this regard a surprising study gives us something to think about. M. Greenberg, A. Stone, and C. Wortman asked a group of people to write a story about traumas *they had never had.* Here, too, they found a general improvement in health. So it is not just about venting emotions. People enjoyed writing a good story. The aesthetic factor in creative writing seems to be essential. In fact, according to Pennebaker, writing gets the best results when the story is coherent: It serves to bring order into the chaos of our lives. And it is also crucial, when we write, to find our own style—not to write in an academic or impersonal way, but in a way that is intimate and expressive of who we are.

Can gardening and horticulture be a form of creative expression? The answer is yes—they are a form of work or exercise in which we express ourselves with living forms. The Natural Growth Project in London is devoted to treating torture victims. These people have had terrible traumas and carry the burden of nightmarish memories. They need much time for rehabilitation. Helped by two psychotherapists and an organic gardener, they are asked to express themselves freely through gardening. The result is that the contact with the natural processes of plants, combined with the possibility of being creative, somehow makes it easier for them to face their terrifying memories and consequently elicits emotional healing. The beauty of plants and flowers and the possibility of self-expression help them to heal the wounds of cruelty.

And what about music? Music therapy does not consist only in having patients listen—that is passive music therapy. In active music therapy, patients are invited to *make* music. They play an instrument, perhaps an easy instrument like a xylophone or a drum, and improvise, sing in a chorus, or accompany songs. The effects are, at the same time: *social*—in playing together they no longer feel alone; *emotional*—they are able to express depression, anger, fear; *cognitive*—they improve neurological function and alleviate their sense of confusion and disorientation; *physical*—playing and singing means movement and coordination. Results have been excellent with Parkinson's patients, hospitalized children, and even with terminal patients and their families. The results are always the same: better pain management and improvement in perceived quality of life.

Another creative channel is photography. To give someone a camera is like saying: Now you can express *your* point of view, now you can show us the way *you* see the world. Photography is less objective and factual than we think. Put a camera in twenty people's hands, ask them to portray the same subject, and they will express surprisingly and radically different points of view. Melbourne Royal Hospital in Australia ran a project of this kind, in which schizophrenic patients were given the chance to express themselves with photography. They felt less marginalized, and both their hope and their ability to participate in society increased.

Dance, particularly expressive dance, helps free people from their blocks and manifests energy and the joy of living. Our emotional habits stiffen our muscles so that they trap emotions, memories, and past conditioning. Our whole emotional history is locked in our tensions and postures. Dance melts these tensions and liberates energy and therefore helps us get in touch with our body and feelings, improves our capacity to express ourselves, increases self-esteem and self-confidence, and develops interpersonal communication. It helps relieve stress and often stimulates the secretion of endorphins, the pleasure hormone.

Then there is the most expressive art of all—drama. I have often noticed sudden improvement in those of my patients who have taken up amateur theater. No surprise. Acting loosens, stimulates, and transforms. One of the most interesting projects is perhaps the one by the University of Nevada: a study on seniors' theater. Participants can express themselves through a theatrical production. Many things happen at once: Because they have to remember a part, they exercise their memory; they relate with the other actors and the audience, and thus overcome loneliness; by acting various characters, they can express latent aspects of themselves; by acting on stage stories that are not their own, they (at least temporarily) forget the problems that afflict them.

## Interconnectedness

Faced with this harvest of activity we might feel confused: How can we be sure that the healing agent is beauty and not some other factor, such as being with others or learning a new skill? The honest answer is that we cannot know for certain. Imagine a cello student playing in a jazz ensemble. What is it that makes him feel well and helps him move about in the world with greater ease and competence? Is it the arduous discipline of studying the cello and the complex motor tasks it requires? The interaction with colleagues and friends? The trusting relationship with his teacher? His success with the audience and the consequent raising of self-esteem? The physical exercise demanded by hours of movement? The aesthetic perception of what he is playing? The creativity in improvisation? Or the victory over his father, who wanted him to work in a bank?

Probably all these elements in various proportions. But how do we separate them from one another? We simply don't. A Tibetan Buddhist saying maintains that all the events in the universe are like a lame man, who cannot walk without leaning on someone else. No event can be understood in isolation from the others, but can be explained only by leaning on other phenomena. So, too, with beauty. It never exists in a void: It is always mixed with a thousand other factors and experiences. Yet beauty is right there, and it nearly always has central importance in creative expression.

Therefore all of us who want to be healed and grow in our lives would do well to ask ourselves a basic question: How can I create beauty in my life? The answer is never an abstract one. We have to find what our heart inspires us to do. We must ignore inner and outer voices that try to discourage us. Usually we will need some study and discipline. Then we can begin to respond, in our own way, to the tantalizing call of beauty. Will we dare to be creative?

# Nature and Music

Not surprisingly, the healing effect of beauty is clearest and most complete in the benevolent influence of nature. Throughout the centuries, and in many societies all over the world, men and women have seen in it a living soul, a superior mind, wisdom, a capacity to nourish and support, divine qualities, and a godlike essence.

## Ecopsychology

At times a little exposure is enough to activate the powers of nature. We saw in the preceding chapter how trees outside the hospital window, by the simple fact of being perceived, accelerated patients' recoveries, or how birdsong can comfort and uplift. These are not the only examples. An American study found that green space is inversely proportional to crime. Based on police reports, researchers conducted a study on ninety-eight town condominiums and found that the more green areas, the fewer crimes of both violence and theft. Enter "Vitamin G" (for green): We learn more and more how beneficial green spaces are, not just as places for social contact and physical exercise, but also for the beauty they offer.

We also have a series of studies on children. Nancy Wells, an environmental psychologist at Cornell University, looked at 337 children between the first and the fifth grade. For each child, she noted the number of plants in the families' homes, how much green they could see from their windows, and whether or not they had grass, dirt, or cement in their backyards. She found that those who had more exposure to green were far more capable of facing stressful situations and had longer attention spans.

If just seeing a little green from the window already makes us feel better, what happens if we immerse ourselves for days and days in the wilderness? This indeed is the theme of ecopsychology: What makes us sick is precisely our distance from nature. We are stressed, anxious, alienated, depressed, unhealthy, without really knowing why. Maybe it is because we are far from nature. The ecological unconscious—our connection with the natural environment—is repressed and excluded from the field of consciousness. Deep down, we feel separated from a wisdom and a beauty which we cannot afford to lose, in fact from the source of all life. This deleterious split causes malaise and confusion. Going back to it is like coming home again.

Take the case of Claudia, for example. For a long time she worked in the city: "I used to work in a small gray office. And that meant for me a gray life. Now I live in the country. From my window I can see a precipice, then a church, trees, birds. There is a farm, and I see the horses drink from a river nearby. Then there is a wide plain, with only a mountain in the middle. That is beauty for me. And if I see beauty while I study or work, I am three times more efficient."

Or look at Gianna, a middle-aged woman who lives a life rich with interests and experiences, loves art and nature, and above all the sea. When I see her after she has spent a day at the seaside, she is a different person. Right now, she is fighting the aftereffects of a serious disease. For her, perceiving beauty, whether it be a poem, a landscape, or a dream, "makes the heart flutter." She tells me about when she saw a sunset at Saint-Malo in Brittany, where the sun sets in the Atlantic: "It is high tide. The wind is blowing, seagulls are flying about, the sun enters the sea, and the water is becoming red. It is a sunset with colors I have never seen. The scenery of Brittany I carry inside me; it is like drawing from the fountain of life."

The metaphor of the fount recurs often in descriptions of the aesthetic experience. The beautiful does not bestow its benefits merely in the moment—it continues to be a source of nourishment and support for the rest of our lives, as long as we do not forget it. It is our spiritual treasure and heritage.

Think of nature's great wonders—the sea, its rhythmic waves, the salty scent of its breeze, the vast expanses of water; the mountains, the invigorating air, the bluest of skies and grand panoramas; the colorful fields of wildflowers; brooks and waterfalls; the peace of forests; the extraordinary colors of autumn; the deserts, with their silence, purity, and space; and the starry sky: These are our greatest source of mystery and awe.

And what about the smaller scale? Think of the architecture of a shell, the designs on an autumn leaf or a butterfly's wings, the shapes and colors in a flower's heart. No one remains the same after being in touch with the power and beauty of nature. Nature is our home. To go back to it is to get in touch again with ourselves, to rediscover what we are made of.

## Divorce from Nature

For many of us, these wonders have been replaced by a completely different environment: the noise of traffic, the smell of pollution, the harshness of neon signs; gray cement façades; the impersonal, hypnotic atmosphere of supermarkets; the ubiquitous presence of the TV or computer screen. In such unnatural conditions we get sick, and our sicknesses are the unheard cry of an organism begging for a return to its true habitat and seeking lost harmony. Have you ever watched animals at the zoo and in circuses, especially the most evolved animals? Confined, far from their natural habitat, many of them suffer; they are visibly depressed, scraggy, confused. Might this not be true for us, too? Maybe we, too, have become unhappy circus animals.

The strongest example comes perhaps from noise. Noise is a source of stress. It can be seen as ugliness in its acoustic aspect. In certain quantities it is tolerable, but beyond that it is dangerous. The word "noise" derives from the Latin *nausea*—and not by chance: It is an aggression to our organism. One of the most common effects of noise pollution is an increase in blood pressure. Many animals are also traumatized by our noise. For instance, excessive decibel levels stress certain species of birds and force them to sing more loudly to attract a mate. And what of the terrible mass suicide of whales, probably pushed to this extreme behavior by the indiscriminate use of sonar by the American navy?

Compare that with nature's sounds: Perhaps not all of them cheer us up. Thunder and hail may frighten and disquiet us. But think of rain, the rhythmic pounding of waves, the rustling of leaves in the wind, the murmur of a stream or the roar of a waterfall, the croaking of frogs or the singing of crickets. These are sounds which pervade and soothe us, if we would only listen to them.

## Nonplaces and Horror Pleni

The widespread malaise of today's world has been described and analyzed in many ways. I would like to quote two analyses that seem to me especially enlightening.

One is that of nonplaces, as described by the French ethnologist Marc Augé. Nonplaces have no history or personality: shopping malls, supermarkets, airports. To be admitted to a nonplace you have to prove your innocence or at least endure an anonymous check (passport, credit card, parking ticket, security). You are alone among other individuals who are also alone, and you are surrounded by impersonal messages: "Please do not leave objects unattended," "Join our T-shirt promotion." You are disciplined by precise rules (put the cart back, display all metal objects, etc.). You are encouraged to buy. Time is suspended. Even where it is important to know the exact time, such as in airports, you live in a kind of spurious present that belongs to no time of the day and no season of the year. How deeply do these places affect our consciousness?

Another analysis is that of Gillo Dorfles, art critic and philosopher. According to Dorfles, we have reached the condition of *horror pleni* ("the horror of fullness"): the dismay we feel, or ought to feel, in facing the profusion of stimuli with which we are bombarded every day, including images, songs, objects, words, Web sites, jingles, ads, movies, phone messages, TV shows, e-mails, newspapers, street signs, graffiti, posters, neon signs. This overabundance generates confusion. The repetitiveness of messages and the relentlessness of pace worsen the situation, because they compress stimuli to an extreme degree, taking away breath and pause. It's just too much of everything, in too little space and time. Moreover, the new tribalism—mass meetings in clubs, sports arenas, and rock concerts—contributes to the excess of fullness, reducing space between one person and another, and thus diminishing individual independence. Everyday we get more stuff. What we lack, instead, is emptiness, which would allow us to taste, think, or just be.

Those are two descriptions of phenomena that have never happened before in the course of human history, that make the experience of beauty harder, and that, more than in any other epoch, alienate us from ourselves and from nature.

### *Folly and Sanity*

From the point of view of ecopsychology, the consumerism of our society, the compulsive search for abnormal quantities of artificial products, is a form of mental illness. The products that surround us can be seen as the embodiment of folly—bags of candy sporting gaudy colors and weird names, artificial food loaded with aggressive and habit-forming flavors, television ads invading us with hysterical rhythms and demented scenarios, violent video games that turn out to be true crime manuals, fast food to be eaten in anonymous venues, glossy magazines about nothing, designer clothes, one item of which would pay to feed a whole village in a developing country for a year, cell phones emitting sudden and bizarre sounds which we unhesitatingly and dutifully respond to.

Think of all our wild consuming and compulsive habits, then think of the sublime majesty of nature. In this light our consumer society looks like the huge delirium of a mind that has lost touch with its very ground. In fact our mind *has* moved far away from its natural environment, where it has evolved for millions of years, and, detached from its roots, it builds for itself an unreal, insane world.

You may find this view rigid and extreme. Yet the core of the message is profound and true: We can return to nature, and there find ourselves again. Much good work has been done in this direction. In the United States and elsewhere, for instance, programs have been developed such as Outward Bound that are suited to a variety of individuals: business men and women, military personnel, teachers, juvenile delinquents, psychiatric patients. Participants stay for a few days in the wilderness, sometimes alone (with adequate precautions), and have to manage by themselves. The result is healing and personal transformation. Getting physical exercise and becoming more self-sufficient are among the main factors, but I am sure the beauty of nature plays a big role.

### Nature Is Near Us

Of course, the aesthetic experience is also possible outside a natural environment. We must not demonize the city, since urban beauty of all kinds can feed and stimulate us. We grow fond of cities, and especially at certain times of the day—like dusk or early morning, or in a particular kind of weather, such as an exceptionally clear day mist—cities can reveal their beauty.

Nevertheless, nature certainly has a unique healing power. And I have always been struck by the way nature, almost like an intruder, enters our artificial world. It is as though it were trying to remind us it still exists, it is still alive. In my bathroom, because of the damp, the wooden door frame started to rot a little. One day I noticed in one of its cracks two tiny white and delicate mushrooms, very beautiful. I felt a great tenderness for them. The next day there were two more smaller ones, like a family of four. Another time, returning home at night, I came across a family of badgers alongside the road: parents and their children. At other times I have seen the magnificent geometry of a spider's web attached to a roof beam, poppies growing out of a crack in a wall, two intertwined snakes falling suddenly from a garage roof, a large female toad crossing the road with her lazy husband on her back, and the classic example of nature sharing our life-space: the magnificent swallows' nests under the eaves. Whenever I see sights like these I am reassured, as if healed of a worry. I feel part of the web of life, quite another story to "man, king of creation." Not part of a hierarchical system with humans at the top, but of a network of relations. No bosses and subordinates, only multiple elements in continuous interaction. Riccardo, a forty-year-old man, says: "I was going home along a country road. I was surrounded by nature, even though I was not in the wild, as I was not far from the built-up area. The full moon lighted my path, and I felt that the trees, bushes, grass around me, the moon, everything, was alive. I understood why the ancients thought nymphs and spirits lived in the woods and springs. This world seemed so different from ours, much wiser and more wholesome. I felt it pervade me and vivify me."

### The Power of Music

Nature is beyond the human realm. It has not been created by us, and that is why we see in it signs of a higher intelligence, nourishing support, and extraordinary resources. Music, instead, is human. It is perhaps the most effective way of changing a mood or reviving a memory, of making our organism strongly respond, of understanding another culture, of transporting us to an altogether different universe. A great number of the people I interviewed have mentioned music as a source of beauty. Together with nature, it was the most popular factor.

That music can also heal is an obvious fact, were it not that we often forget it. In its origins, one of music's prime functions may have been to heal and evoke the sense of the holy. Only later did it become a means of entertainment. More recently, it has also revealed its destructive potential—when it is vulgar, disharmonious, aggressive.

But the essence of music is to harmonize and heal. The most famous story on this subject is perhaps that of the Benedictine monks in southern France. After the reforms of the Second Vatican Council in the 1960s, seventy out of ninety monks became mysteriously ill. They were lethargic, depressed, unable to carry out their normal tasks in the monastery. A series of doctors tried to explain the causes of their illness, all unsuccessfully. Then came Alfred Tomatis, the famous expert in audiology. Tomatis straightaway noticed that the only substantial change in the lives of these monks had happened when, after the reforms, the new abbot had radically reorganized the daily chants. Whereas before the monks had chanted eight or nine times a day, for periods of ten or twenty minutes at a time, now they hardly chanted at all. The absence of chanting had made them ill. Tomatis prescribed a return to the past order, and within weeks all monks recovered.

Since then we have made much headway. Several studies have shown that singing in chorus has results of great significance. It seems to be made for people to feel good. Psychiatric patients, individuals with serious family problems or those who have recently mourned a loss, the handicapped, chronic pain sufferers, the el-

derly, Alzheimer and dementia patients, are among those who benefit the most. But the results are seen in everyone. First, singing is
a social activity, and thus helps participants feel they belong. Think
of the wonderful sensation of singing in unison with a group of
people. There is no better example of social inclusion. Second,
singing is an aerobic activity that brings known benefits to our
health, linked to increased oxygenation of the tissues. Third, controlled breathing helps us rid ourselves of anxiety, stimulates mental activity and concentration. In one study, participants said they
received these benefits from singing: social (87 percent), emotional
(75 percent), physical (58 percent), and spiritual (49 percent). Is it
any wonder the English government has allocated 41 million pounds
to ensuring that every primary school child sing regularly?

In these studies the word "beauty" is not used. But singing is an
artistic activity, its basis is harmony, and what attracts us in singing
is precisely its beauty. As always, we have to do with a complex
phenomenon in which it is difficult to gauge the relative efficacy of
various factors. It seems obvious to me that here, too, the aesthetic
component is present and active.

Singing brings spectacular results. Other examples are perhaps
less sensational, but just as important:

- In some hospitals and hospices, harp music is used to comfort the dying. In these anguishing and difficult situations,
  the sweet, dreamy sound of the harp brings them serenity
  and peace and eases the transition they are about to make.
- In an American study, newborns or babies a few months old
  who had to have an electroencephalogram—invasive and
  irritating for a baby—were more easily calmed by lullabies
  played to the rhythm of their breathing than by sedatives.

- Like images, music is also used in many hospitals to reduce anxiety and improve patients' mood. With their intimidating, impersonal atmoshere and the pervasive presence of suffering, hospitals may make us sick rather than healthy. Yet it does not have to be so: It is possible to generate a beneficent, healing atmosphere in almost any place.

- Some homes for the elderly have adopted programs in music, along with literature and art, with a view to enriching older patients' lives and increasing intellectual stimulation.

- Music has produced excellent results for pain management in some hospitals and hospices. It has been shown that if the emotional and spiritual needs of patients are not recognized and at least partly satisfied, physical pain will continue, almost as a cry of protest requiring care and attention. With its strong and benevolent impact on a patient's inner life, and with its capacity for soothing without speaking, of involving without forcing, music pacifies and regenerates. No wonder it helps reduce the request for painkillers.

- In some pediatric hospitals, music has produced excellent results, for example, with premature and underweight babies and also babies needing transplant operations, or those with heart disease or cancer.

- We know that the immune system is the guardian of our health. It must look out for and defend against invasion by entities foreign or dangerous to our organism. Until a few years ago the immune system was thought to be independent from our existential situation. The field of psychoneuroimmunology has shown, on the contrary, that it is sensitive to various factors. Music stimulates and strengthens the immune system, making it more efficient.

While paintings are created once and for all, music can be recreated again and again. Is the effect of live music any stronger than that of recorded music? The actual presence of musicians surely makes a difference. One day the two great English writers, Aldous Huxley and Christopher Isherwood (both resident in Los Angeles), asked Dave Brubeck, the famous jazz pianist, to come with his orchestra to the Veterans Hospital and play for a group of catatonic patients. These patients would lie or sit motionless for days on end, out of touch with the world. But as soon as the band began to play, to the great surprise of the doctors, several of them started to tap their feet to the rhythm of the music, and one even took the trumpet from the hands of a musician and started to play in his own way. These people, for years reduced to an apparently vegetative existence, were reawakened and reborn. After this experience, the same music, by the same musicians, was played for the same patients—but it was recorded music. And it had no effect.

Does this episode mean recorded music is of no use? Not at all. It just underlines the potency of live music where the presence of the players vibrates along with the music and reaches the listeners directly. But do not discount recorded music. Any kind of music can evoke beauty for a big number of people.

At this point, however, we run into a serious objection: In many cases, it is hard to understand the effects of beauty. Other possibly beneficial factors are mixed together in ever-changing combinations. In fact, in the case of studies such as the ones quoted in this chapter, you could argue that various healing elements work at many different levels. For example, in the case of nature, fresh air plus physical movement are largely responsible for recovery and well-being. In the case of singing, maybe the crucial element is the improved breathing. As for music, the actual presence of musicians may count as much or more than the beauty of the pieces played. In the visual arts, colors by themselves, irrespective of aesthetic values, may be beneficial. Even so, we cannot help but notice that beauty is a common element in all these examples. Ugly music does not heal. Some paintings and photographs may make us feel worse, not better. And nature brings relief and well-being, particularly when it is experienced as beautiful.

## A Way of Life

The interventions we have been looking at in this chapter are sometimes called "complementary" to traditional medicine. You use music, for instance, to alleviate pain—but you still have to go through the medical routine of tests, drugs, surgery. It is unlikely that a piece of music will cure cancers, even if Professor Fabien Maman in France has been able to dissolve cancerous cells with music. And a beautiful painting hanging on the wall cannot be the only sedative for a postoperative patient. In such situations the interventions are a support, not the main cure. But remember, these interventions arrive on the scene when the disaster has already happened; that is, when the tissues have already been compromised by years of bad psychological habits, stress, bad nutrition, pollution, and other grave offenses.

We should perhaps get used to thinking of beauty as a preventative cure, or better still, a way of life. Small, occasional doses of beauty can have significant effects. But what would happen if beauty were a guiding principle, a reference point in our actions and choices? What if it became the main theme, or one of the main themes, in our existence—if beauty, as opposed to disharmony and vulgarity, were the very context in which we live? Would our pathologies be equally numerous, aggressive, and lethal? We would do well to find comprehensive answers to these questions. As soon as possible.

# The Invisible Ally

Every Friday, I take my ten-year-old son Jonathan to choir practice. Just getting there is an ordeal. The music school is on the hillside of Fiesole, in a glorious spot, but accessible by a single road so narrow that only one vehicle at a time can pass. Thus, if you find a car coming the other way, either you reverse or the other reverses. If in the meantime another car has arrived behind you, and another behind the other driver, the difficulty is fourfold. If you are facing someone who is waiting for you to make the first move, and you cannot, because the road is too narrow or you are in a curve, then you are trapped.

The last fifty meters are crucial. On one particular occasion, I was in trouble. Jonathan, after eight hours of regular school, was tired and irritable. And I, for different reasons, was already in a bad mood. All I needed was to be blocked on the road. The seconds ticked by, more cars arrived. I felt oppressed and claustrophobic, even unhappier than before.

When I finally got to the school, I could not find a parking place anywhere, and the way the cars were parked bore no resemblance whatever to classical music. I had to make do, park messily, and hang around so as to be able to move my car when needed. I wondered: Why does it all have to be so intricate and laborious? I reflected that our entire existence is built this way—one frustration after the next, one more nuisance to cope with, when what we need is a break. The tiny everyday difficulties seemed enormous and ready to squash me. I was not at peace with the world. And, yes, my response was way out of proportion. But who can argue with feelings?

Luckily, beauty saved me. As I had to wait, I hung around outside the room in which the young choir was singing. The choir mistress and the pianist are great teachers, and the kids were in perfect pitch. I listened. They sang their repertoire, and at some point they came to Mozart's "Goodnight"—a simple but lovely song. To hear it sung by a group of children was extraordinary. It was the opposite of the car scenario. This perfect, simple music, sweet and melodic, reached my heart and filled my whole being with delight. Not only did it cancel the frustrations with one clean sweep, it made me look at life as an adventure full of surprises. If I had to imagine how I want to be received in Heaven, I would choose this way: by a children's choir singing Mozart.

### Two Systems

It took a moment for me to make the transition from malaise to well-being. Somehow everything clicked: The tension in my neck, my shallow breathing, my miserable state of mind and dismal ruminations, my dark view of the world, all gave way to physical well-being, and an altogether different mode of being and interpreting the world around me—one much more hopeful and open to pleasure.

We can perhaps put it this way: Events do not happen in isolation. Our bodily response, our perceptions, our worldview, all are part of one same system. And, as psychoanalyst Andras Angyal once remarked, there are at least two systems that seem capable of organizing our bodymind: health and illness.

In the illness system, each situation, event, object, or person becomes an element that takes vitality away from us, causes disharmony and confusion, makes us feel unwell. Even what is beautiful and good becomes a torture: A beautiful woman loves me, but I am consumed with jealousy; I am successful, but I don't deserve it; I eat a delicious dish, but I know it will give me indigestion; the weather is glorious, but I know it won't last.

In the system of health, each situation, thing, or person becomes an element that increases our vitality, makes us learn, gives us meaning and well-being. Even what may seem negative makes us grow. A woman who by conventional taste is unattractive, I see as beautiful. I have little money, but I feel rich nonetheless. An impasse becomes a stimulus. The weather is awful, but even the rain and wind are a blessing.

## The Construction of Reality

We know why we can oscillate from one system to the other. More and more, psychologists are showing that what we think of as reality is instead a construction of our mind. We construct a concept of ourselves and our body, of other people, of man and of woman, of space, memory, and time. We even construct nature and see it according to our own ideology: These are not objective realities, but ideas, therefore subject to change. We live in a house we have built ourselves, and sometimes it is uncomfortable. To become aware that our life as we perceive it is, at least in part, our own creation, and to know we are able to redesign it, can give us a great sense of freedom. We understand that we are not imprisoned in a given situation, because it is an idea in our mind and that idea holds us under a spell. Once we realize that the stuff our reality is made of is mental, we can change it: The same person may seem friend or enemy to us, a difficulty may be a trap or a lucky break, a trait of ours may be a weakness or a strength. The world is as we see it: And we can change the way we see it.

In order to attain this freedom, we need a certain degree of mental fluidity and field independence. At times we are truly attached to our suffering, our anger, our discouragement, and our ideas. It is as though someone had glued them to us. Actually it is even worse: We think we *are* all that stuff. We have to be able to release ourselves from that influence. Meditation is a big help for many people. Relationships can also give us a hand. For the religious, prayer is invaluable. Bodywork may serve us in changing our patterns. And then, of course, beauty can be our ally. It can cause a true catharsis, a release from the past. A man says: "I had left the theater where Shakespeare's *Troilus and Cressida* had been playing. The actors were wonderful. The atmosphere was electrifying. Walking home at night along empty city streets, I felt renewed, as though my old ideas, my old self, had slid off me like an old snakeskin."

### Beauty Is Health

Beauty has the extraordinary capacity to take us from one way of functioning to another in an instant. We are all familiar with the black-and-white image of two human profiles, where the negative space can be seen as a vase. The passage from seeing the vase to seeing the profiles is not gradual, or vice versa, but instantaneous.

And you cannot see both at the same time. It is the same with the passage from the system of illness to that of health and vice versa. We can say that the perception of beauty is a definition of perfect psychological health. The moment we perceive beauty in its fullness and we are filled with it, in that moment, even if only for that moment, we are not paranoid anymore, we are not depressed, we are not obsessive, we are not bitter. We are as we were meant to be. It may be just that one moment, but *we have reached perfect health.*

In my interviews, I have often found that beauty appears as a miraculous element that resolves a critical situation. The switch is sudden and total. One philosophy is abandoned, another one is adopted without any need of deliberation. It just happens. And it is not just a feeling or an idea by itself. It is a whole system encompassing an array of sensations, attitudes, and thoughts. And that is the essence of healing.

### "Another Part of Me"

Often people describe this change as "another part of me" taking over. They are talking about another part they did not know before or had forgotten. A part that is stronger, better, and wiser, is activated by beauty, and gives new strength, a novel way of seeing things, an influx of vital emotions.

But what is this "other side," and how is it manifest?

To understand it, we have to think of certain moments in our life—when, for instance, after a period of depression, we find new powers; when a new idea unexpectedly comes, an inspiration; or we wake up in the morning with the solution to a problem; or when, in an emergency, great mental energy is suddenly available to us. All this comes from the "other side," our hidden face—the face of our latent resources. It is our deep self which comes to our aid. It is an invisible ally, accompanying us in our predicaments, reassuring us when we are frightened, giving us strength when we feel weak, encouraging us when we are disheartened.

In Indian mythology, Kutsa is Indra's friend. Kutsa is the human being in his earthly form. Indra is the divine form. Together they board a carriage that travels to the sky. At the beginning of the journey the difference between the two is obvious. One is radiant and strong. The other one is all too human: weak, grayish, hesitant. And heavy. But at the end of the journey, Kutsa can no longer be distinguished from Indra: He, too, has become divine. The invisible ally does the same for us. It takes us to another level, it carries us beyond our present limitations.

Our invisible ally may come to our rescue at any time, at any place, in the many vagaries of our path. A woman says: "There were fireworks, and my two children were having great fun. I enjoyed watching their ecstatic faces more than the fireworks. They were really beautiful. They reminded me that there was more to life than financial worries and arguments with my husband."

Sandra is about thirty. She loves nature and is especially fascinated by waterfalls. One day when she is on holiday in Iceland: "From the road we saw a waterfall in the distance. While my husband was parking the car, I started walking. That waterfall drew me like nothing had ever done before. The water came down a sheer wall and formed a small lake in a landscape without vegetation. I was spellbound. I could not bear to wait for my husband. I started running, even felt scared because I couldn't stop. I only stopped when my feet were in the water." When Sandra finds beauty, it is as if a new part of her were activated: "I get in touch again with the most authentic part of me, one that I had denied, as though I had wanted to punish myself, as though that part was not okay and I had to change myself to be accepted. Beauty is the road for finding my truest part."

### Finding the Soul

Often in our life we are distracted, we forget what really counts. We chase pipe dreams, let ourselves be scared by ghosts, lose ourselves in the labyrinth of the irrelevant. We lose ourselves, our soul. We feel impoverished and estranged. In the Grail story, a king is sick, and all around him nature is dying: springs dry up, plants shrivel, animals die. All kinds of people surround the ill king and try their best to help him: scholars, doctors, knights, magicians. But they seem to miss the point, all their know-how is powerless. The king is cured only when a young stranger of humble birth, Parsifal, asks him: "Where is the Grail?" Then nature blooms again, the springs flow, the animals recover their vigor. Sometimes it only takes asking the right question.

It is like saying: "Where is my soul? What is essential, what is so precious, so vital, that if I lose it I become a living corpse and the world around me a ghost town? Where is my soul?" That is perhaps the only question worth answering. Where *is* my soul? Each one of us answers in his or her own way. That is our life search, our continuing effort to solve our maddening puzzle. In any case, beauty has probably a lot to do with our plight and may be, if not the answer itself, a potent aid that leads us to discovery.

According to one tradition, the Grail is a cup the angels forged out of an emerald from the sky that fell from Lucifer's diadem when he was chased out of Paradise. It is represented at the center of the Round Table, where the twelve knights are seated: a symbol of the sky, in which the twelve constellations of the zodiac perpetually rotate. Finding the Grail means rediscovering our soul and thus our connection with the cosmos—our place under the stars.

It is really very simple: To lose beauty means to become ill. To meet it again, face-to-face, means to find again the part of ourselves we should never forget. It means to be healed.

FOUR

THE HEART
OF BEAUTY

# Sharing

To what extent are we alone with our own experiences?

Do we each exist in an individual bubble, a world of private perceptions, feelings, and images which no one else will ever know? Do we live alone, side by side with others who are also alone? Perhaps. Our subjective world is subtle, ever-changing, indescribable. Maybe we should just accept the sad truth: Our inner experiences are incommunicable, our life is a lonely dream. What we feel and think happens, and then vanishes forever, never to be shared by anybody else. And that would apply also to beauty. Aesthetic experiences, in this hypothesis, would be intense but private events no one but ourselves would be allowed to know.

But think again. The other possibility is that beauty lives and breathes in relationships. To see a film or a landscape or listen to a piece of music is an almost entirely different experience if we are with another person. Compelling research is now showing us how social we really are; how our brain—our whole organism—is made for relationships. In the course of our evolution we have learned to read the emotions of others, participate, and share. Our very survival depends on these capacities. In fact, from this perspective, not one of our experiences can be fully understood outside the context of relationships.

True, we cannot ever be sure we are really sharing our experiences. Yet every now and then we have the clear sensation that what we are feeling, someone else is feeling, too, that our experiences coincide, and that this fact, of itself, has value, especially when the experience is important to us. Such as in the case of beauty.

## The Other

In my interviews about beauty, sharing often emerged as the main theme, not just a supporting factor. It seems that sharing is the starting point, not the consequence, and that the other person's presence makes the experience of beauty possible. Relationships are often the field in which aesthetic experiences can arise, just as fertile soil allows a seed to germinate.

Here is an example. I am at the Hermitage Museum in St. Petersburg, with my friend Sasha. We arrive just before closing time, but Sasha knows his way around this huge building. He heads for the room with the Rembrandts—his passion. We focus on two paintings. The first shows the return of the prodigal son. The whole story culminates in the moment, charged with pathos, when the father meets the son who has come back home. Everything takes place in that intimate atmosphere painted with Rembrandt's preternatural light. In the embrace, you see the son from behind, while the focus is on the father. His face shows the mixture of love and relief: He thought he had lost his son forever, but the son is back. It is a beautiful expression. Sasha is the father of two daughters; I have two sons. Being fathers ourselves, I believe, helps us feel this emotion in its depth and beauty.

The second painting tells the story of Abraham and Isaac. Carrying out God's command, Abraham is about to kill his son Isaac. At the last minute, an angel arrives. *We* know that the angel will stop Abraham, but they do not know it yet. Abraham has a blank look, as though following orders in a state of hypnosis. In one hand he is holding the knife with which he must kill his son. The other hand is pressing violently on his son's face. Isaac is lying down, overpowered. You do not see his face, but every contour of his body expresses the tragedy: He realizes that his father is about to kill him. You understand from the image that Rembrandt has no sympathy for Abraham—for him, Abraham is one who stifles his own emotions and whose obedience to God is destructive. There is nothing holy here: This is not true spirituality, but blind and abject fanaticism. You see that the relationship between the two is forever compromised. How will they ever again be able to look at each other, after Isaac's life is saved? How will Isaac be able to trust his father again? This painting expresses violence and brutality. It is the exact opposite of the previous one. And yet even horror can be great art.

Both paintings are beautiful, and I feel a new perspective open in me. The first painting shows me with unequalled depth the immense beauty of love for one's child. It reveals the breadth and meaning of this emotion, which I recognize in myself. The second painting shows me the terrible danger of suffocating our deeper feelings. It tells me, though in a paradoxical way, how important emotions and relationships are in our life. It gives me permission—in fact, urges me—not to stifle my heart.

I exchange few words with Sasha. And yet I am sure that his enthusiasm allows me to understand them more completely and convincingly than if I had visited the museum alone. Later I tell

Sasha's wife that we have been to the Hermitage. "Ah! You have been to see Rembrandt!" she says, with a tone as if to say: "You have been to see an old friend." It is this warm familiarity that Sasha has for Rembrandt which allows me to understand and appreciate these paintings so much better.

During this visit, after Rembrandt, as we still have a little time, we look at other masterpieces, such as Monet's *Waterloo Bridge* and Matisse's *Five Dancers*. They are paintings I have always loved, so to see the originals is a great pleasure. Yet months afterward, my memory of Rembrandt is much more alive. I saw his paintings with someone who passionately loves them—and this resonance has left in me a stronger trace.

### A Common Ground

All of us can recall moments in our lives when we enjoyed beauty with another person or other people—and when an atmosphere, a common feeling, arose such that the experience of beauty could not be split from that of being together. We can also recall other moments when we were in the presence of beauty, the other person was not, and we wished he were: Now, in this amazing landscape of forests and lakes, or listening to this music, or under this night sky ablaze with stars, how I wish you were here with me.

Can a large body of people share beauty? Is fashion a form of sharing? In fashion everyone likes the same item: a color, a style of dress or sunglasses. Here, too, a field is formed in which many individuals, as if by magic, find they all like, say, tops that show the bellybutton, or nose rings, or pointed shoes, or the color orange, or whatever. But too often fashion exploits our fear of being different, and therefore it may produce regimentation and uniformity of taste. This constraint restricts our aesthetic range. Our enjoyment becomes superficial and illusory. We know it will yield to the next fashion. Its only advantage is the relief of being approved. But it is an imposed, and therefore oppressive, duty: "You *have* to like this dress—this style of makeup—this car" and that does not facilitate opening to beauty. On the contrary, it obstructs it. Fashion is a society's desire to experiment with beauty: It can be creative, eye-opening, and liberating. Depending on how we assimilate it, though, it may become dictatorial and constrictive.

Sharing beauty is a more intimate matter. At the Hermitage I had no wish to be persuaded about anything. I have always liked Rembrandt, though he was not one of my favorite painters. Had I not been deeply touched, I would have been able to make some general remark, out of politeness, to a person kind enough to show me his city. But instead, a vast expanse opened in me. To have appreciated that beauty with Sasha allowed me to understand him better and to feel closer to him.

This is not the whole story, however. We could also say the opposite: True aesthetic experience happens only in silence and solitude, where we are free, away from society's conditioning, other people judgments and expectations, our own fears and social strategies. It is then that the discovery of beauty helps us form our own taste, and therefore leads us to be truly and freely ourselves.

Beauty is discovered in solitude. Beauty is born with sharing. The two statements are not contradictory, but complementary. My impression is that for most people one process facilitates the other, although we may need to emphasize one or the other at different times in our lives. We have already seen how the aesthetic experience is authentic only when it stems from our own genuine response. Here we will focus on the power of beauty to encourage sharing between people, unite them, and allow them to better know and enjoy one another. A woman tells me: "I listened with my fiancé to the *Incarnatus*, from Mozart's Great Mass. It is a glorious song, simple and sublime. In a flash it takes you to what is essential in life. I already knew it and appreciated it and wanted him to hear it, too. In seeing his reaction, how touched he was by its beauty, I was once more struck, and the piece moved me even more intensely. Thus the *Incarnatus* became our song, a milestone in our relationship."

The aesthetic experience is transmitted in a subtle, mysterious way. It almost feels like telepathy. When this happens, the two or more people who are involved find their relationship grows stronger.

To understand why this is so, we must go back to basics. When two human beings face each other, they immediately—and without realizing it—look for a common ground or a point of reference, which then becomes their basis for communication. The common ground can be anything at all: the experience of having had one's wallet stolen on the bus, a liking for chocolate, a passion for bridge, the same political views, or owning the same brand of car—anything can bring two people together.

It is imperative they find a common ground, otherwise the whole encounter is much more difficult. Imagine being with a person who has nothing in common with you—no interest, no experience, no value. Communication is labored, perhaps impossible. This is why when we meet another human being, we go through the ritual of seeking some kind of convergence. If we do not find it, we may even panic and, at the least, will be bored or embarrassed. To find a common ground, even if only in complaining about the weather or the slack postal service, gives us a sense of relief and makes any sharing possible.

At times the common ground is a theme we deeply care for:

such as the yearning for social justice, a religious faith, the desire to help other people. Clearly, the encounter will be as deep and meaningful as the field that is being shared. It is one thing to share annoyance over bad weather or parking fines, quite another to share love of the mountains or religious faith.

Beauty is an outstanding common ground because it stimulates such deep and intense experiences. Let us take a few examples. Maurizio is a forty-year-old doctor who likes walking in the mountains, especially the Apennines in the summertime. He speaks of a memorable walk: "It was an incredibly happy day—to be with my best friend and to see such glorious sights . . . We were on foot the whole time, walking in a mountain landscape. It was so beautiful because I was with someone who was sharing nature with me, including the smallest things. We would stop to contemplate the mushrooms on the bark of a tree, or we would notice a badger run away . . . Had I been alone, it would not have been like that. Being with him gave me much more joy."

Susan was born in the tropical zone of Australia. She regards herself lucky, because there she learned to appreciate beauty, developing great sensitivity to the colors, shapes, scents, and sensations of the tropics. One day she took a walk with a friend to a riverbank: "We were in a mangrove area, with lots of wild birds. We were on the boat ramp jutting into the water. We lay back and started watching the clouds and were both under the same spell. It was satisfying on every level. Then it started to rain on us. And we were just standing in shelter and watching—the sun started to shine and there was a beautiful rainbow, but none of that was particularly important. It was more the light on the water and the raindrops pitting the surface that were marvelous—you could be there forever.

"And the very fact that we both knew each of us was in the same space made me feel very close to her. We were sharing something magnificent, and to share beauty is to share soul to soul. I feel I can trust that person. Sharing beauty is the natural foundation for trust."

## Context

Can the warmth and the vitality of a good relationship—friendship, intimacy, parenthood, teacher-pupil—actually *amplify* the experience of beauty? Not only make it possible, but also boost it? I think it can, and I will use an example to explain how. One day, like a sudden meeting on the street, a gift from the past reaches me. It is a disk with a film score, promised to me a long time ago by my friend Judy. The film, *Swing*, is about a boy who comes into contact with the world of gypsies, and it shows their customs and way of life. I liked the music, and looked for the CD in several shops, but never found it. Judy said she would find it and send it to me. In the meanwhile she became ill with bone cancer, a terrible disease that deformed her body and caused her great suffering. I heard she had found the disk before she died, but life went on and I just forgot about it. Fast forward to the present day. Because of misunderstandings and misplacements and postponements, the disk arrives—after three years. I am by now less interested in gypsy music, so I am not in a hurry to hear it. More time passes. One day I happen to play it in the car.

It is a fascinating and mysterious music with a hypnotic, seductive rhythm. It evokes a free and passionate lifestyle. Suddenly, while I am listening, the unpredictable happens. I feel Judy's presence in the music, I feel as if I am perceiving her kindness. It is an almost tangible presence which I sense to be inherent in the music, as though it had been packed in with it. She, my ill friend, had kept me in mind, had remembered that I liked this music, and set about finding the disk. At first I had made nothing of it. Now I realize: Between that act of kindness and the moment I am listening to the music, three years have passed, yet that by no means lessens the intensity of its effect—on the contrary, it increases it. I am amazed at the capacity of kindness to travel in time and space. I am full of gratitude, even more for the thought than for the music itself. And, as often happens with beauty, here comes a surprise. The music starts to sound magical. No longer just pleasant music, but a bewitching sound. The kind thought has acted as an amplifier, and the music becomes far more beautiful than it had been for me before.

The general rule here is: The context determines and colors our emotions about beauty. What would have happened if Judy had not become ill, but had found and given me the disk, telling me what a nuisance it had been to look high and low for it? Or, what if the disk had arrived anonymously in the mail, say, as publicity for the film? I am sure I would have heard the music in a different way. Instead, I listened to it with feelings of warmth and gratitude, and its beauty was all the more intensified and valued.

Every experience of beauty—weak, fair, intense, marvelous— happens in a context. It is like meeting a person. Do we meet in the waiting room of a railway station, at the park, at the stadium during a soccer match, or at home in a welcoming environment? If I had heard that music while in an angry mood, or while distracted, or worried, would it have been the same?

Friendliness, warmth, and gratitude amplify beauty. They intensify it and make us appreciate its every detail. Sometimes they transform it, making it a hundred times more extraordinary than it would have been in a colder situation. To receive beauty with an open heart means we do not miss one bit of it.

Beauty does not happen in a vacuum, then, but in the context of our relationships, which have the power to intensify it, let us understand it better, imprint it in our memory. And beauty in turn can make a relationship richer and more alive.

### Transparency

Why is it that beauty, perhaps more than any other factor, can unite with sublime ease two people, bring them effortlessly close to each other? I believe the reason is this: When we appreciate beauty we are open—that is, we are not pretending, not playing our roles, not taking refuge in some theory, not having an ax to grind. We are defenseless, we are true. In this state it is easier and more natural to be with others. We allow them to see us for who we are.

In the perception of beauty free of conditioning—free of what we learned at school or what experts have told us, free of fashion dependency or the fear of looking silly—we feel that what we like is very close to us, that it somehow represents our identity. If I find beauty, for instance, in the jazz of Charlie Parker and Dizzy Gillespie, or the yellows and reds of autumn leaves, or the bare architecture of a little Romanesque church, then all this speaks for what I am. If I reveal my true preferences, those that move and change me, I expose myself. I find it significant that most people point to their heart as the seat of the aesthetic experience. The heart is the seat of intimacy. Sharing beauty resembles a declaration of love.

Beauty is not an accessory or frill but a central factor, a medium for revealing who we are. If we then meet another person who feels what we feel, our relationship will be simple and direct, because the obstacles that existed before—fears, suspicions, expectations, resentments, power games—have been momentarily swept away. It is then that transformations are possible, understanding is fluid. We let emotions move us, and happily overthrow our clichés, our tired old mental habits.

Thus an encounter is possible, in fact we may discover unanimity—literally "to be one soul." To be, for a while, timelessly one with another person—this is a highly valuable experience, and those who have had it, want to repeat it; those who have not, vaguely feel a need for it.

The Celtic tradition speaks of *anam cara*: the soul mate. Before birth our soul was one whole, then it was split in two. At birth these halves went different ways. Now they must find each other again. The soul mate is someone with whom we have an immediate understanding, crystalline transparency, a total absence of barriers and defenses. Our *anam cara* is the one who helps us learn life lessons, understands what we feel, responds to the very same beauty as we do.

I do not know if soul mates really exist as a metaphysical category. But a deep, intense yearning to find one is a wish many of us have. To state it simply, there are people with whom we have a greater affinity. To find them has enormous value. And, as several studies show, it is the capacity to be fearlessly open and to allow ourselves to be seen which is at the basis of friendship and love.

### Being in Tune

Aesthetic intelligence is this, too: the capacity to tune into other people's perceptions, give others the chance to convey to us their experience at that moment. If our tastes are similar, the experience will be intensified and deepened. If you and I both like Bartók's Sonata for Two Pianos and Percussion, or Malawi tribal music, then in listening together we may discover new aspects, love it with even greater depth.

If, on the other hand, our tastes are different, aesthetic intelligence consists first in the ability to let the enthusiasm of another affect us. In this way we are enriched by her, and she becomes a guide in territory unknown to us.

This happens also the other way round. Just as some people are receptive to aesthetic resonance, so others find it easier to help people perceive beauty where they least expected to find it. This ability is vital in education, where parents, relatives, and teachers may have the privilege of transmitting an aesthetic perception.

### Sectarians and Outsiders

At the worst, if this does not happen, aesthetic intelligence will consist in tolerance, in acceptance that someone may see beauty where we do not. Such acceptance is crucial because it honors the real nature of beauty—which is extraordinarily varied and surprising. It hides in the least obvious places. It takes ever-new and ever-different forms. It is no one's monopoly, but the prerogative of everyone.

Aesthetic tolerance is not easy. Snobbishness and intolerance are rife. *Sectarians* may proclaim that what others like is garish and vulgar, appointing themselves as the real connoisseurs of beauty. This gives them a sense of exclusiveness and superiority.

Conversely, if we do not have self-confidence, we may think with dismay that the vision of beauty is denied to us and that only others may really understand and appreciate beauty, that we are forbidden entry to paradise. We are the *outsiders*. This condition brings self-pity and unhappiness. No doubt, sectarians and outsiders abound.

Aesthetic intelligence stops us from being rigid in our position. It enriches by giving us new ways of being, by widening our experience and understanding, by showing us that beauty is for everyone, by moving us to love more deeply.

I can think of nothing that unites two people so powerfully as beauty, whether in friendship, family relations, or as a couple. In particular, beauty can create magic for the couple. Occasionally I read in the paper about the presumed effect of one food or another on people's erotic attitude: chocolate, oysters, tortoise eggs, arugula. Maybe so. My vote goes to beauty. Find something you both consider beautiful: a film, a song, a place. What can be more erotic? Beauty savored together puts two people in harmony and dissolves defenses and hesitations. Beauty is the most powerful aphrodisiac.

# The Beauty of the Soul

Picture the following situation: A beautiful woman is standing on the road beside her car. She is unable to change a flat tire. Would you stop to help her? And what if the woman was not beautiful? The data for this study show that 67 percent more people (men and women) stop in the former situation. A beautiful woman (that is, one considered beautiful by the majority of people) has a much better chance of getting help. Furthermore, a good-looking person, man or woman, is served before others in a shop and is regarded as more credible by a jury, and therefore more likely to get away with crime. Various studies have shown that "beautiful" people are also more intelligent, find work more easily, have more success if they run for election in public office, and are richer. The figures on earning power are pitiless. To be a good-looking man in the United States and Canada means to earn on average 5 percent more; to be "ugly," 9 percent less. For women it is less of a factor: +4 percent and –6 percent). But this is nothing compared to China: –25 percent for "ugly" men and +3 percent for good-looking men; and for women –31 percent and +10 percent. Yes, life is not fair, in fact it is, at times, cruel. But this is the way it is, and this will be our starting point.

## To Appear and to Be

One may protest: It is not outer, but inner, beauty that counts. In the light of the above results, and of life as we know it in the West, this seems at first contrary to fact. Not to say pathetic. With brutal realism, a bumper-sticker warns: "Inner beauty won't help you get laid." It comes as no surprise that Americans invest more money in beauty (cosmetics, plastic surgery, etc.) than in education: It is a promise of love. Physical beauty arouses emotions, moves money, creates power, brings down empires.

Talk about beauty of the soul (or inner beauty), and you will be seen as an idealist. For most people outer beauty is what makes the world go around; inner beauty is at best a nice idea.

## Moral Beauty and Moral Ugliness

But not so fast. It would be unforgivable and superficial to drop the idea of inner beauty altogether. We need only think a moment: The word "beautiful" can apply not only to the visible, but also to the invisible and subjective. Think of a wonderful character, a beautiful mind, a great person. Far more than we realize, beauty of the soul is a criterion for understanding and evaluating an individual. Perhaps, after all, physical beauty is not the only important factor. Imagine being married to a beautiful person with an obnoxious character. Are you sure that only physical beauty counts?

Maybe the best way to understand this point is to think of moral ugliness. In the face of a terrible crime, such as newspapers report every day—murder, child abuse, terrorism—we feel revulsion, at times rage, and we exclaim: How horrendous! We apply an aesthetic category. When someone takes advantage of the weak, betrays a friend, ignores a wounded person, we regard these acts as ugly and the people who committed them as repellent.

If moral ugliness exists, moral beauty must exist, too. Newspapers do not emphasize it, because it does not make a big impression. Monsters, sadists, warmongers, evildoers—that is what sells papers. Yet moral beauty is alive and well. In fact, both kinds of beauty exist—outer and inner. The former is more obvious, more likely to attract attention, more immediate, gratifying, and short-term. The latter is subtler, deeper, usually needs more time to be perceived. And often it is not fully disclosed to the distracted eye. Physical beauty is a sprinter—it covers short distances faster. Beauty of the soul is a marathoner—it shows up over long distance.

Beauty of the soul includes, for example, intelligence, honesty, coherence, generosity. It is a beauty that has nothing to do with cosmetics, is not dependent on elegant clothing or the latest model car, and cannot be bought. But if we can see beyond appearances, it can guide us and transform our lives.

Several studies have shown that our perception of a person's physical beauty is influenced by what we know about that person. If we have not met him before, then our aesthetic judgment will be purely exterior. But if we know him, he will seem more beautiful to us if we appreciate some of his nonphysical aspects, such as his willingness to cooperate, his intelligence and trustworthiness. In a course of field archeology, participants were asked to evaluate the physical beauty of all the other participants at the beginning of the course and then again at the end. The two sets of evaluations—at the beginning and at the end—differed considerably: The evaluations depended on how well acquainted the participants were with one another, and how able they had become to see beyond appearances.

### The Human Face

Sure enough, inner beauty can become one with outer beauty. It can be expressed through the body—the look in the eyes and the facial expression, as the great portraitists, painters, and sculptors well know. I am thinking, just to make an example, of the Duke of Montefeltro as portrayed by Piero della Francesca. You see the profile: You can feel in him the dignity and splendor of being human. Or Rembrandt's self-portraits—he painted more than ninety during his lifetime, and turned this art form into a stunning reflection on the human predicament and the passing of time.

Photographers, too. One day in a bookstore, I was leafing through a photographic book by Cartier-Bresson. All the photos were portraits. Magically, every photo was a window to the inner reality of the person: Sartre, Gandhi, and many others. How on earth did he do it? An ordinary photo is often flat—you see a smiling face and little else. Here every face revealed a whole world. The book was expensive, so I did not buy it, but for days I continued to think about those photos; they went on working in my mind, as beautiful things often do. Finally, I just had to go back to the store and to buy the book. Too late: It was sold out.

And, speaking of photographic portraits, I recall the famous one of Winston Churchill. The photographer Yousef Karsch got Churchill to agree to being photographed straight after a talk at the House of Commons in 1941. But that morning, Churchill was extremely busy and irritated. He gave Karsch only two minutes. When he was about to shoot, Karsch went up to Churchill and took the cigar out of his hand. Churchill pulled a still more annoyed face. At that moment, Karsch took the photo. The picture beautifully shows the fearsome power of his bulldog expression. It became an icon of the man who would defeat the Nazis.

Faces: What an astounding show! As a psychotherapist, I see, every day, faces that express emotions: young faces full of freshness and innocence; older faces with signs of many battles; strong faces, weak faces, graceful, disproportionate, crazy, intelligent, luminous, dense faces. Faces full of fright, of horror, of pain, of love and happiness. And I never cease to be amazed at the remarkable ability of the human face to reflect inner states and, at times, to manifest inner beauty. It is a capacity we take too much for granted. I knew someone afflicted with macular degeneration; she was losing her eyesight. The world appeared to her as a horrid, meaningless nightmare. But the worst part of her sickness was being unable to see the expressions on people's faces: She saw only blank outlines. She felt this handicap made understanding and communication almost impossible and condemned her to isolation.

### The Paradox of Inner Beauty

Sometimes beauty of the soul is illogical and paradoxical. It goes against common belief, social habits, perhaps even our interests of the moment. An Indian story tells of the king Yudhishtira, who is walking along the road with his dog. Suddenly he hears a loud, numinous noise, sees an extraordinary light, and in the light he sees the god Indra seated in a carriage. "You can enter Paradise in your human form, Yudhishtira. Come with me." The king straightaway asks if he will meet there his wife Draupadi and all his friends who died in battle or as a result of conspiracy. Indra assures him he will, but as the king is about to step into the carriage with his dog, Indra stops him: "Not the dog. Paradise is no place for dogs."

But Yudhishtira does not accept this ban. "If I can't take my dog, I won't go." Indra tries to persuade him: "Think of Paradise and all it can offer you—prosperity, well-being, beauty, immortality." But the noble king will not be swayed. The dog is devoted to him, he tells Indra, and it is wrong to abandon those who love us and want our protection or are too weak to fend for themselves— even if it is only a dog. It would be a betrayal. Desiring happiness is not reason enough to forget those who are entrusted to us.

At this point, the whole scene disappears: It was an illusory vision for the purpose of putting the king to a test. In its place appears the god of justice: "You renounced the happiness of the gods for the sake of your dog! This is true Paradise, and now happiness is yours." Thus the king enters Paradise.

But he is put to one more test. He does not meet his wife and friends as he hoped and was promised. "Forget them!" says Indra. "In Paradise there is no room for personal affections. You must forget your past."

But the king cannot accept this either, and he renounces the beauty of Paradise, which would mean nothing for him without those he loves. He sets off to look for his wife and friends. He must descend into hellish places. Alas, they are in a dark and desolate land, full of stinking, toxic fumes, poisonous plants, biting insects, and ferocious animals. At some point he hears the voices of his wife and friends, who are groaning in pain. "Stay with us," they say, "your very presence gives us relief from this terrible suffering."

The king must choose: He can turn around, go back to Paradise, and enjoy eternal beauty, or he can stay forever with his wife and friends in this place of suffering. An even harder choice, but Yudhishtira has no doubts: "I will stay here always with the ones I love!"

In no time at all the whole scene changes again. The horrible visions disappear—they, too, were illusions to test him. Yudhishtira is surrounded by gods who finally welcome him into real Paradise where he finds his wife and friends (and his dog as well). True beauty is not selfish, superficial enjoyment of pleasure, but the beauty of justice, freedom of choice, faithfulness to one's values, loyalty to those one loves.

Inner beauty is harder to see because fewer people are aware of it and few people manifest it. All of us to some extent try to be what we are not. We have a social mask, because if we were to show who we really are, we would feel too vulnerable.

Inner beauty is related to innocence and transparency, and so it is much easier to see in children, who have not yet learned to hide it. We adults are slower and more awkward because our inner beauty is clouded, stifled by caution, anxiety, the weight of roles, and maybe also by a degree of compliance. Nevertheless, it *is* beauty. In my workshops, I occasionally do a simple exercise. I ask participants to sit facing another person and to look at that person: look at the expression on her face, the look in her eyes, the lines on her forehead, the mood in her lips. Meanwhile, they have to think: This person has big problems, troubling faults. After a little while, I ask them to look at the same person once more, but this time they have to hold another thought in mind: She has inner beauty, the hidden beauty of the soul—love, intelligence, patience, courage, and so on. Perceptions change as if by magic. It is an experiment we can do subtly with everyone in our daily life without telling them. And also with ourselves: to see and acknowledge our own inner beauty—our qualities and potentialities.

## Beauty and the Beast

Traditional tales remind us of this skill. Remember *Beauty and the Beast*, a universal story with many variations. The Beast is anything but a desirable fiancé: Would you marry a snake (Chinese fairytale), a lizard (Indonesian), a monkey (Japanese), a frog (Irish), a pig (Turkish), or a three-headed monster (Russian)? A girl has to marry a repellent being to save her father, who is in trouble. Only later will she find out that the beast is, in fact, a handsome young man, victim of a spell, whom she has saved by her love and her capacity to perceive, beyond his physical ugliness, the soul's beauty.

In my interviews it has not been hard to find people who appreciate the inner beauty of others, especially of loved ones. A mother, for example, says of her son: "I recall many moments of my son's childhood when I saw his beauty—moments when he was happy with himself. For instance, at the final of the regional tennis championship, he was scared stiff, and managed to overcome his fear. Or times when he was happy about life. Whenever he was passionate about something, a vein in his neck would bulge with excitement. He seemed very beautiful to me in his excitement and enthusiasm."

Friendship is also fertile ground for this sort of perception: "I can remember a time a friend listened to me. Nothing transcendental— I was a bit down, we were in the car, and he just listened, without giving advice or judgment. It was a difficult period for me, and everyone else was too busy. But this friend was present, listened, that's all. In that moment, I saw his beauty—his willingness to be with me."

Many people I interviewed told me they can see such beauty when a person is not hiding, not pretending or defending herself, but simply showing who she is. It is simple. To reveal our inner beauty, we do not need to prove we are clever, show how much we know, or how many honors we have accumulated. On the contrary, these would all be screens: We just let people see our difficulties and faults, without filters and pretenses. Our inner beauty will then be more likely to show. A woman says: "The soul is beautiful. Everyone has a beautiful soul, even criminals. Human beings are beautiful when they do not have resistances, when they let others in, like children do. It happens in seconds."

This is the opposite of outer beauty, for which you have to have done your exercise, kept to a diet, dressed well, worked on your hair, and so on. Inner beauty is already there, all you need to do is not hide it.

Some people admire the moral beauty of literary or cinematic characters—figures who are imaginary, yet have great strength. Even though they are fictional, they can represent the most beautiful and inspiring qualities. A woman recounts: "Imagined beings are a distillation of actual humanness—even if they are martians! Literature is full of them. For instance, when I was a teenager, I met the character Antigone in Jean Anouilh's play. It changed me deeply. She is a very strong character, and I recognized that strength in myself. It almost frightened me and has made my life difficult. That strength is not easy to deal with. Her inner beauty had to do with fierce courage and loyalty. That is a wonderful thing, but it's also far too much for a human being, and that is why she must die.

"Another example is a film character—Dersu Uzala. In Akira Kurosawa's film, the setting is Siberia, and Dersu is a small, indigenous man of that region. The film is about his encounter with a Russian engineer. Dersu becomes his guide and friend. He is an amazing man. And everyone who has seen this film loves him, because he is a true human being. He is humble, he is humorous, he is true. That is what inner beauty is for me. It's when somebody is true."

### Depth

So to see a person's inner beauty is to read reality in a different way. We are with a person. We pay attention—a necessary condition (for the greedy, the distracted, the hurried, inner beauty is invisible). We put aside our demands and ideas regarding this person, as they stop us from seeing what is there. We drop our fears (no one said it was an easy exercise). And we look at him with an intuitive eye. Then maybe we will catch a glimpse of this person's inner beauty.

Is it possible to help someone's inner beauty be manifest? The answer is not simple. The best in each of us usually comes out when conditions are right, when we are given the right amount of attention and encouragement. But often inner beauty is not given the attention it deserves. If, however, we see it, encourage it, and value it, we are likely to help it manifest in its full strength.

Sometimes inner beauty needs attention and encouragement. At other times, the dramatic challenges of life bring it forth. Think of Anne Frank or Etty Hillesum—their beauty manifested in the horror of Nazi times. Or think of the people who, in a sudden choice, sacrifice their lives to save someone in danger, like the firemen of New York on that fateful September day. Or think of all the people who, in spite of extreme hardships in their life, manage to be kind, serve other people, be creative and resourceful, or just bring up a family. Every undertaking, every plan, often encounters difficulties. At times, unforeseen obstacles and failures strengthen us, bring to light our inner resources, and pave the way for inner beauty.

This whole subject is full of surprises and contradictions. The American psychologist Nancy Etcoff has done several studies on feminine beauty and has written a valuable book on the subject, *Survival of the Prettiest*. Here, too, the data are hard and cruel. Apparently, beauty has little to do with taste or cultural conditioning. It depends on precise geometrical proportions of the face and body, present at all times and in all cultures. At the end of the book, however, Etcoff mentions an example which seems to indicate a deeper, more puzzling dimension of beauty: George Eliot, the great English writer and poetess. When Eliot was fifty years old, Henry James fell in love with her: "She is magnificently ugly—deliciously hideous. She has a low forehead, a dull gray eye, a vast pendulous nose, a huge mouth, full of uneven teeth, and a chin and jaw-bone *qui n'en finissent pas* . . . Now in this vast ugliness resides a most powerful beauty which, in a very few minutes, steals forth and charms the mind, so that you end as I ended, in falling in love with her."

To see inner beauty is sometimes easy, sometimes laborious—like working out an enigma. In exceptional moments no problems exist, such as when we are in love: Life becomes easy and bright. But this state vanishes. And then we can learn to see someone's beauty and that can radically change our relationships. There is no one from whom we cannot learn *some*thing. Every human being has his special gift to offer, a beauty not found elsewhere. In this view, no one is banal.

Falling in love sometimes jumps clear of all the common expectations about beauty. With grand and heroic indifference, it ignores what the majority considers beautiful. A story by Alberto Moravia, "Scorfani," is about a very ugly man. He is rickety, has a huge nose, his eyes are "the color of a dog running away," his face is narrow and yellow. They call him "scorfano," meaning ugly fish. He is resigned: No woman will ever like him. But luck turns his way: a woman, ugly too, finds him beautiful and falls in love with him. One day they go together to the circus. There, a bully sneers at him, he gets angry, but is too thin to be beaten. The bully picks him up and puts him on the back of a passing baby elephant, opening him to ridicule. But his girl is still in love with him. She keeps thinking he is beautiful. Nothing, not even weakness and ridicule, can stop her from seeing his beauty. Nothing can stop her from loving him.

To understand that inner beauty exists helps us understand the wider phenomenon of beauty—or perhaps makes it more mysterious. Either way it lets us see that beauty is not governed only by objective, measurable criteria. It suggests an unexplored land, throws doubt on all our certainties, and reminds us yet again that nothing is what it seems.

### To Be Seen as We Are

When the beauty of the soul is seen, it is invariably considered to be the true identity of a person. It is not an extra layer, an exterior ornament, a chance phenomenon. This beauty, the moment it is perceived, is taken to be the real thing.

And when people are seen for who they are, they feel affirmed. This is the great secret of good psychotherapists. Often psychotherapy is a method for keeping people dependent or trapped in their own limitations. This happens when emphasis is placed on all that is weak, meanspirited, or pathological in them. They themselves are accomplices in the game, since psychotherapy is viewed as an occasion for talking about their troubles without putting themselves on the line. A diagnostic label surely does not help: On the contrary, it pushes the client further into the role of weak and sick person.

Many years ago I became aware of how psychotherapy could make a person shrink rather than grow, when I saw one of my clients in the street, without him seeing me. In our sessions he usually behaved as a weak, shy loser. Yet now I saw him strong, radiant, and energetic in the company of his friends. What was going on? Because I was intent on listening to his suffering, and because I focused on his weakness, I forgot to look for his strength and beauty, and he did nothing to show it to me.

Much the same happens in daily life. Hurry, stress, difficulties, worries, all conspire to bring out our meanest aspects. Moreover, we often secretly judge and criticize others, because doing so makes us feel stronger and more just—but that is an illusion. On the other hand, seeing someone's beauty usually takes time. And patience. And trust. And the willingness to see it. But then, we find that the people around us, whom we easily take for granted, are so multi-faceted, so much more interesting and mysterious and surprising than we ever suspected.

# The Good and the Beautiful

The beautiful and the good: What do they have to do with each other? Are they identical, like twins, or remotely affiliated, like distant cousins? Or are they total strangers? The good is what supports life, makes us feel well in body and soul, and facilitates social cohesion and concord. The beautiful has intrinsic harmony, balance, or an arrangement of forms that pleases and gives joy. We may regard them as widely different aspects of our life. But we may look at them as the same reality, expressions of each other. Think of heaven, the ultimate good: It is full of harmony and beauty. Think of hell, the house of evil: It is ugly and it stinks.

## Disgust

To understand that beauty and goodness have common roots in our psyche, it is useful to consider disgust—the ultimate form of repulsion. You may think of disgust as a disagreeable and irrelevant topic, but it is not. In fact it is an extremely interesting subject, as it shows a few intriguing facets of human nature.

Disgust is an aesthetic response: It is our reaction to ugliness in its extreme forms. Usually we feel disgust for excrement, vomit, unclean food, and decay—such as a corpse or physical sickness in its most revolting aspects. It was thought to be an instinctual reaction. After all, it is the best defense against infections and poisoning. But children do not experience disgust: so it is an acquired reaction, which we learn between the ages of four and eight. According to Paul Rozin of the University of Pennsylvania, physical disgust is a way for human beings to differentiate themselves from the animal world. Unlike animals, we keep away from rotting food, excrements, and decomposing tissues. We are civilized, we are human. Thus an aesthetic category helps us define what we believe we are.

Similarly, we experience sociomoral disgust, as Carol Nemeroff has called it, the ethical revulsion provoked by senseless cruelty toward the weak, atrocities, and other offensive attitudes and behaviors. We make a connection between what is physically repugnant and what is morally outrageous. We have already seen how the sense of taste is connected with beauty. To find evil disgusting—ugly in the extreme—is a common response in many cultures, and many languages all over the world use words denoting physical disgust also in reference to moral revulsion. This point is extremely relevant to our discussion, because it shows that moral judgment has to do with our sense of beauty and ugliness.

### A Complex Relationship

Contact with beauty makes us less angry or anxious, helps us feel whole, brings out our best qualities, leads us to happiness. In practice, this is what usually happens. But it does not *always* happen. Exceptions abound:

- sometimes beauty makes us uneasy
- it may cause us to feel inferior and miserable
- instead of increasing our self-confidence, awareness of beauty may intensify our insecurity
- rather than fulfillment, it may evoke nostalgia or regret
- instead of feeling at peace with the world, we may become more restless, even destructive

Usually beauty has a positive and integrating effect. When this does not happen, it is useful to ask why. Our relationship with beauty is sometimes disturbed and painful: Why is that so? If we want a clear answer, we need to understand our hurts, our obstacles, our fears.

In my work, for instance, I have more than once met people who felt unworthy of beauty. This problem often has to do with guilt feelings and a low self-image. Unless we honestly face these feelings, happiness remains a mirage.

For other people, beauty means the recollection of someone who is no longer in their life. In this case, beauty is a reminder of pain and memory is a prison.

Another fairly common problem is hostility toward beauty—or toward goodness, perfection, order, intelligence; this attitude often masks a rebellion against excellence.

For others still, the encounter with beauty is disturbing because it puts them in touch with a new dimension of reality. And what is new is unknown and therefore *may* upset, hurt, or trouble us.

So, beauty can be like an X-ray photograph. A test that pitilessly tells us how we feel about life and how open we are to experience. It can show us our own deep fear of surrender and the irrational, our hostility to culture and intelligence, our sense of inferiority, our unease with sensuality and pleasure. This may be a painful revelation. But it is a most useful means of showing us our weak points and where we need to work on ourselves.

Then we have the problems that are inherent in beauty. For instance, it is natural to think that an attractive person with lovely eyes and a sincere look is good. But maybe that person routinely uses her beauty to seduce and deceive. Moreover, attractive people arouse jealousy and possessiveness.

Beauty unleashes our wish for possessing objects, especially when we can realistically get our hands on them. But beautiful objects are often luxury items which incite envy, feelings of guilt, and social division. Beauty is so desirable, we want it all for ourselves. We want to put it in a safe, for fear it will be stolen. In the case of a person's physical beauty, we want to possess that person, who then becomes the main source of beauty in our life. Not surprisingly, we become jealous.

At times we feel beauty is something we must *be*, rather than have. Desirability, love, success, pleasure, are all associated with bodily beauty. That means we will do everything we can to emphasize and preserve whatever beauty we may have: Our emotional survival depends on it.

The cult of physical beauty can make some people (who believe themselves to be ugly) feel excluded and inferior to the point of self-hatred. Making physical beauty a value can distort social relationships. It makes them unjust, superficial, in a way violent, as all forms of discrimination are.

Moreover, beauty allows some people to belong to an elite—for instance, the elite of those who understand contemporary art, or have a wonderful body, or play the violin like Paganini. Others are not admitted to the elite: The in-people will feel proud and power-ful, but the out-people will feel envious and hostile.

Finally, beauty is associated with sin—the forbidden fruit—or with all that, for one reason or other, we cannot afford. Remember? "Everything I like is immoral, illegal, or fattening."

### Selling Beauty

Throughout the centuries beauty has become more and more controlled by the market, obeying the merciless rules of competition. The result is a tendency to impress the possible buyer and to generate aesthetic obsolescence. In our consumer society this trend is in dramatic crescendo. For example, consider two objects, each an expression of a different era. One is a thirteenth-century cathedral, the other a contemporary sports car. The former was built over a span of about a century. Those who planned or worked on it knew they would never live to see the final result. Theirs was a choral effort, undertaken to celebrate the glory of God. Once completed, the cathedral remains standing for centuries. A flashy sports car is made ready for the market very quickly after being designed, in order to outdo the competition; publicity grabs people's attention, selling, besides the car itself, the promise of success, an exciting lifestyle, the thrill of speed. Its lifespan? Let us say a couple of years, until the next model is on its way.

Therefore beauty is packaged so as to stand out and attract potential customers. It becomes louder and more intense. Consumer society, by commercializing beauty, has made it more seductive, as well as more widely available—but at the same time more superficial and less mysterious.

In all these ways, beauty declines. We cannot peacefully open to it. Somewhere in us attachment takes root, and therefore also anxiety, suspicion, fear. Beauty perceived in this mode is always partial and somehow diminished. Our relationship to it is uneasy. Instead of being serene and thankful, it becomes greedy and suspicious. If we do not understand the beneficial aspect of beauty, its inherent goodness, we will have a limited concept of it, and beauty will become peripheral.

Also, we will not be able to see that whoever creates ugliness commits a crime. Disfiguring the environment, for instance, is a crime, although it mostly goes unpunished. Producing software with violent content *is* a crime, even though at present in our society it is mainly a means of making big money.

### The Split Between Beauty and Goodness

On the other hand, the good, when divorced from the beautiful, is impoverished. It becomes stiff and boring. It becomes dutiful action, what we ought—but have no desire—to do. It means being a good student, the perfect father, a flawless wife, an honest worker. It is right but unattractive, useful but unexciting, proper but uninspiring. If we, instead, can see that an act of kindness or an honest stance or a courageous act has its own inherent beauty, we will make it more interesting and valuable for ourselves and everybody else.

If beauty is separated from goodness, we end up both loving and fearing beauty. Suspicion creeps in: This may be a trap. Beneath the appearance of beauty may lurk a deadly danger, so we inhibit our surrender. The most eloquent expression of ambivalence is perhaps Ulysses and the Sirens. In Homer's *Odyssey*, the sirens are monstrous beings who devour men after seducing them with their irresistible music. Ulysses knows it. He does not want to be their prey. But his curiosity is too strong—he wants to hear their music. So he asks his men to tie him to the mast, and to plug their ears with wax. As the men row, the ship sails close to the Sirens; Ulysses can hear them. Their song is marvelous and compelling. Ulysses is bewitched. He begs his men to stop and to untie him. But they cannot hear him. The ship sails on, till at last they see the bones of sailors who, seduced by the Sirens, landed on those deceptive shores and were devoured. Only later does Ulysses emerge from the spell, the only man ever to have survived the enthralling music of these monsters.

Yes, beauty does sometimes have this tempting and sinister aspect. Yet perhaps the trouble lies not in beauty, but in our relationship to it. Are we able to imagine a beauty that is unequivocally good? A beauty that does not harm, divide, exploit, or belittle? A beauty that heals, unites, empowers, makes people happier and more intelligent? When we feel that beauty is good, then we embrace it unhesitatingly, and we feel whole.

The crucial point here is that unless we see the goodness of beauty we will not understand beauty, and unless we see the beauty of goodness we will not understand goodness. If that does not happen, we have a psychological and cultural split. As psychologist James Hillman has shown, the split between beauty and goodness is deleterious and painful. We experience it as we would feel the disharmony and separation of our parents: We are fond of both and would like them to get along. Their fights and separation greatly hurt us. Our relationship with both becomes difficult, and even if we are more attached to one than to the other, we may be uncertain about our loyalty. Any hiatus within ourselves causes pain, useless effort, reduced potential. When division is overcome, we feel greater coherence, better flow of energy, greater possibilities.

Can the painful schism between beautiful and good be healed? Panaceas do not exist—only partial, gradual remedies.

First, we may become more fully conscious of our own relationship to beauty. What are our emotions, wounds, hopes, and conditioning in this relationship? Next, as we have seen in the chapter on the aesthetic range, we can learn to see more aspects of beauty in more and more situations. That way it becomes more difficult to fall into habits, fixations, or prejudices.

### Goodness Made Visible

So far we have seen the risks and the possible side effects. But one thing is certain: Beauty makes most people feel calm and harmonious. "When I come across beauty, I feel like a better person," said one of my interviewees. "I realize that it is possible to be good." This is a recurring response as well as an age-old concept. For Plato, beauty is the visible aspect of goodness. According to him, goodness makes itself beautiful in order to be recognized. Beauty is noble and harmonious, it uplifts and inspires us when we perceive it. Morally and emotionally speaking, it tunes us if we are out of tune, as if we were a musical instrument.

A thirty-year-old woman says: "I was very angry, full of dark, malevolent thoughts. It was one of those days when I was cross with everyone, felt tense and closed. At one point I found myself near a small park and sat down on a bench. There was a little lake, children were playing, birds chirping. The sound of children playing is one of the loveliest things I know. Very soon I was calm. The bad thoughts disappeared. I felt more kindly toward everyone."

Another woman expresses a similar idea in a peculiar way: "I feel that beauty ennobles me. Truly, it is as if after having seen a beautiful landscape, for example, or a good film, I feel pure, as if the debris and cobwebs and dust, and the useless bits and pieces, all vanished. I feel renewed and better disposed toward others."

A man, a computer expert, says: "All I need to do is read one of my favorite poems, or go for a walk in nature, and I feel it impossible to do harm—any act of impoliteness, any hostile word, any unpleasant attitude, is deleted, and it becomes impossible even to imagine it. This condition lasts a while. It is as though someone had deactivated spitefulness in me."

Just as ugliness is likely to make us feel unbalanced and aggressive, beauty decreases violence and restlessness. If by "good" we mean a social, nonaggressive attitude, then we have some supporting data. For instance, music lowers restlessness and aggressiveness in Alzheimer's patients. Babies whose mothers listened to Mozart's music during pregnancy are less aggressive and more tranquil. Conversely, aggressive music has violent effects. Those who go to heavy metal concerts consume more alcohol and behave more aggressively, when compared to hip-hop, reggae, or country music audiences. Several studies show that the practice of an art—music, dance, painting, drama—helps prevent and reduce juvenile delinquency, improves communication and social skills, and lowers the likelihood of dropping out of school. An experiment carried out in a gym exposed students to either disharmonious, irritating music or harmonious, serene music. Afterward, the students were asked if they would help distribute pamphlets for a charity organization. Those who had been exposed to the harmonious, serene music agreed more often than the others. They were more willing to help.

The living environment, too, is crucial. Simply by painting the ceiling of a playroom for children in more pleasant colors, researchers found that the children's readiness to cooperate had improved. Another study showed that certain characteristics of a home, such as order, security, and privacy, influence the socio-emotional health

of the child. In fact, it is an experience we all know: The arrangement of space, harmony of the décor, colors, proportion, are all
elements which can influence our emotions.

Reading a book can also calm us. Many studies show that reading therapy reduces the intensity and frequency of aggressive episodes in difficult kids. We cannot say for sure the effect is due to
the book's beauty. In reading therapy much depends on identification with the characters and on catharsis, and group-work done
after the reading is often very useful. In any case, a fairly obvious
criterion in the choices for reading therapy is that they be beautiful books.

Wilderness and nature programs, too, have proven effective
in reducing and managing aggressiveness of participants. When
they are alone amid the majesty and beauty of uncontaminated nature, aggressiveness starts to dissolve and sometimes disappears
altogether.

Last but not least, new technologies come to our aid in understanding the relation of beauty to goodness. Brain imaging can
show where the aesthetic experience is located: Indeed, when we
perceive beauty, the cerebral region that is activated is the same one
as when we make moral choices and judgments or is contiguous
to it. In other words, beauty and goodness are roommates in
our brain.

### Beauty Brings Out the Best in Us

These are just a few studies, and the concepts of beautiful and
good are so vague and generic, they will not allow us to draw conclusions. But we can say with reasonable certainty that when we
perceive beauty, whatever that is to us, it eliminates, at least temporarily, conflict and hurt. Then we are more kindly disposed to oth-

ers, we can feel empathy and understanding. And we are more likely to be fair and generous.

This is no small matter, particularly if we see its potential. *Beauty brings out the best in us.* As we shall see, it makes us more intelligent, able to understand and know more. It improves our relationships with others, with society at large, and with the environment. It makes us better human beings. So far, we have managed to put this important fact to use only minimally.

We must remember that in the studies cited in earlier chapters, the subjects were exposed to one or two episodes in which they had contact with beauty and *that* only in one or two of its many aspects. But we cannot hope to generate change, simply with a piece of music or a poem. We need to think on a large scale: What would happen if beauty were the central core of education in the human lifespan?

We may try to imagine exposing adults and kids to the arts—for instance, listening to or making music, learning to draw and paint, acting, singing; learning to see beauty in mathematical theorems; coming into contact with nature—the rhythm of waves, the wonder of the stars, the miracle of flowers, the colors and structure of leaves, and so forth. And what about the search for inner beauty in everyday life—the beauty of qualities such as gratitude, sincerity, or altruism? And the search for beauty in the mundane, in all that is obvious and maybe even boring in our lives?

All of this is already available in our culture. But it is not a central theme, and it is up to each individual to find it on his or her own. That is not enough. In order for our aesthetic intelligence not to atrophy, a much stronger engagement is needed, so that beauty, instead of an occasional pastime, or a pleasant but transient novelty, becomes the basis of our life, a value shared by all.

No one claims this is an easy task. Sometimes beauty is on the surface, before everyone's eyes. Sometimes, as we have seen, it is hidden in unexpected places. We need the patience, the dedication, and the imaginative strength to look for it.

It is also necessary to appeal to the heart, which sees and understands what is otherwise inaccessible. My son Emilio, sixteen, has two violins—one a seventeenth-century prized violin, given to him by my elderly aunt who was once a violinist. The other is a cheap assembly-line product. The difference between the two is unbelievable. The first is almost a living being and can make a beautiful sound. Emilio is lucky to have it. The second is an inert piece of junk.

But is it? Emilio uses the cheap violin when he travels, so as not to risk damaging the good one, and when we are guests at the home of my aunt, the ex-violinist, Emilio complains about the poor violin. But one day I hear a wonderful sound, a vibrato that seems to be expressing a deep and moving emotion. I cannot believe my ears— where is this wondrous sound coming from? You guessed it, from the bad violin. My aunt is giving Emilio a lesson. But at ninety-four, she is almost blind. The entire lesson consists in playing only one note in the most beautiful way possible. No exercises, tricks, or techniques. No melodies. One note, but the best note. How can Emilio draw out that beautiful sound from a humble piece of factory wood? It's simple. She said to him: Emilio, think of a girl you are in love with, then try telling her what you feel for her with only one note. The result is that, even from a dead piece of wood, Emilio magically manages to get a beautiful, moving sound.

I am astonished and curious. I ask him: Emilio, who is the girl that makes you feel such beautiful sentiments? But maybe it was enough for one day. Emilio has expressed the song of his heart, yet

he is shy of his feelings, and anyway, what business is it of mine?
Perhaps my curiosity was excessive. And so he promptly tells me
to get lost.

### Ho*ho: The Unity of the Beauty

I would like to end by speaking of the Navajo Indians. For these
people beauty is central. A person is not rich for the money he has,
but for the number of songs he knows. The artist is not an eccentric
living on the edge of society, but is the norm. As the anthropologist
Gary Witherspoon says in his excellent book, *Language and Art in
the Navajo Universe*, for the Navajo the creation of beauty and the
embodiment of oneself in beauty are the highest achievement and
the destiny of each human being. The experience of beauty is at
once "intellectual, emotional, moral, aesthetic, and biological."
They have a rich production of carpets, their most important craft,
as well as music, sand painting, vases, moccasins, baskets, paintings,
and silversmith craft.

The Navajo language uses the word *hoxho*, which means health,
beauty, goodness, harmony, and happiness, all at once. Here the
dualism between the beautiful and the good, prevalent in our culture, disappears. Beautiful and good are the same thing. And so also
success and happiness. The prefix "ho" means whole and infinite,
and thus gives the idea of harmony with the environment and the
universe. Navajo thought does not make any distinction between
humans and nature. In this culture people are encouraged continually to walk amid beauty, speak in beauty, act in beauty, and live in
beauty.

That is an example we may want to think about.

# Beauty Is Primary

A baby a few months old (therefore with no cultural conditioning) looks at faces projected on a screen. Some of the faces were chosen as beautiful by a large number of adults. The baby looks at all the faces, but his gaze lingers on the beautiful ones. When two images are shown side by side, one beautiful and the other not, he concentrates on the former. The baby invariably opts for the beautiful face! According to J. H. Langlois, who designed this experiment, this means that beauty is not in the eye of the beholder and is not dependent on taste or fashion. On the contrary, it is objective, the same for everyone, beyond personal preferences and cultural or social influences. It is inherent in the very structure of our nervous system. How else can you explain that tiny babies reliably choose the same way as most adults?

The essence of this experiment, in my opinion, is that appreciation of beauty is an immediate point of reference. It precedes thought, education, life experiences, and contact with other people. It is a given, a primary fact of our being.

Beauty enhances and improves our life—making it deeper, more pleasant, and stimulating: Everybody agrees on this point. But there is more: It not only betters our life, but forms its very foundation. It is primary—a vital need, like food and air and sleep.

Beauty has been, from the beginning, the compass that helps us find our way. Think about what you care most about: a person, an activity, a place, whatever you like. Then try to show me that beauty is *not* central to your choice, that it has *nothing* to do with it. I bet you cannot.

The child-aesthete of this experiment (that is, all of us) gradually grows up. His aesthetic orientation toward life does not die. Perhaps it is repressed or forgotten, but never altogether extinguished. In fact, it determines his aspirations and choices: of games, interests, friends, clothes, house, job, entertainment—anything which falls within his range of conditioning and possibilities. Everybody, to some extent, and more or less consciously, has since childhood been a seeker of beauty.

We could say that our moral choices are aesthetic, too. The child has grown up, he is now a man. He is faced with the possibility, for example, of getting his hands on a large sum of money without being caught. He knows that this theft will cause innocent people to suffer and that he stands to gain a lot. What will he do? Or, he has to choose between telling the truth and lying, between his own interests and those of the community, between doing a thorough job or a messy one, between hostility and friendliness, or between recycling garbage or, when nobody is watching, dumping it.

### Meaning

In all the choices life throws us, one usually stands out as the right one, and it is also felt as the most beautiful. If we choose that one, our conscience will be at peace, and we will not have the unpleasant aftertaste of knowing we have made an ugly choice. As the great Russian poet and Nobel Prize–winner Joseph Brodsky said: "Aesthetics is the mother of ethics; the categories of 'good' and 'bad' are, first and foremost, aesthetic ones . . . The tender babe who cries and rejects the stranger or who, on the contrary, reaches out to him, does so instinctively, making an aesthetic choice, not a moral one."

We have already seen how beauty is the factor that stimulates our joy of living. One further and complementary explanation we can give for why beauty is so vital for us is that it is a guarantee that life is not a senseless series of happenings, nor meaningless chaos, but has order and significance. It is what makes us truly human and founds civilization in the broadest sense.

Everything we see around us is destined to die or disintegrate: This is entropy, a measure of disorder and loss of sense. It is a terrifying fact, because it devalues and empties all that we do, all that we stand for. We try to think about decadence and death as little as possible, because it dismays and frightens us. But anxiety over this subject lurks in the unconscious and urges us to seek a remedy. Thus our life becomes a constant search for order just where we are continuously threatened by precariousness, chaos, and dissolution. Through beauty we discover that order is possible, that life has sense, and that one splendid moment can stop time and conquer death.

Let us imagine a city: A hideous city, where no order exists, only disharmony and ugliness. Houses and roads have been built chaotically. Big highways run all over, carrying the anonymous noise of traffic; there are no parks, the walls are covered with graffiti, garbage is visible on every street corner, degradation reigns everywhere, and smog pollutes the air. The planning of this town takes no regard of people, their needs and dreams. A sense of impersonality and alienation pervades it, so that even after we have visited it, we still feel its disharmony inside us.

Now imagine a beautiful town—with lakes and streams, parks and tree-lined avenues, a clear organization of streets, buildings that reflect our loveliest dreams. It is a city built for the dwellers, not the exploiters. It has a main square, harmonious, functional roads organized according to a single intelligent principle. Living there gives a feeling of inner harmony. It is easier—we feel part of the environment in which we move. It is a welcoming, guiding, and protecting scenario.

To live with or without beauty is like living in one or the other of these two cities. They reflect our inner structures: In the one case, strong and harmonious; in the other, weak and disorderly. To live with or without beauty also means to inhabit a world with meaning or one with only selfishness, insecurity, abuse. Beauty becomes synonymous with what we feel is right and good. Disharmony of shape and sound represents our inner fragmentation and discord.

## The Evolutionary Advantages

Beauty is primary because it comes from long ago. In many ways beauty is woven into our evolutionary history. Let us see how this is so. Many of us naturally and spontaneously admire the talent that produces beauty, whether it be a violinist playing a virtuoso piece, or the artisan who blows glass in Venice before a load of tourists, or an ice-skater performing a dance, or the novelist who enchants us with her use of words, or the Olympic diver whose acrobatic movements we love to watch in slow motion.

Why is it that talent in its many forms arouses our admiration, to the point of making us at times think it is divine? The answer seems obvious. Those who evoke our aesthetic sentiment are always welcome. If they can do it with unusual ability, we are even more enthusiastic. But there is another reason why we feel so euphoric, a reason rooted in our evolution.

In recent years evolutionary psychology has often asked: What is the meaning of our search for beauty, a longing we see in all times and cultures? What adaptive value does it offer? Our preference for beauty has evidently been useful in the course of our evolution or it would not be part of our psychological makeup.

The simplest answer comes from research into sexual behavior: We look for a mate who is beautiful, because that signifies youth, strength, health. This potential mate is fit for reproduction, for finding food, and for taking care of the young. And we like people who are not only beautiful, but also intelligent and skillful. Talents make for evolutionary advantage, and they extend to all sorts of intelligence and skills: It is the creativeness and resourcefulness in someone who sculpts wood, sings, plays a musical instrument, or dances—these are all signs that tell us: I can manage to survive in a hostile and dangerous world, I can take care of you and have children who are healthy and intelligent like me. I can give shape and sense to our lives. This is the thesis held by Geoffrey Miller in his book *The Mating Mind*.

That is, according to Miller, why we are so fascinated by excellence in any field. True, this is a partial explanation, because beauty may not be difficult or complex or require exceptional ability. Moreover, not everything that is hard is beautiful. And yet the fact remains that we are fascinated by talent, and this probably shows the extent to which beauty is rooted in humanity's history, how it has been part of us from the beginning. We are aesthetic animals.

Now we will see an alternative explanation. But in order to understand it we must go back to children and their innate need to bond with their mothers. It is no coincidence that a connection exists between beauty and the first relationship with the mother: The expression of the face is essential. Four-month-old babies prefer photographs of people looking directly at them to photos of the same people looking away. In another experiment, when mothers were asked to look impassively at their babies, the babies reacted with agitation and crying, yet recovered immediately as soon as their mothers smiled at them. I do not hesitate to call this an aesthetic experiment.

The ethnologist Ellen Dissanayake ascribes our aesthetic sensibility to our longing for mutuality—that is, our organism's inherent need for relationship with another, evident from early infancy. This is what gave rise to lullabies, rhythms, songs, and "baby talk"—the mother's musical language found in all cultures. They are all experiences related to the child's pleasure and sense of safety. According to Dissanayake, mutuality is one of the four basic psychobiological needs that generate our need for art. The other needs are: the sense of belonging to a group, the need to understand and create meaning, the need to make artifacts with our hands and thus to show our competence. Dissanayake examines cave paintings, decorations on utensils, dances and ceremonies, body ornaments, ritual clothing, music and song, statues, architecture, and games, and she shows how the different arts are intrinsic to our physiology and to human life. Whereas for Miller the relevance of beauty is born of male competition, for Dissanayake it originates in sociality and the need to demonstrate competence. These are very different, yet not mutually exclusive, explanations.

Music in particular can help us understand beauty's ancient

roots. We may think of it as an art which humanity has gradually created, developing musical instruments and the capacity to play over a span of several thousands years. This has always been the common belief. But according to Steven Mithen of the University of Reading, music is even more fundamentally steeped in our body and evolution. According to him, making music with song and dance was crucial for the survival of hominids—long before the beginning of human culture and civilization. In his book *The Singing Neanderthals*, based on the study of our anatomy and neurology and on archeological findings, Mithen holds the thesis that the musicality of our ancestors began when they became bipedal— about 1.8 million years ago. Hands were freed from their walking function and became instrumental for finding, gathering, and breaking food, and thus also for hammering. The evolution of the brain received a powerful impulse from this new development, and the first rhythms came into being. Also, erect posture produced an anatomical change, by which the spinal bone marrow no longer entered the cranial box from the back, but had to enter from below, and this meant that the larynx was lowered, the vocal cords became longer and therefore able to produce less shrill, more melodious and varied sounds: Thus the first songs began. We are musical organisms, we are born with rhythm and melody in our DNA. Music, song, and dance have been essential in our bonding in groups, and this social competence has given great advantage to our capacity to survive.

Few things are as deeply rooted in our organism as rhythm. I realized this a while ago when I was giving a course at the school where I teach. I was on the upper floor, a pleasant room from where you enjoy a beautiful view of an olive grove. The group was receptive, the workshop was going well. At one point I heard: *Bumm!* A loud, dull, decisive sound. It did not take long for me to understand. On the floor below was my colleague, a drum enthusiast. Whenever possible he uses drums in his courses. *Bumm! Bumm!* We could not help but hear the rhythmic sound. It was not deafening— on the contrary. But you could hear it. As if by magic, my students started tapping the rhythm with their heels, hands, or heads. They were all well-meaning and wanted to keep paying attention, but the rhythm took over. Their organisms responded to it, whether they liked it or not. I could feel the group sliding away from my control. It was more powerful than any concept I could mention, any subject, no matter how fascinating. *Bumm! Bumm! Bumm!* I got by as best I could and after a while the drumming stopped. We were relieved. But it had lasted long enough for me to realize how overpowering the ancient call of rhythm can be.

And what of the figurative arts? Imagine you are entering a cave. You must make your way in the dark, in mud, in the damp, through narrow, sometimes oppressive passageways, further and further underground, for hundreds of meters. At some point on the rocky walls you find paintings that represent various kinds of animals in stylized form: bison, lions, rhinoceroses, horses, as well as regular geometrical figures. According to David Lewis-Williams's *The Mind in the Cave*, cave art expresses the visionary experiences of our progenitors. They showed beauty in a secret, secluded place and they expressed the sacredness of life—its terrifying and fascinating mystery. Painting has been with us since the beginning of time.

In cave art we find testimony of another ancient art form: bodily decoration. I confess that for a long time I had a moralistically suspicious attitude toward makeup. It seemed to me a way of hiding who you are. And yet no. Makeup is the manifestion of the universal tendency to paint, decorate the body, of the pleasure of inventing new forms of attractiveness. It is a true artistic manifestion. From Australasia to the Americas, from Africa to India, from China to Japan to Indonesia, from clowns to carnival masks to punk, there is no place where you cannot find some form of body painting. Its immediate goals are several: to take on the powers of an animal, declare social standing, defend against evil spirits, proclaim and pass on values, attract a mate. The deep motivation is to create and celebrate beauty, sometimes with astounding colors and visionary shapes. In this case, too, we see that beauty is born together with the birth of humanity.

The same can be said of literature, if by this we mean storytelling. What is more fascinating than listening to a story? This, too, is a universal passion, which started with the discovery and management of fire and the development of language. Many now say that the creation and telling of stories is an adaptive activity. All the peoples of the Earth, even those apparently most primitive, tell and listen to stories. Those who could not or did not want to, died out. This activity has had a huge advantage for the development of our mind and personality: It trains us to understand others and put ourselves in their shoes, to think up different ways of facing a situation, and to explain the world around us. There could be no better exercise for our brain. Some studies even show that people who read books are happier than those who do not. Here, too, we see how the search for and creation of beauty are part of our being, a primary survival tool.

### Aesthetic Animals

Though it may be too soon to say so with certainty, it seems that many animals are interested in the perception and creation of beauty. Perhaps we humans are not the only aesthetic creatures. The fact that till a short time ago animals were studied more for their problem-solving ability than for their aesthetic sense highlights our culture's prejudice about animals—and about beauty! But we now know that chimpanzees, when given paintbrushes, have a great time painting and often protest if interrupted. Elephants, too, paint, holding the brush with their trunk. Birds sing not only to mark territory or attract a mate. Some of them, such as the magpie, in fact, sing just for themselves, as when we sing in the shower. Furthermore, some birds have a phenomenal memory—the brown thrasher (*Toxostoma rufum*), an American sparrowlike bird, can recognize more than two thousand types of song. All this does not necessarily show that animals have an aesthetic sense—but it gets pretty close.

The most famous example of an aesthetic animal is the bower bird, an apparently insignificant little bird that lives on the islands north of Australia. In this habitat, food is plentiful, so the ability to procure it is not an evolutionary advantage. But beauty is: The bower bird builds a little house according to the most rigorous architectural rules. Then it fills the structure with small colored stones, twigs, feathers, berries, the iridescent husks of insects, all arranged in an orderly and attractive manner. If someone changes the pattern, the bower bird will put things back the way they were before. It is all done to attract the female, who will choose a nest of her liking.

The bower bird creates beauty. Other life-forms already have it: Flowers, butterflies, and birds take advantage of their spectacular beauty of form and color to attract a mate and reproduce. To be aware that beauty is not a human prerogative, but on the contrary is present and relevant in so many animal and vegetable species, allows us to see that it is not a chance whim of our history, but one of its basic themes.

## Hardwired to Seek Beauty

A better understanding of how beauty is part of our deep structure comes from human ethology, the science that studies human behavior as one would study the behavior of any other animal. The ethologist Irenäus Eibl-Eibesfeldt, author of the formidable *The Biology of Behavior: The Basis of Human Ethology*, has studied the last tribal populations still living in a natural state. According to him there is a universal preference in the human species for big eyes, small, delicate noses, high cheekbones, a wide smile, a well-developed skull, and a nonprotruding chin—all the features which differentiate us from the other primates. These preferences have been the main factor in the natural selection of the traits in our actual appearance. The search for and choice of beauty has helped us to differentiate ourselves from similar species. We have been guided by an aesthetic model, which has led us to the present refinement of our physical traits. The search for beauty has literally made us human.

In our pleasure at a beautiful landscape, we can also find traces of our evolutionary origins: Why are we attracted, as a few studies and countless calendars from all over the world testify, to natural scenes replete with flowers and greenery and blue skies with a few white clouds? Better still if we can see the landscape with a wide perspective, while at the same time trees, cliffs, rivers, or other barriers give us a sense of comfort and protection. The answer is easy: Because we are attracted to places which promise fertility, well-being, and safety. All these considerations show us we are, as evolutionary psychologist Denis Dutton expressed it, "hardwired to seek beauty."

The evolutionary hypothesis about beauty is convincing, even if it cannot give a complete and coherent explanation—but then, who can? It is nevertheless true that besides beautiful, young people with symmetrical faces, we also love old and asymmetrical ones. And besides the places full of lush, green plants, colored flowers, and water courses, other natural places that are dead and desolate may also give us a strong sense of beauty—like the Naimibia desert with its expanse of dry sand, dotted here and there with blackened trees, in the midst of surreal emptiness.

The mystery of beauty will perhaps never be definitively elucidated. But more and more we are realizing how *vital* it is. The joy it can give is ancient. Each time we experience the aesthetic sentiment, we are in contact with the deepest roots of our history, with a process that has accompanied us in our evolution and made us human.

All these data and hypotheses I find very interesting for understanding the centrality of beauty in our lives. But what convinces me most is another thing: It is the evidence I see with my own eyes or feel inside myself. When I see a person in touch with beauty, I see it is a reaction of her whole organism. I see her pulsate, shine, blossom. I immediately see that enjoyment of beauty is a basic aspect of our being—like breath, food, sex. When it is I who have an experience of beauty, I am straightaway aware of it: The happiness evoked is elementary, spontaneous, pure, and physical. The well-being it brings is comparable to the all-encompassing relief we experience when we are thirsty and we drink, when we are exhausted and we sleep, when we feel lonely and we meet our beloved.

This is why, when beauty is missing, we feel its lack as an unpleasant and even painful condition, although our uneasiness often is unconscious and opaque. This is why beauty makes us feel happier to be in the world. One woman, for example, says: "I was at a street corner. It had just rained. There had been a wild storm and the street was full of large puddles. The air was clear and gave the sensation of newness and cleanliness you sometimes get after a storm—as if life were beginning anew in that moment. As I was waiting for the light to change to green, I was looking at a big puddle that reflected buildings and a bit of sky. I have always loved reflections in puddles. Suddenly a car passed slowly in front of me. It did not splash me, but the image in the puddle, so clear and perfect, was fragmented into a myriad of images and flickering reflections. It felt like the world was dissolving in that moment, revealing its illusory, dreamlike nature. Then slowly, before my enchanted eyes, the puddle once again became a calm mirror. And the real world quietly, faithfully, recomposed itself as before. Seeing this humble spectacle, I felt great joy and pleasure. I was happy and grateful to be in this world.

"It was a banal chance event. Yet then I saw that I had rediscovered the beauty I had forgotten. And beauty is anything but banal. I saw that I cannot live without it."

### A Vital Need

We cannot do without beauty. If we do not have it, we die—at least psychologically.

To live without beauty means, from this point of view, to be deprived of oxygen. Then we will breathe with difficulty, pant, gasp, die. To live without beauty, because we are incapable of seeing it around us, and thus to think we live in a world in which it does not exist or is not possible, will lead to desperation.

And if this criterion is forgotten, we will live in a world that makes no sense. No longer is there good or bad, beautiful or ugly. Moral indifference reigns, and all values are reduced to zero. Without our inner compass, we live in a disorderly, arbitrary world, where absurdity, incoherence, and brute force are the law.

An individual who is devoid of aesthetic intelligence feels weak and his personality has no binding principle. To have no access to beauty is like being in a foreign country without a map: You do not know where you are and cannot decide where to go. You are confused and disoriented. Belief in the existence of beauty, in its availability and value, characterizes (when it is not dictatorial and intolerant) a healthy and strong personality. In short: Beauty is primary.

To sum up: We have seen how deeply interwoven beauty is with our evolutionary makeup, with our organism, with the very foundations of our psyche. Some of the theoretical models we have seen are widely diverse, yet they do not contradict one another. In the vast maze of hypotheses about the human condition, beauty pops up almost at every turn.

Beauty, as we have seen, is often ephemeral and uncertain, at times linked to antisocial tendencies, arrogance, and greed. But ask anyone you want if he associates beauty with good or evil, with love or hate: Very probably he will say "with good" and "with love." Beauty is what we want for ourselves and the people dear to us. It is what seems supremely desirable and is inextricably linked to the survival of our species, as well as to our own individual emotional survival. This is why beauty has to do, though not in a perfect and complete way, with goodness, with love, and with the heart.

FIVE

~❧~

# KNOWLEDGE

# Mind and Beauty

I am in a meadow filled with crocuses. These delicate, shy flowers open for only a couple of hours a day, and last about two weeks. To see them again, I will have to wait a whole year. They are extraordinarily beautiful: Their petals are violet with tiny white streaks, the center is yellow (pistils) and orange (stamens)—a perfect color combination. These are the year's first flowers. It is still cold, and, here and there, a few patches of snow remind me that the demons of winter have just left. The crocuses announce that spring is coming. I am here to photograph them.

I love photographing flowers. It helps me see and know them better. I look in the viewfinder and see them floating in the camera screen, framed by black: an otherwordly vision. I use a microscopic lens that lets me focus on a small part of the flower and see the tiniest details.

There are about a thousand crocuses in this field, and I have arrived at the moment when they are opening to the weak February sunlight. I am looking for the flower with perfect petals and the richest center. I look at them one by one. I am in no hurry. They are all immensely beautiful and different from one another: Each one is an individual. It is like looking at a thousand faces in a crowd, one at a time. I choose the loveliest ones, then finally what seems to me the most beautiful of all. I focus and observe, speechless. The petals show subtle, elegant arabesques. The pollen appears as golden spheres. The stamens are an opulent labyrinth, soft and fleshy, almost an invitation to dive in and lose yourself.

If you are not careful, you can trample these little flowers. But if you stop and watch closely, you find a treasure. Looking at this vision, I feel awe. Even though I have seen many crocuses before, they seem to me each time as beautiful as ever. In some undefinable way, I feel I know and understand some truth that is extremely hard to communicate. If I had to put it into words, I would express it this way: We live in an intelligent universe, teeming with creativity and genius, endlessly inventing beautiful forms. This is one of the many examples of natural beauty in its most common forms. I think of the dancing lines of a shell, clouds that constantly take new shapes, the delicate matrix of a dandelion, a spider's web, the colors and patterns on butterflies' wings, a field of wild blue chicory flowers in late summer.

### The Intelligence of Nature

I believe I understand what Leonardo da Vinci meant when he wrote in his notes that nature is the teacher of teachers. These beautiful forms do not evoke only emotions in us. They teach us intelligent harmony. We know exactly what it is, even if we cannot put it into words. It is a way of being that enters us, propagates in our inner world, infusing it with beauty. It is the blessing of intelligence.

Indeed, when we are with an intelligent person, if all goes well, through a beneficial resonance we feel more intelligent ourselves. We rise to her level. Being in nature similarly allows us to absorb the intelligence of beauty.

So what does nature teach us? Nature's lesson is not academic, and does not, it seems to me, have a content we can explicitly describe. It teaches us something much deeper and more important. It shows us that we live in a world supported by harmonious order, that we live in a *cosmos*—from the Greek word for order. This order silently organizes our thoughts and emotions. After having contemplated a landscape or flower, after having touched the bark of a tree or looked at the dewdrops on a blade of grass or the magical line of a mountain range, we feel different. We feel that our world has gained, as if by resonance, an inner coherence.

Put this way, it may sound simplistic and vague. Yet at the moment when I perceive this reality, it is certain knowledge, clear and precise. The hard part is to express in words what is beyond words. We can point to it, but cannot truly describe it—unless we are talented poets.

### Ineffable Knowing

In my interviews about the aesthetic experience, I ask: Do you think you understand something you were not able to grasp before? Does beauty give you new knowledge? The answer is immediately and invariably yes. But if I ask for an account of this knowledge, then uncertainty creeps in, even for the people who are most articulate and in touch with their inner world. They run up against the ineffable.

Often the responses are general, or seem to describe emotions: It is like going home or being in a world alive and permeated with intelligence; fear vanishes; I feel one with what I am contemplating;

time stops; goodness really exists; war is crazy; we are beautiful inside; I feel an infinite peace.

Here the trouble starts, because it is easy to confuse an emotion with a thought. I know this from professional experience. I ask a person what emotion he feels, and he tells me what he thinks. I ask him what he thinks, and he tells me how he feels. If we stick to the age-old distinction between thought and feeling, we are at a loss. This distinction has, for thousands of years, molded our way of understanding the psyche and of evaluating our decisions. On the one hand, we have the mind: cold, analytical, objective. On the other, we have emotion: hot, fluid, irrational. If emotion wins, we may be blind. If reason wins, we risk being cold and out of touch.

This distinction is sensible and true. But it leaves out a basic point: Emotions themselves are a way of knowing. We have survived and evolved as a species precisely because our decisions are not cold, logical choices, but emotional preferences mixed with instinctive judgments. Emotions contain information. Consider this recent discovery: Neurons, brain cells, have been discovered also in the heart. Just as thoughts are rarely devoid of a feeling component, maybe emotions are, after all, carriers of knowledge. The heart, as Pascal reminded us, has its reasons, of which reason knows nothing.

It would be wrong to dismiss the aesthetic experience as just a series of pleasant emotions. Knowledge comes into it, too; in fact, is at its very core. But the truths beauty reveals to us are subtle, hard to pinpoint and hold on to. In a Jewish story, a rabbi is overcome with the yearning to learn the language of animals: He wants to start with birds, then move on to all other animals; he hopes he will be able to hear even what worms underground are saying to one another and also plants and flowers. In this way, he thinks, being in touch with all creation, he will be closer to God. At one point the miracle happens. His teacher, a wise and holy man, infuses him with this magical power. The two of them are traveling through a wood in a carriage, when suddenly the birds' chirping takes on a new and surprising dimension, and the rabbi, pricking his ear, understands what they are saying to one another. It is a magnificent gift, as suddenly everything acquires a beauty and depth he never knew before. But soon the rabbi loses it. In his longing to know, he becomes distracted and therefore does not hear his teacher's words anymore. The songs of birds lose their depth, and become as he had always heard them—simple sounds without meaning.

## Another Mode

Perhaps we can say that beauty gives a new dimension to our knowledge. It is like learning the language of birds in this story. We know more about reality. It is an ineffable knowing, hard to define and easily lost, yet real and concrete. If you are not convinced, try this thought experiment. Imagine this scenario: One morning you wake up and, like the rabbi who no longer understood the language of birds, you no longer perceive beauty. Music has become just sound. Flowers are colored outgrowths. Masterpieces of painting are no more than blotches of color on the canvas. You do not see in your beloved the beauty that once enchanted you. All beauty is reduced to zero. If you can imagine life this way, proceed with phase two, and ask yourself: Besides the emotion of beauty, have I also lost any information about the world? Have I lost essential knowledge?

In a way this is a general rule: Every experience teaches us something. If I travel by train, for instance, I learn how to buy and punch a ticket, take the right train, find the least crowded compartment, recognize the countryside I see through the window. I realize I should not expect too much of the food they serve, and I learn when to get off, and so on. If I go to the hospital, I learn about human suffering and sickness, find out how to tell the doctors from the nurses and one ward from another, I get acquainted with the hospital timetable and rituals, etc.

If I have an experience of beauty, it is itself a vehicle for a new understanding. Beethoven told Bettina von Brentano that his music could open us to the superior world of knowledge. The stained-glass windows in cathedrals were made for the purpose of teaching sacred history to illiterate people in an environment that would evoke admiration and awe. In the ragas of Indian classical music, the pauses are as important as the music, because they represent timelessness. In Islamic art, it is prohibited to represent God or the human being in concrete form: You see only geometric patterns of great beauty, which serve to untie the mind's knots, to stop attention from being fixed on this or that entity, and thus leave the mind open to the divine. All that is knowledge.

You may object that if every experience teaches itself, then it is useless to say that beauty brings knowledge. It would be more exact to say that *any* experience, in fact living itself, meeting new people and situations, brings knowledge.

But beauty is a vehicle for knowledge because it delights us. An Indian story may help us see the point. Two men go to a mango plantation. They want to start a business and buy it, but first they need to know more about it. One gets right down to counting the mangos, rows of trees, number of trees per row, number of mangos per tree, estimating the average weight of the fruit. It is a lengthy calculation, and he gives it his full attention. The second man instead makes friends with the orchard owner. Then he picks a mango from a tree and eats it. Exquisite! He enjoys its intoxicating fragrance, the sweet taste, the fleshy texture, feels it melt in his mouth. For a few timeless moments, nothing else exists for him but the mango with its sensory intensity; he is totally absorbed in it, forgets figures, business, calculations, prospects, and so on. Now, which of the two men got to know the essence of the mango?

Which one knew more directly, intimately, and completely what a mango is? (Not: Who did better business? That is another, and an open, question.) Doubtless the one who smelled it and tasted it knows it better. The Indian sage Ramakrishna used this story to illustrate the difference between discursive, rational knowledge on the one hand, and contemplative knowing on the other.

Knowledge given by beauty is not based on notions. It is not about facts, as in, what are the fluctuations of oil prices or when is the next solar eclipse? It is an indescribable, intuitive knowledge, much more intense and all-encompassing, that makes us feel part of life, draws us nearer to the essence of what we know, leads us to understanding through direct involvement. It is a knowledge that transforms us.

The experience of beauty teaches itself, as all experience does. But its content, by definition, is much more passionate, alive, and intimate than other kinds. It uplifts us, frees us, shows us happiness. Thus it brings more substance with it. Thomas Mann wrote that beauty is the sensible form of the spirit. This statement belongs to the philosophical and literary tradition according to which truth and beauty are interdependent, if not identical. Remember? "Beauty is truth, truth beauty." Keats's statement would be hard to prove. However, as a psychologist, I can tell that most people who have an experience of beauty come out of it not only regenerated by waves of joyful feelings, but also endowed with a sense of a deeper knowing. A woman reminisces about giving birth. She was tired, but happy. Lying on the bed next to her baby, it seemed to her she knew life's great mystery: "I knew everything." I asked her what she knew. "I knew all there was to know."

### Cognitive Facilitation

Would you agree, then? Beauty transmits knowledge. Even if you do not agree, you may accept that beauty *facilitates* knowledge. It is like a catalyst that makes mental processes more fluid. In fact, it enriches and multiplies them. If I truly enjoy beauty, I feel happier and more open, a disposition which facilitates learning and thinking. This is well known to those who teach art in schools. I am not talking about art history—that is just an academic subject—but the creation and appreciation of art. Students who actually recite Shakespeare know it better than those who simply read it. The ones who play Mozart know him better than those who study music history from a book. Students who practice the art of pictorial composition in their own painting, better understand Raphael, Vermeer, or Matisse, than the ones who just read about them. And that is not all. According to a recent study in the United States, schools which include in the curriculum at least 20 to 30 percent art appreciation and expression have much better academic results in *all* subjects.

Here is another example: The scholastic system that gets the best results from students is the Hungarian one, according to a study carried out in seventeen countries on fourteen-year-old students in scientific high schools. This success was attributed to the fact that, in Hungary, from kindergarten through to the end of schooling, teachers use the Kodaly Method of musical education. In this system, pupils learn a musical instrument and sing every single school day. The other two populations which show excellent scholastic education are the Dutch and the Japanese—and in both cases music has a crucial place in the curriculum.

A longitudinal study at Boston College compared two groups of children, who were tested and found on average to be equal on a variety of scores. Then one group of children took a course in music (the Suzuki Method for violin and piano), while the other did no musical training. After three years, the children in the music group were superior to the others, not just in manual capacity and musical perception, but also in mathematical and verbal performance and in their total cerebral mass.

It is not only a matter of music, however. What about drama, dance, painting, sculpture, pottery, writing? In the United States, the schools that have given a significant role to active teaching of the arts have had academic results 31 to 50 percent better than other schools, as measured by the SAT. Moreover, the personal capacities and qualities developed in artistic expression—such as greater sensitivity and self-confidence, respect for others, ability to collaborate—extend to all subjects, not just the artistic ones.

According to Dee Dickinson of New Horizons for Learning, the arts are important because they cross ethnic and social barriers. They are symbolic systems, as important as letters and numbers. They integrate body, mind, and spirit and offer students the chance to express themselves. They facilitate "peak or flow experiences"; that is, expansion of consciousness. They stimulate the motivation to learn. They develop both independence and collaboration, and thus improve socialization. They exercise intellectual abilities, such as analysis, synthesis, and problem-solving.

Here, too, we face a difficulty we have repeatedly met. To what extent are these extraordinary findings the result of activating multiple capacities—the skill of communicating, manual ability, sensitivity to small differences, self-expression, and contact with one's emotions? And how much depends, instead, on contact with beauty? We cannot discount this basic fact: To cultivate the arts means to learn to use our body in new ways, acquire new abilities, create new neural circuits. But it would be a mistake to forget that it all happens for the sake of enjoying and expressing beauty—that all this activity is dominated and colored by aesthetic appreciation. We do better not to try to separate one factor from the other. In real life and experience, all aspects are inextricably linked. The essential point here is that the cultivation and expression of beauty produces stimulating effects on our cognitive abilities.

### The Beauty of Ideas

Beauty and knowledge are linked in yet another way. Certain ideas strike us as beautiful. They are beautiful because they are simple, strong, and elegant. Thus they can touch the lives of many people and greatly improve them. Great ideas strike us with their innovative power. They underlie our way of thinking and living, and they become the leading forces of our own and other cultures.

Consider, for example, the Christian idea of loving one's neighbor; or nirvana as liberation from attachment and ignorance; or the idea of God as a mind that governs the universe; or the key role of men and women as expressed by humanism; or the idea of democracy; or the Copernican revolution; or the importance and value of reason for dispelling ignorance and clarifying issues; or the idea of evolution through the natural selection of the best adapted; or that of the unconscious—the human mind as an iceberg whose large underwater mass determines our thoughts and behaviors. We can all think of the guiding ideas that have most influenced us.

We find these leading ideas powerful in their simplicity, and beautiful in their revolutionary strength. For instance, one woman, Martha, was fascinated by the ideas expressed in the Magna Carta. In this document King John of England in 1215 expressed in writing a number of liberties and rights of the individual citizen, such as personal liberty and habeas corpus: No one on Earth is allowed arbitrarily to impinge on your freedom. This idea is a pillar of Western civilization and it changed forever the way in which we perceive ourselves and one another. Martha went to see the original in England in Salisbury Cathedral, and was deeply moved by this experience: "Since I was a little girl I have been passionate about human rights. I was interested in the French Revolution and the American Constitution. The feeling of human rights that go beyond any concrete material situation . . . When I was face-to-face with the original of the Magna Carta, I felt in touch with a dimension that did not have to do only with me, but with eternity."

### Mathematical Beauty

For some people, mathemathics is another name for beauty. They admire its abstraction and elegance. Bertrand Russell experienced ecstasy before the beauty of mathematics: "Mathematics, rightly viewed, possesses not only truth, but supreme beauty—a beauty cold and austere, like that of sculpture, without appeal to any part of our weaker nature, without the gorgeous trappings of painting or music, yet sublimely pure, and capable of a stern perfection such as only the greatest art can show. The true spirit of delight, the exaltation, the sense of being more than Man, which is the touchstone of the highest excellence, is to be found in mathematics as surely as poetry."

Alex, in his forties, has a passion for mathematics, in fact, he cannot even conceive himself without it, because he sees it as the structure of thought and perceives it everywhere—in the shapes of a tree's bark or in music, even in the rules of ethics. To help me understand the beauty of mathematics, he comes up with this easy example: When Carl Friedrich Gauss, the greatest mathematician of the nineteenth century, was still a child in elementary school, the teacher, in order to silence the pupils, asked them to add up all the natural numbers between 1 and 100. All students started patiently to add $1 + 2 + 3$ and so on: a long, boring task. But Gauss immediately saw that to get the answer you could couple the numbers that added up to 101; that is, $100 + 1$, $99 + 2$, $98 + 3$, and so on. There are fifty such couples. Therefore, $50 \times 101 = 5050$. The formula is $n(n + 1)/2$. That is simplicity. That is elegance. Alex says: "The feeling of perceiving beauty in mathematics is like getting a joke. It's very simple, there is this change in your mind where you cannot not get it anymore. It feels like the release in an orgasm. I don't know if that's specifc about mathematics, but there is something more beautiful about mathematics than anything else, and I think it has to do with the fact that the objects that induce it are as abstract as possible. There is an abstraction in mathematics that makes this feeling not tied to any perception, it's pure feeling. Almost all feeling of beauty is tied with perception, but mathematics, especially if you go deeper and deeper in what is perceived as greater and greater beauty, is not tied with perception. There is no vision, no sound, no tactile feeling, but there is still something beautiful.

"When I see something that is very deep and very beautiful, it makes me feel small. It's like being at the top of the mountain; I am above everything else, but I shrink down and the city below becomes vast before me and I have this feeling of being one in ten million. If I step up, there are more people and I get smaller. And the same in the vastness and the beauty of the desert. In mathematics it's much bigger, you can get really small."

The Oscar for mathematical beauty perhaps goes to the Golden Mean, the geometric proportion found in the temples of Ancient Greece, in the growth of leaves, in the structure of shells and galaxies. Other often-quoted classic examples are: the demonstration of the Pythagorean theorem with four right-angled triangles drawn in the square—the work of Indian mathematician Bhaskara (born 1114); the method adopted by Eratosthenes for calculating the circumference of the Earth by measuring the shadow cast by the sun at the same moment in Alexandria and in Syene; Archimedes' theorem, according to which the volume of a sphere is two-thirds that of the smallest cylinder that contains it; the marvel of the dodecahedron—the perfect solid, seen by Pythagoreans as the symbol of the universe; Euclid's demonstration that prime numbers are infinite; the application of coordinates to ellipses and parabolas, realized by Descartes.

H. E. Huntley, who wrote the book *The Divine Proportion: A Study in Mathematical Beauty*, says that there are eight ingredients in the experience of beauty in mathematics: resolution of uncertainty, realization of an expectation, surprise, perception of unsuspected relationships, brevity, unity in diversity, sensorial pleasure (in geometry), and a sense of wonder.

And according to Burkard Polster, author of *Q.E.D.: Beauty in Mathematical Proof*, the synonym for beauty and truth in mathematics is the proof: *quod erat demostrandum*, as one wished to prove. That is the moment when everything squares—when, seeing the ineluctable necessity of mathematical thought, one reaches the apex of aesthetic enjoyment.

Beauty can also be an indicator. Do you remember that favorite children's game "hot and cold"? The child looks for a hidden object. You know where it is, and you guide the child with clues. "Cold" means she is far, "hot" means she is close. Beauty at times does the same with us, as if it were saying: "Hot, hot, you are getting close to a truth." Many scientists have adopted beauty as a guide. Einstein, for example, when he had to evaluate a theory, would ask himself whether God would have made the universe that way. One of his most common phrases in this regard was "This is too good for God to have overlooked!"

On the other hand, beauty is not a foolproof guarantee, and we cannot go the extreme of saying that beauty and truth coincide, even if it sounds good. Facts are sometimes ugly, irregular, unpleasant, and simply will not conform to our aesthetic theories. To believe in a theory simply because we like it is a kind of intellectual dishonesty.

A number of scientists have been led by beauty to formulate their theories; sometimes successfully, sometimes not. Some theories are beautiful but not true. Wonderful theories have been murdered by ugly facts. Nevertheless, beauty has a cognitive dimension: It lets us know something we did not know before. And knowledge has an aesthetic aspect: What is true emanates, in the eyes of many, an indescribable beauty.

### Contemplation

When appreciation of beauty extends in time and gains in substance, we have contemplation. Contemplation first of all means not going anywhere: not being under pressure, not having to do anything, not being distracted or pursued by anyone. You are undisturbed and quiet. Second, it requires a complete lack of purpose.

Not in the sense of futility: This is a positive lack. You contemplate a landscape, for example—see gold-tinted, multiform clouds, a colorful flowery meadow. In that moment, the vision gives you happiness. You do not think of trying to possess the meadow, nor wanting to prolong the moment of beauty forever. You do not fear this moment will end, and no one is trying to force you to love flowers and clouds. You just enjoy, as the man enjoyed the mango in the Indian story. You do not form hypotheses, but are passive and receptive—you receive the field of flowers. You have all the time in the world. You are absorbed by the vision, as if under a spell. You pay attention without effort. Perhaps a sense of sacredness pervades you. Above all, you become convinced that this is a way of total and profound knowledge, higher than any other form.

Someone may judge this attitude with suspicion: It is lazy, unproductive, even asocial. Indeed, contemplation is often regarded with suspicion in our active, extroverted society. It is not cultivated, nor taught in schools. It is neither praised nor rewarded, it earns neither money nor fame. And yet we could consider contemplation as the other side of action. It is the charging of our physical and spiritual batteries. Animals do it, too, in their own way. Watch your cat when it just sits there, looking in the void, just being. Maybe, as a culture, we are forgetting to recharge our batteries, and we have to learn anew the profound art of contemplation.

Ananda Coomaraswamy, the great Indian scholar who, within his tradition, wrote various essays on beauty, kept highly visible in his study a quotation from Thomas Aquinas: *Pulchritudo splendor veritatis* (beauty is the splendor of truth), meaning: All that is true is not neutral, but shines. Beauty is the glowing evidence of truth.

According to the Indian tradition (as interpreted by Coomaraswamy), the beauty, *rasa*, which we perceive in contemplation resides not in what we see or feel. It is not in the notes of a sonata or the verses of a poem, not in the brushstrokes of a canvas, the fiery sunset, or reflections of the moon on the sea. These are not beautiful *in themselves*. In actuality, they are just impersonal air vibrations, wavelengths, lines, and colors. They simply take us back to the indescribable beauty that is within us: our true, timeless Self, the Atman. They show us who we are and have forgotten we are. External and internal stimuli are pointers that show us a beauty which is already there waiting.

Some pointers work better than others. Also, they work at some times and not others. And certain pointers work better for some people than for others. But the result is the same. Swept up in the jumble of our lives, we have forgotten who we are, what we have inside. We have been hypnotized by a complex and distracting dream. The moon, the sunset, painting, poetry, music, take us back to this basic truth. The ecstasy they evoke in the depth of our being is nothing else but our truest Self. They reveal to us that which we have always been.

# Revelation

The soft sound of music from the room downstairs reaches my ears. My wife, Vivien, is playing the piano. The sound is barely audible, because she is shy about it, afraid of making mistakes, and tries to play so no one will hear her.

I strain to listen. The piece she is playing—or trying to play—is familiar to me. She plays it over and over again, slowly. Now I hear it, now I don't. Then I recognize it: It is one of Bach's Two Voice Inventions.

I know this music, I have heard it countless times. Vivien plays piano reasonably well, but with this piece she is still unsure, still learning and needing to repeat it. Yet that is just where I find beauty, because I am hearing a Bach Invention gradually taking shape, and it is like recognizing an old friend, a piece of music I love. In this moment it seems more beautiful to me than if it were played by a talented concert pianist.

## Gradual Unveiling

How is it possible that hearing this piece played with uncertainty, interruptions, repetitions, perhaps a few mistakes, and just audible, lets me appreciate its beauty even more? Naturally it is because I love Vivien. But the main reason is gradual revelation. As when I watch a landscape slowly emerging from the mist or the moon disclosing itself from behind clouds, I am puzzled and amazed by this music while I slowly make it out. To hear it reconstructed bit by bit allows me to appreciate it more deeply.

I reflect on the work of Professor George Balan, founder of musicosophy, a form of musical meditation invented for a profound and complete learning and appreciation of music. Balan invites you to listen to a piece many times and to single out the main themes. Goethe said that architecture is petrified music; for Balan, music is liquefied architecture. To discern its inner structure helps us perceive its beauty. We have more than a fleeting, emotional response. The truly beautiful is not manifest, but is the inner structure of a work we slowly learn to recognize.

One form of music especially helps us in this kind of meditative reflection. It is the variation. The composer takes a theme, at times not even his own, then begins to play with it, rewriting it in different forms. Beethoven, for example, began with a fairly banal theme that an alcoholic musician, Anton Diabelli, had given to him and to others, with the request for variations. Beethoven took this theme as his starting point and composed twenty-eight variations, each with a different style and atmosphere. In fact, one of them is supposed to represent a drunk trying to walk without falling over, but slipping at every step: Diabelli himself. Beethoven takes you through one realm after another, exploring the whole range of human feelings and possibilities, from the earthly to the sublime.

Variations often appeal to children, because they are a novel way for them to understand music. I remember when my son Emilio was six and already started learning the violin. His teacher played him the theme of "Ah, vous dirai-je, Maman," better known to us now as the nursery rhyme "Twinkle, Twinkle Little Star." Not everyone knows that Mozart wrote a series of variations for piano on this theme. When Emilio heard his teacher play the theme on the violin, he reacted indignantly: "This is baby music." But the teacher did not stop. He went on to the first variation. Emilio was fascinated. Then he played the second variation. Emilio was amazed—he fell off the chair without even noticing. Then he climbed onto the teacher's knees so as to listen more closely. Why? In this case, too, it was because he did not merely gloss over the theme, but, despite his own pride, listened keenly to the same theme played in ever new ways.

A similar appreciation occurs when you learn about the intermediate stages of, or attempts at, a masterpiece. For instance, a famous photograph by Dorothea Lange shot in the 1930s shows a desperate unknown woman with her children. In her eyes you see pure pathos; the photo communicates her poverty and desperation. It is a photo that shakes you and touches your heart. We have other photographs of the same subject, shot immediately before. In one, the scene does not fill the frame, in another, the woman's expression is more distracted. They are not as good. But seeing them allows us to understand and admire the successful photograph; it helps us get inside the mind of the photographer. And the same happens when we can read earlier versions of a poem or see drafts of a painting. They show us the gradual construction of beauty.

### The Timing of Beauty

Consumerism has accustomed us to have easily and immediately whatever we want—and then to gulp it all down at once. In our hasty times, everything has to happen right away: Success, sex, money, knowledge, happiness—we want it *now*. No time is allowed for probing and delaying. No time for doubt, exploration, or just playing around. We are in too much of a hurry.

Maybe we have to discover again the art of being slow, because that is often the rhythm of realization and enjoyment. A distant memory comes to mind. When I was a child I went with my family to visit the United States: In those times you traveled by ship and the crossing took about a week. I remember our arrival at the port of New York. It was dawn. The ship sailed slowly, almost solemnly. At first you could see only dark, indistinct shapes. Then, out of the mist, the skyscrapers and the Statue of Liberty emerged, an unforgettable sight. And it was all the more beautiful because it did not appear suddenly. No instant gratification there. After seven days of sea, we saw these dreamlike, shadowy forms gradually reveal themselves to us in all their majesty.

Myth, even in its elementary aspects, accomplishes a similar task, as when a story about the gods explains the seasons following one another or the constellation of stars or when a myth sees in the dark spots on the moon the form of a woman, a frog, a hare, or a forest, as several traditions have had it. There is no haste in this process. The fortune-teller, who sees in the tea leaves at the bottom of a cup, an airplane, a butterfly, or the letter J, is also looking for coherent forms. In the pleasure of recognition, the "Aha!" by which we perceive a coherent form where before we saw only chaos, brain scientist Vilayanur Ramachandran sees a fundamental principle of the aesthetic experience. According to Ramachandran, the visual system enjoys finding hidden objects, just like the brain likes solving problems. Indeed the beautiful is not always a given. We must discover it in the vast riddle of existence.

All this takes time. And the chance to slow down is like widening the cracks through which beauty can pass and reach us. It is the same old task: Beauty is all around us, but how can we let it reach us?

One way is simply to lengthen time. Hurry usually obliterates all forms of beauty. Instead, it is a matter of listening harder, looking for longer, tasting slowly. That is when we understand more.

Yes, beauty is the adversary of hurry and flurry. It can be known in its intimacy. It wants to show us how it is generated, what it is made of. It can reveal itself to us and have us know it well. We have to assemble and dismantle it, so we can see how it is held together. We have to look at each and every one of its parts. Seeing earlier tries, failures, and imitations, may also help. Will we give it as much time as is needed to know it as it deserves to be known?

## Pattern Recognition

Knowledge emerges gradually, creates connections, uncovers links, as when we connect the numbered dots in the well-known children's puzzle. From an initial series of incomprehensible signs on a page, we make out a precise figure—a house, or a horse, or a man with a balloon. This is hardly an experience of beauty, but we can see in an elementary way how gradual revelation of meaning gives pleasure. It is the same with camouflaged animals. At first you see only a leaf, then you also see a butterfly, whose wings reproduce the leaf patterns. Or among a bunch of twigs, it turns out one of them is an insect. In the recognition of such forms we feel a curious sense of enjoyment.

The ability to recognize forms, connections, and structures is basic to the human brain. It is thanks to this capacity, among others, that we have survived and evolved. We are naturally attracted to recognizable shapes, and chaos appeals less to us—in fact, it irritates or disorients us. Chaos theory has even managed to find order in chaos! The ability to distinguish forms helped us, for instance, to find animals' tracks or discover the right path, to estimate distance, to read a face. In the program of research into extraterrestrial intelligence, the same principle applies: Astronomers try to find a coherent structure in the radio waves coming to us from the remotest sites of the universe. Do any of the sounds have order, coherence? They could signal the presence of an intelligent mind in the cosmos. Structure equals mind, equals meaning, equals life.

Beauty is not synonymous with coherent structure and information. Some structures are banal and repetitive. But often the forms of nature, besides having their own coherence and order, are beautiful. A booklet titled *Li*, a Chinese word roughly meaning dynamic form, illustrates some of the forms you can find in nature. The book is full of black-and-white illustrations: swirls, such as fingerprints or the mazes in the brain; angles and corners, as in crystals and snowflakes; ramifications, as in rivers, trees, algae, and neurons; concentric circles, as in a tree-trunk cross-section, rocks like agate, or ripples in water; the broken lines of cracks in dried mud or in rocks; fern-like formations, as in ice-crystals and some fossils; labyrinths, as in eddies, whirlpools, or some crystals; net-formations, like dragonfly wings or spiderwebs; waves, such as those in desert sand dunes formed by the wind; spots, like the skin of the leopard or some frogs, toads, and insects or the eggs of some birds; cloud-like shapes, spirals, or polygons. And many more. The book shows us the great variety and beauty of shapes in nature, and how our mind enjoys contemplating these forms.

Sometimes we find beauty in the most unexpected forms. One day I went to pick up an X-ray of my son Jonathan's hand. I walked out into the street and opened the envelope. I looked at the transparent radiogram and saw the invisible structure of the hand. Spellbound by its diaphanous beauty, I ignored the radiographer's report. I could clearly see the hand with all the tiny finger bones, and the palm, where the bones looked like separate little islands floating in space. The entire hand in its architectural structure was exquisitely elegant.

Probably the X-rays of all hands are beautiful. But right then I was thinking that Jonathan plays the piano, and plays it quite well. His specialty is his touch, precise and sensitive. This thought made the X-ray seem even more beautiful to me. It was as if the secret of his touch came from the delicacy of those little bones, so accurately and intelligently structured. It seemed to me a work of engineering genius, not just Jonathan's hand, but the human hand in general. I could see how, in a way, it summarized our evolution. For us humans, unique among primates, the thumb is in opposition to the other fingers, and this adaptation has allowed us to achieve many feats that would otherwise have been impossible, such as making tools or manipulating food. This development has stimulated our practical intelligence and allowed us to take the quantum jump that made us, for better or worse, fully human. I thought, too, of many other activities to which the human hand can turn itself: stroking, squeezing, giving pleasure or pain, writing, molding clay, chiseling and drawing, performing surgery or transmitting healing energy, cooking or doing conjuring tricks. In this X-ray image, I could see millions of years of our evolution and intelligence.

Did these thoughts amplify my experience of beauty? Maybe. But what struck me most was that this X-ray revealed to me the inner structure of the body as a world of pure harmony. My thoughts went back to when Jonathan was still in the womb. We went to do an ultrasound and saw him for the first time: the structure of his body, skull, spinal column, pelvis, limbs—all perfect, in that field of sound waves that showed us forms which were otherwise hidden.

I know that scientific photography is not done with the purpose of amazing or pleasing us, or evoking emotion, but solely to show what is there. And it is as if this lack of effort on the part of the photographer freed her in her job of documenting reality as it is: photos of shells, flowers and leaves, crystals, cells and tissues, planets and galaxies.

### Hidden Beauty

Some pictures go further. They are not trying to create a work of art, but are more consciously aesthetic. They seek to extract hidden beauty. For example, the work of cymatics: This is the photography of materialized sound waves. A sound is made to pass through minute sand particles, which then assume ordered forms, beautiful and complex. Or else the photographic study of vortexes, showing us water's ever-changing forms, reminding us why the great Lao Tse saw in water the clearest manifestation of the Tao, the divine principle of the universe. The work of Masaru Emoto also comes to mind. His idea is that water reacts differently to different stimuli. He exposes it to Mozart's music, for example, or to the word "peace," crystallizes it instantly into ice, then photographs it, obtaining shapes of great beauty. But if he exposes it to disharmonious or offensive music or to words evoking hate and evil, the crystallized structures are chaotic and disharmonious. We think also of the harmonograph, a kind of pendulum that responds to musical vibrations by drawing ever-new, and at times striking, harmonious forms.

More examples. Rie Takahashi, biologist at UCLA and pianist, has invented (with the help of Jeffrey Miller and Frank Pettit) software that translates the molecular structure of proteins into music. Apparently, this music is very beautiful—some of it is reminiscent of Chopin—unless they are proteins associated with a disease. Huntington's disease, for instance, generates an unpleasant music, comparable to a broken record. In this perspective, life's code is musical, and beauty is at the heart of living matter.

At other times sounds already exist, they just have to be amplified. An American geologist, J. T. Bullitt, has created software that transforms the Earth's vibrations (too weak and slow to be perceived by the human ear) into audible sounds: seismic waves, "terrestrial tides," oceanic storms. Once he simultaneously reproduced the sounds of the seismic stations all over the world and accelerated them by 250. The whole procedure was reproduced by a ring of eight loudspeakers: the Deep Earth Dome. He wanted to simulate the impression of being at the center of the Earth. "I could not believe what I was hearing! It felt as though I could embrace the entire planet." Bullitt thinks this is the *musica universalis* some philosophers refer to.

Finally, an art form can help us understand the mathematical structure of nature. A Harvard mathematician, Peter Lu, traveling in Uzbekistan, visited the country's mosques, which are filled with visionary geometric figures. These forms show all seventeen types of symmetry. Lu visited the Darb-i Imam mosque, built in 1453. The tesserae of its mosaics, made of stars and polygons, are extremely beautiful, and they can be generated infinite times, creating ever-new decorations. Lu realized that at the basis of these creations are mathematical concepts, unknown in the West up to thirty years ago. These concepts can also be used to describe the structure of quasicrystals—mineral formations that do not follow the laws of classic crystallography.

If I think about all these examples, I understand why, looking at the X-ray of Jonathan's hand, I felt transported to a world of translucent beauty. It is because I penetrated matter and found that its inner structure is beautiful. Matter has weight, you can touch it; sometimes it is inert, thick, opaque. But in the X-ray I saw its essence—its secret, intelligent structure. This took me for a few moments out of time to an immaterial, ethereal world. Then a car horn tooted at me, and I realized I was in the middle of the street. Suddenly I was back in the concrete world, the one where you may get run over. But in my inner world I was still carrying that luminous harmony—and the regenerating belief that beauty is inherent in the invisible structure of the world.

Here is another episode. This time I was on a flight from Tokyo to Rome, and at some stage I was flying over northern Russia, at 11,000 meters. Watching from the window, I saw rivers, lakes, forests, and fields. Everything was frozen and appeared in various shades of white and gray—no colors.

I found it an enchanted landscape. It was as if an ingenious mind were at play, inventing forms: wondrous doodles, a phantasmagoria never repeating itself. It looked like a show created by a highly original imagination, like a complex and fascinating story. But not a story in words: It was abstract, and there were surprising happenings, plots and subplots, characters, encounters, loves, battles, and coups de theatre. It was a story impossible to tell in words. But it was every bit as interesting as one you might read in a novel or see in a film.

To see things from high up gives us a different perspective. It is likely that down there, on this icy land, lived people who had no idea what their home looked like from above. They saw it from up close, with all its imperfections and problems. There was probably beauty in that, too, maybe much beauty—a lovely countryside, people with goodness and inner values, works of art. For me, at that moment on the plane, all that was invisible. What I saw was forms from far away. It was a colder kind of beauty, because it had nothing to do with relationship. I had no connection with the people down there. This vision of forms from a distance allowed me to see a new aspect of beauty, a beauty that is reaching us as impersonal patterns, abstracted from human life.

### Meaning and Order

We are, all of us, seeking sense, or, to put it more technically, we are looking for negentropy. Negentropy, or negative entropy or syntropy, is a measure of order and meaning. It is the synonym of information. It is easy to understand. Take the words of a poem, mix them up randomly, and the result will be a jumble of words: Entropy is increased. Take each of the words, mix up the letters, and you get a nonsensical mess: Entropy is further increased. Put it back together again, and you increase syntropy.

We are all after syntropy; we want to give sense and order to what we perceive. This helps us orient ourselves, understand where we are, where we want to go, what we can and wish to do. Few situations are as unpleasant as the panic in which we do not know where we are, do not remember who we are, and cannot make sense of our present situation.

Information, we have seen, is not the same thing as beauty, but makes it more likely and meaningful. To give, or give back, form or meaning to something that does not have it is pleasurable and often takes an aesthetic note. Luciano, a thirty-year-old man, looks for all kinds of objects that people throw in the garbage or forget in the attic: He considers them priceless treasures. He takes these objects, and, with patience and method, fully restores them. Not because he wants to sell them, but just for the fun of it. Lately, for instance, he has been busy with a child's bicycle, a toy school-bench, an early-twentieth-century birdcage, a coffee machine, a TV set from the 1970s, and his great passion, the mythical Vespa scooter from the 1950s. His wish is to bring forgotten objects back to life. He is not interested in the secondhand stalls that sell restored objects. What he likes is the process of gradually bringing out the original form from material that has been wrecked or has decayed.

Someone gave him, for instance, a pair of skiis from the 1940s, complete with bamboo sticks, found in a cellar that had been flooded in 1966 by the Arno: "It was a big job. First I had to clean them of all the dry mud, then I sandpapered them to get back to the original wood, then I treated them for termites, and finally varnished them, keeping their original color; and I oiled the old leather bindings with linseed oil. It gave me huge satisfaction: They are a beautiful object, far more so than modern skiis, because they are handmade, wood only, and with their own true pattern—no stickers or ads.

"The whole job took place while my father was very ill. He had been in the hospital for some months. For me to restore these skiis was like hoping that my father would also have a new life. As I worked on them, I would think of him."

Sometimes the hidden structure is in the mind, though it may seem to be in the surrounding environment. A sixty-year-old man, a jazz pianist, one day suddenly perceived as strikingly beautiful the faces of people in a workshop. What impressed him most was that they were all perfectly symmetrical, classically and impersonally beautiful, like Greek statues: "*So* beautiful," he says emphatically, "but the aesthetics of symmetry had taken away their personal beauty." Oddly, he no longer recognized these people by their faces, but only by their clothes. Among them was his wife, in whom he saw a beauty he had never seen before. Only later did he find out he had had a stroke, which had opened a pathway to a fresh perception of beauty. This makes us wonder whether there really was symmetry and the stroke helped him see it by inhibiting certain perceptive habits, or whether it was a symmetry created by the mind and superimposed on reality. Or whether it even makes sense to ask this question.

In conclusion, it all boils down to this: We can find beauty anywhere. Sometimes it is obvious, sometimes it needs some commitment on our part. Sometimes it jumps out at us suddenly, other times we come upon it slowly. To succeed in making connections, noticing structures, seeing coherence increases aesthetic pleasure, and is perhaps a necessary condition to find beauty. In that way we have a revelation. We discover a hidden aspect of the world.

Beauty comes from knowing the world around us in unexpected ways. If we think we already know all we need to know, we only end up shut in a sterile, inert, unchanging world. No prison is more oppressive than that. Better to inhabit a world where we can see the new even in the old, the banal, the rejected. No scenario could be more inspiring.

# Secret Echoes

I am in the Tuscan town of Arezzo for a lecture, and, as always, I have arrived early. Before it is time for the event, my friend and host Andrea says: "Now I will take you to one of the most beautiful squares in the world." I cannot help thinking of the greatest squares I know: Piazza del Campo in Siena, Piazza San Marco in Venice, Piazza Santissima Annunziata in Florence, Piazza San Carlo in Turin. A very high standard indeed. I am sceptical, but willingly go with him.

We reach Piazza Grande in no time at all, and straightaway I realize he is right. I had forgotten this beautiful square. It is not rigidly coherent and symmetrical, as the buildings enclosing it are all different from one another. Yet the overall effect is one of great harmony. The elements—colonnade, baptistry, houses, paving— are in concord with one another. As always happens when I am in a beautiful square, my sense of space changes. I am pervaded by a feeling of peace.

"Shall we go and say hello to Piero, too? He is nearby," says

Andrea. The Piero he means is Piero della Francesca—Andrea knows he is a favorite of mine. This great painter depicted his characters with a magnificent dignity. The story we look at in the church near the square is his most famous one: The Legend of the Cross, according to which Jesus' cross is made from the Tree of Knowledge of Good and Evil in the Garden of Eden. You see various episodes of this story, and all the characters have a wonderful meditative composure—as though they came from the square I have just seen.

Piero della Francesca's frescoes are high up on a wall. You cannot see them well without binoculars. But my familiarity with them helps a lot. Piero paints legends, his subjects exist and move in timelessness.

The Arezzo art experience apparently comes to an end, and after leaving the church, I lecture, have a quick dinner, and go to the station. But here I run into a hurdle. My train is five minutes late. After five minutes, a further delay of ten minutes is announced. After another five minutes, a fifteen-minute delay is announced, and so on until finally we have a three-hour delay. The voice giving the announcements is digital and the entire station is automated, so there is no one around to whom to complain or just talk. It is a cold night, the bar is closed because the station is being renovated. I am tired and frustrated. I have to take a different train and get off at the wrong station, returning home in the early hours of the morning. I have forgotten the square and its beauty.

But no. Next day, the square comes back to me. Without deliberately evoking it, I see it again with my inner eye. That square is closed to traffic. I find this symbolic: It is like a mental space unreachable by ugly thoughts, where harmony and serenity reign. It is working inside me, changing me, opening me to a dimension of harmony quite beyond daily frustrations, like trains that never come or impersonal stations that work like a trap.

The experience of the square, I find, has a vitality of its own. Whether I want it or not, it lives on in my inner world. It teaches me a balance beyond life's frustrations. Now I really understand the beauty of the place. Piero della Francesca's noble characters with the high Renaissance hats and solemn gait, those regal women living in the eternal present, accompany me in my life and visit me in my dreams. The square is no longer the square from real life, the one where people drop junk, where killjoys scrawl graffiti on the walls, and dogs urinate. It has become the square of the ideal town. It is a place of the spirit, to which I have been given an access I did not have before.

## Unconscious Elaboration

I have learned from my own experiences and from my interviews that the aesthetic experience often can have a delayed reaction. For instance, I usually do not know straightaway whether I like a film; I need to wait a day or two. I have noticed this is a common process. I recall seeing a documentary about Federico Fellini. It showed people leaving the cinema after seeing his film *La Dolce Vita*. The journalists asked the critics for a comment. One by one they said something like: "It is too early, we need to wait, let the experience mature." I then understood this did not happen only to me.

What happens to our memory as time moves on? We think of it as an archive, and for this reason we call the recording of computer data "memory." I am afraid it is a misleading metaphor. Imagine that the data stored in your computer have their own life. A spell changes the numbers. The texts you have written mix with each other, conjure up stories, or turn into songs. The photos become animated, then a film, the characters take trips all over the computer, start writing e-mails themselves, and the people in your address book suddenly have a will of their own and decide to play videogames. That is how a computer would work if it had human memory. That is how our unconscious works. Any experience we record does not stay the same, but interacts with other experiences, creates in us certain moods, evokes reminiscences, rouses fantasies, makes up stories. Memory is neither neutral nor mechanical, and hardly accurate—it is not like a filing cabinet of archives. Memory is a creative activity.

### Priming

Whether it is in changing behavior, modifying feeling, or altering memory, even the most banal stimulus counts. Lately, studies on priming by John Bargh and others of Yale University have managed to show us a surprising aspect of our mind. Priming consists in exposing a subject to an apparently irrelevant stimulus, which nevertheless influences his subsequent behavior. For example, I take a verbal test (without knowing anything about the aim of the experiment) which uses words that suggest old age: "elderly," "gray," "wrinkles," "lonely." When I leave the room, I will walk more slowly than those who took the same test using other words. This is because, without knowing it, I feel older. Metaphors also count. Before the experiment, the subject meets a laboratory assistant who is holding a pile of books and a paper cup of coffee. In some cases it is an iced coffee, in others, boiling hot coffee. The assistant asks the subject to help him by holding the coffee for a few moments. Of course the subject does not realize this is already part of the experiment—for him it is just a chance episode. Then the experiment officially starts: The subject has to read some information about a person and give an opinion about her. If he previously had held the hot coffee, he will think her to be less selfish and more sociable—warmer—than will those who had held the cup of cold coffee.

In another experiment, if there is a scent of detergent in the air, say, lemon-scented detergent, and the unknowing subject is given crumbly biscuits, she will be much more careful not to drop crumbs than if there is no such scent.

This research gives us a new perspective on the functioning of our unconscious. The astonishing insight here is the extent to which apparently casual and irrelevant stimuli can change our attitude. What would happen if, instead of the detergent smell, or instead of the cold coffee, another stimulus altogether were at work—a videogame where we steal cars and saw off people's arms, or, say, Beethoven's Sonata opus 111? To what extent will violent, unpleasant, shocking stimuli or, on the other hand, beautiful, calming, and harmonious ones, be able to enter our unconscious and there continue to exist and act? A man tells me: "Some time ago my friends and I stopped over in a city as we were traveling. We were all cheerful. We did not know what to do. We went to see a pornographic film. It showed people participating in an orgy. It was the most depressing experience I could imagine. The actors were evidently poor devils, their faces wore a look of false pleasure, maybe they were forced into it. There was a feeling of violence—not explicit, but a violence to human dignity. It was disgusting, and about the least erotic thing you could imagine. Afterward, that experience stayed impressed on my mind for quite a while, and interfered with my sex life. The images came back in my mind at the least appropriate moments. And yet I am not in the slightest a moralist. Even though we had not lasted more than ten minutes in the cinema, the feeling of disgust continued for several days."

This is an experience of ugliness—just for a change. In studying this kind of experience, we see how ugliness can depress and harm us, just as beauty can uplift and benefit us. What interests me most here is to highlight the fact that the experience does not end when we have had it, but, for better or worse, keeps living within us.

So an unconscious process takes place. First comes the aesthetic experience itself, the initial impressions. But that is far from the whole story. What I have seen or heard lives on. Haunting or healing, puzzling or reassuring, enlightening or shocking, its beauty goes to work. The square is not just a scenario of stone and walls, but a subjective, living entity that thrives in my inner world, taking me to a realm of perfect proportion and preternatural serenity.

The psyche, then, is alive: It changes, creates, makes connections, idealizes, assimilates, enriches itself, matures. Is this a banal statement? We all know that the psyche is in continuous motion. Yet we rarely pay attention to this aspect. We behave rather as if we were always the same. Indeed, many people, including several authorities, believe we thrive on homeostasis—the continual search for equilibrium. But is that really so? The time comes when we understand that stability is not destiny. We see it is possible to change and grow. We realize that our lives—even the dullest—are stories full of surprises, quantum leaps, stasis followed by transformations, breakthroughs to freedom. The moment we assimilate this basic fact, our own conception of ourselves and our existence changes.

## Welcoming Beauty

The experience of beauty does not stop suddenly, but goes on by itself and keeps working inside us. This is not unique to the aesthetic experience. All our experiences enter us and do not stay still, but are processed in the unconscious. They end up as part of our personal history, ultimately changing us. But some more meaningful experiences, among them those of beauty, touch a deeper vein in us and thus have immense potential.

Why experiences of beauty have such a capacity for penetration is perhaps explained by the value we attribute to them. As I have seen in my psychotherapy work, beauty, when perceived and heard, hugely affects people. The intensity and depth with which beauty strikes us can be enormous, akin to that of pain and love, perhaps the only other kinds of experience which can leave an impression of similar import. The greater the power and value of the experience, the more fully it sinks into our psyche, and the greater is the magnitude of further unconscious elaboration.

Moreover, we must consider the origin of these experiences. Often they stem from nature: The sound of waves at the sea and the scent of salt sea air, for example. Or the shape of a tree standing out against the sky. Or the iridescent colors of a dragonfly. Or a rushing stream by trees and rocks. Understandably, these perceptions leave a strong impression on us: After all, our origins are in nature.

Or else the aesthetic experience comes from art: a movie, a song, a novel. In this case, too, it is natural that we be open to an impression, that this impression does its secret, precious work inside us, and that it offers us new teachings about life and ourselves and makes us think in a new and different way. That, after all, is the more or less declared aim of art. And, as we have seen earlier in this book, art was born with the dawn of humanity.

The aesthetic experience, we have seen, also comes from the encounter with others. Here, more than anywhere else, it is clear that the impression is deep and penetrating: The beauty of a person, his or her body or soul, stimulates countless interactions and emotions. We learn about others, we *are* the others. They live in us and we in them.

Naturally, much depends on how open we are to beauty, how far we let ourselves be taken by it. In the presence of beauty, at least two attitudes, on a continuum between extremes, are possible: On the one hand, we can be closed to beauty and keep it at a distance. We might feel it brings troubling insights and changes, and we dimly sense this impact can be upsetting. It is undeniable: Beauty is a risk. We risk being vulnerable, changing in ways we dare not imagine, and this is a cause of alarm. Beauty can be uncomfortable. If we stop it in its tracks, it becomes an ornament or a piece of merchandise, at best a cultural object: A beautiful body, a flashy car, a trendy dress, an impressive painting to hang in the living room. Nothing more. Thus beauty is disempowered or fossilized.

On the other hand, it is possible to let ourselves be moved and changed by beauty. Our aesthetic intelligence opens and extends itself. This is a harder but much richer path. In my interviews I have met many people who were in touch with the ways in which beauty had changed them. Others instead spoke in abstract and philosophical terms, finding it difficult to say what had happened in them during an aesthetic experience. They had kept beauty at a safe distance.

## Context

To understand better what the experience of beauty can stimulate in us, it may be useful here to introduce the idea of context. All of us have a mental context within which we live, think, feel, act, and enter in relationship with others. It is hard to define our context, because we are often not even aware of it ourselves, and if we were, we could describe it only in a general way. The context is the matrix of all our concepts and emotions. At times I think that we might be able to describe it by a single sentence, even though it would not do justice to such a complex phenomenon. For example, my experiences could take place in a context in which "The world is dangerous, and I just have to cope" or "I have to grab everything I can" or "I cannot trust anyone" or "I am always the loser," or, on the other hand, "There is always something new to learn" or "I am here to help others" or "The world is to be enjoyed." Every context determines and colors our beliefs, choices, relationships. The context we live in can foster or hinder our experiences of beauty, and these in turn can powerfully and deeply influence it.

It has to do with how we receive and process our experiences. Let us make an analogy. Imagine you are collecting stones. You go about looking for specimens, but then you have to put them one by one in boxes made of dark glass the size of postage stamps: The stones are usually larger than these boxes, so you have to break them into smaller pieces. Once they are in, you can barely see them, and they all look alike, because you see only the outlines through a glass darkly. This is your context: It is poor and constrictive, and it does not do justice to the stones. Now imagine instead that you place your stones on spacious shelves in full view: You can then see quartzes and opals, crystals and gems, rocks with turquoise or purple veins, shale and conglomerate, fossil efflorescences and petrified wood, and so forth. A completely different stage.

How do we receive our experiences of beauty? It depends on the context. If we receive them in an unwelcoming, tight inner space, we will not have a true aesthetic experience, and so we will not be changed. If we receive them in an open context, where we let ourselves be touched and involved, then anything is possible.

Now we will look at examples of how beauty enters inside us and conditions our outlook. A fifty-year-old woman, Catherine, describes her experience of years ago. She went with her mother to see an exhibition of the Australian painter Jeffrey Smart in Sydney: "We looked at the paintings, then went outside. Looking around us, we both realized that everything seemed like a Jeffrey Smart painting. The trucks, the Harbor Bridge, the roads and highways, the skyscrapers and houses, the park. The artist had given us his very vision. We were seeing the world through his eyes." Catherine also tells me of an experience with film: "For many days after seeing the film *Schindler's List*, I would have waves of fear, sorrow, pity, though my circumstances were so different from those shown in the movie. The film was an affirmation of those feelings. Schindler was an extraordinary person—even in the black death of the Holocaust, someone was able to bring out the best in himself and others. This film reminds us that life is precarious. Life is fragile and cannot be taken for granted. Art goes to our heart and speaks truth to us."

In Catherine's examples we see how the aesthetic experience was not limited to the moment in which it occured, but sank into her, taught her something about life and the world she lived in.

Along with the feelings and perceptions comes a cognitive component, not the most intense, but perhaps the most pervasive and longest lasting, because when the intensity of the emotions is over, what we have learned stays and becomes part of our mental equipment, and we will never be the same again.

At other times someone starts from an experience that reassures and comforts him in a difficult moment—in the following example, seeing a rose in the family garden—and he thereby comes to a much vaster conclusion about life and the universe. Serge is a thirty-year-old musician: "I go back to my mother's home, into the garden, which has been there since I was a child, and there I see a perfectly shaped rose. It has just bloomed, and soon it will wilt, but while it lasts, it is perfect, amazing. Since I am in my family's home, I remember the past and my grandparents. The word that comes to mind is relief . . . Ahhhh. It is an affirmation: Everything is right, the world is good."

It may seem a regressive experience. Certainly all the elements are there: return to the mother, to the warm security of childhood, to a soft, comfortable place like a rose garden. Is this a return to prenatal ecstasy? I think it is not, at least not only, that. The belief this person reaches goes beyond a momentary sense of relief and pleasure. It is a return to the essential, to a truth as actual as the more disquieting one we saw in the previous case. Life is fragile and precarious, life is beautiful and good: two sides of the same coin. Both these people, and the next ones, have received beauty, and they let it change their context—their basic mood and underlying philosophy.

Let us now look at the example brought us by David, a man in his fifties, with a great facility for the aesthetic experience. He has extremely intense reactions to beauty. The first time he saw the Guggenheim Museum in Bilbao, the famous Frank Gehry building with walls that seem like waves and lines reminiscent of jazz, he burst out crying. That moment changed his relationship to architecture, and the ordinary buildings you can see about, seemed no more to him than big boxes, compared to the flowing forms of this masterpiece. Nature also affects him, even in its most unexpected facets: He is moved even by the charcoal skeleton of a burnt tree. And so, too, with film, literature, even food—not the fancy kind, but simple, genuine food like fruit, bread, or cheese. What moves him most of all, however, is music—gypsy, rock, jazz, classical, Indian. The first aesthetic emotion of his life happened while listening to his mother play Liszt on the piano—he started crying. Now music is his regular companion: "I feel something that starts in my stomach, rises and erupts out of my head in an explosion. It does not happen rarely, and I don't have to try. It is like a drug for me. If I am feeling lethargic or tired, for instance after eating, I listen to music and I just take off. When I am driving, I am sometimes so moved I have to stop. In those moments, I feel: Now I am ready to die. Yes, I think: Okay, now I could even die.

"I am not religious, I do not believe in God or reincarnation, but I think that if God exists, it is in these things, everywhere. If it's anywhere, it's everywhere."

David's experiences are fierce emotional shockwaves that shake him and at the same time nourish him. But the point to which he arrives is a philosophical one, it is his context. The experience of beauty for him is an extreme experience and as such it leads him to think of death and God. Here it is not about theoretical or religious beliefs, but about the context in which this person receives his experiences: A spacious and free context in which every perception of beauty can vibrate and manifest fully.

Yet another example, this time from Eugene, a professor in an

American university. He says: "There was a period when I was very depressed. My girlfriend had left me and I was the victim of a malicious lawsuit, all I owned had been sequestered and put up for auction; the situation was terrible, and meanwhile I had ruptured a disc and could not even move. I was very sad and depressed. And I could not perceive beauty. I just couldn't. Then one day I saw how beautiful the San Francisco Bay was, seen from a pier, with lights all around, and the colors of the water, the blue, and the crispness of the air. It was not the beauty that made me feel better. It was my feeling better that allowed me to see the beauty. The healing had stimulated my capacity to see beauty. I saw the bay, and I thought: 'It's beautiful,' and then: 'Wonderful, I am thinking there is something beautiful; it has not happened to me for months.' I had seen the same things before, but I had not seen their beauty."

Eugene has high emotional responsiveness, but his center of gravity is his mind, which is remarkably capable. In this case, beauty was linked to transformation only a posteriori. It is not beauty that had made change possible, but gradual healing from the traumas he had undergone that had permitted him to perceive beauty again. He regarded perception of beauty as an indicator of healing.

### Process

In conclusion: Aesthetic experiences have a history, which we can elucidate in three seamless phases. First, we have *impact*: How full and happy it will be depends on how open, alert, and sensitive we are; it will also depend on our bias and disposition. We meet beauty: How will we receive it? Second, we have *involvement*: We have been invited to dance: Will we accept or refuse? Will we let beauty penetrate to the core or will we stop it at the periphery? Third, we have *elaboration*: A process has started; the more we have let beauty in, the more it becomes part of our system and the more it will affect and transform our perceptions, beliefs, outlook, and inner points of reference. All three phases are a function of our aesthetic intelligence. It could all happen in a few seconds, in days, or in years.

I began with the experience of a piazza. I will end the same way. This time I am in Mantova. The kind lady who receives me says: "I will take you to see one of the most beautiful squares in Italy." After traveling alongside the lake, we go into Piazza Sordello, a square of great beauty and distinction. It was worth taking this trip just to see it. As at other times, this piazza keeps working in me, coming back into my mind. I feel its space inside me. Some squares make you feel on guard, in others you expect perhaps a big meeting, in others still you feel more rigid and solemn. In this piazza I feel welcomed and *held*. I am happy in a space of culture and harmony, the best context for meeting other human beings. I realize that a piazza is not a passive container, but gives shape to what I am and think. This one is a form where I feel at ease, where I can be my best self. And I realize yet again that the experience of beauty is not an event which starts and then stops, but a process that continues in time and whose echo perhaps never ends. Beauty is not an entity. It is a story.

# Transcendence

Imagine going out on a pleasant summer night. Away from city lights and sounds, away from all interference created by human activity. You reach a place where the air is clean and crisp, the sky truly dark. You can see the Milky Way and thousands of stars, so close and real, almost palpable, and yet so far. Suddenly you are transported to a scale which is incomparably bigger than usual, and the ordinary cares of every day drop away like forgotten dreams. You know these distant worlds may sustain lifeforms and intelligence. And you realize that you are part of the cosmos. The silence, the mystery, the beauty, evoke in you a sense of awe.

## Cosmic Perspective

Alas, this possibility is neither likely nor easy. We are surrounded by smog and city lights. It is symbolic: Our own productions separate us from the magnificence of the starry sky, just as our own fantasies, inner rumblings, and paranoias cut us off from the immense resources of our inner cosmos.

But when we are lucky, it happens. We see the splendid vision, we feel ennobled and uplifted. The starry sky, among the many aesthetic experiences, is universal and primordial. A jazz piece, a play, the elegance of skyscrapers, for instance, are all stimuli that can evoke beauty, but we can live a lifetime without ever having known them. The night sky, however, is an experience we share with all human beings who ever existed. We watch the same stars humans on Earth have been seeing for thousands of years. It is an archetypal experience.

From this perspective, it is perhaps easier to understand the absurdity of treating depression and other problems simply with pharmaceuticals. No doubt, they may be useful in certain predicaments. But offer them to those who see the world as a wasteland or a nightmare, and you promote a lie: Life is squalid or horrible, but at least you can anesthesize yourself. The problem is not solved till we realize we actually live in a universe full of splendor and marvel, inside and outside of us, far and near, on a small and on a grand scale.

By looking at the stars we can repossess our true citizenship. We are not born in Rome, Tokyo, or New York. We are born in a vast universe, our body is made up of atoms which once, very long ago, formed the stars. We are made of stars. Lifting our eyes every now and then to the sky reminds us of who we are and what is our real home.

### The Prison of the Ego

Awe and wonder, however, are an unusual state. We are usually prisoners of a smaller, narrower world. For instance, we are trapped in the traffic and running late, or someone has spoken rudely to us and we are offended; a persistent new pain makes us fear we are ill; we stain a piece of clothing that was special to us, and we are upset;

our cell phone rings in the middle of a concert; we are tormented by the feeling of having offended a person we love. Sometimes we are so locked in our immediate experience, and so overcome by it, that we identify ourselves thoroughly with what is happening. There is no escape: Anger, fear, hurry is all that exists in that moment. Perhaps later we will laugh at our reaction, or will have forgotten it altogether. But right at that moment we are totally at its mercy.

The universe is immense in time and space. Our mind, instead, may be prisoner of an infinitely smaller field. And while it is, our experience in that moment monopolizes our awareness. As much as we might try to free ourselves, it will keep a hold on us. Of course, some people are particularly prone to being captured and dominated by their own experience, whereas others manage to distance and free themselves more easily. Neurosis can perhaps be defined as the inability to go beyond the emotions or thoughts of the moment. *We take ourselves too seriously*. And there begins our weariness, dissatisfaction, unhappiness.

In working with my clients (and with myself) I often have the impression that these emotions are held tightly inside us, like so many objects forcibly shoved into a wardrobe, so crowded and without room, the wardrobe is about to explode. I then help my clients take their emotions, one by one, out of the wardrobe: They are creased and shabby, but if we air them a bit, they take on quite a different aspect. They just needed some space.

Stress is often felt as a lack of time. But it can also be described as a lack of space. Our emotions are imprisoned inside us, crowded to the point of suffocation, as though we were afraid that if we freed them, they would get us into trouble. I think the word "magnanimous," literally great of soul, really means: the capacity to air one's emotions and ideas, to hold a vast, free space inside ourselves, and thus to have some distance from our own experiences, to transcend them, if we wish. When we manage this skill, our perspective is much wider and calmer, we can see far, understand others' predicaments, think about grand and beautiful ideas. And we can at last stop worrying so much.

Our private universe, however beautiful and rich, if it is a closed system sooner or later becomes oppressive. If I am under house arrest, so to speak, I feel more inadequate, angrier, weaker, flatter, sadder. If I am shut in my own world, I tend to expect others to conform to me, think like me, be like me. I find it impossible to realize that maybe they think and feel another way. I see them as strangers or enemies. My entire life is reduced to my fantasies, needs, schemes, and horrors.

For this reason we can say that the ability to get out of ourselves is a vital skill. We must be able, so to speak, to leave our own living quarters. To transcend. Otherwise we are in trouble.

### Self-forgeting

Drinking, taking drugs, or otherwise dulling our senses, are ways of forgetting ourselves. But these are harmful, clumsy methods, though the need that generates them is entirely healthy and legitimate.

Or we can distract ourselves. The whole entertainment industry knows this very well. We need a holiday from ourselves. But distraction and transcendence are two different things. In distraction, you do get out of yourself, but when you come back you are more or less the same as before. It is just airing the prison a little. It is better than nothing (perhaps), but not enough. In transcendence you gain new knowledge, capabilities, energy. Then you return— and you are different.

Various ways can lead us out of our own world. One, for instance, is loving. Authentic, healthy love, free of jealousy and possessiveness, takes us outside ourselves. Service to others, embracing an ideal—like justice or freedom—prayer, reflection, and meditation, are all ways of going beyond our prison walls.

Beauty is yet another way, perhaps the easiest. In beauty we forget ourselves. And here we should clarify a semantic ambiguity. In transcendence we manage to forget ourselves, in the sense of being free of our usual ways of thinking and feeling. But we can also say that we go back to our true self, which years of mistaken habits have caused us to forget. We abandon what is inessential and go back to the essence. This experience can at times give us a sense of novelty and strangeness. But the result is that we find our true being. We come back home at last.

It is as though we had all along been in the company of someone who continually complained, expressed opinions, worries, fantasies, ambitions, dreams, fears, anger, gossip, requests, scorn. This was our immediate circle. And this person went on and on talking like this, wearing us out without respite. That person is our ego. Wouldn't it be nice sometimes to take a holiday and go to a place where this uninterrupted monologue ceases and we can take a break?

Sometimes being in the midst of wilderness evokes the feeling of remoteness from the world of ordinary living. A fifty-year-old man speaks about his experience on the island of Stromboli: "I was climbing the slopes of the volcano, alone. It was hard going. I crossed a stretch of black sand. It took many steps just to go a few meters, because the sand slowed me down. At first I had the feeling of what a struggle life is. You walk and walk and stay in the same place. After half an hour I was exhausted. I had gone twenty-five meters. I had no strength left, so I collapsed on the sand. In doing so, I turned to face another direction, and I saw the cliff with the sheer canyons falling away—they had never been crossed by human beings; I saw the terraced slopes abandoned decades ago; then the stretch of tiny houses, little white dots, the town, the coastline, the first strip of sea near the shore, then the intense color of the outer sea, with a beautiful, diffused light. It was of extraordinary beauty, and peace, perhaps also because the silence was total, and I could hear the beating of the birds' wings.

"It had a profound sensation of inner detachment from everyday life. It was as if all the elements that formed my living habits had been broken down. I saw everything from very high up, far away, and all that lay below was so remote as to give me a feeling of beauty."

### The Eternal Now

The main way in which transcendence manifests is in a different perception of time. Usually we are captive of time: Days, hours, minutes, seconds, pass quickly, inexorably, and devour our life, or else they seem to pass too slowly, especially when we are bored. But in moments of awe, time stops. It disappears. It is not that, happy and satisfied and suspended in emptiness, we say: Time does not exist anymore. We realize it only afterward. It is like a spell. And when the magic ends, we still feel its beneficial effects, after returning, more or less sharply, to normality.

Music often has this effect. Sometimes, after a good concert, for a fraction of a second, the people in the audience remain silent. It is as if they needed a moment to recover from the enchantment. They have been carried away by the music, time has stopped. Now they realize where they are, back in their seats in the concert hall, next to other members of the audience. They have returned from space travel and need a moment to come back into themselves. Then they break out in applause, full of enthusiasm and gratitude.

I remember a concert series many years ago: One man had the unpleasant habit of starting to clap when the music had not quite ended, perhaps to show everybody he knew the piece so well that he could safely start clapping, half a second before the end. But I think he did not understand at all what was going on. He did not let himself be spellbound by the magic. He was not absorbed in eternity. He had not transcended one bit.

In my group seminars I sometimes work on the perception of time. It is most fulfilling. As Larry Dossey has shown in his book *Space, Time and Medicine*, time is a cultural construction, and our contemporary perception of it was formed in the eighteenth century with the invention of the pendulum clock. It is an exact time, dictatorial and inexorable, and growing even more so. In England, I have seen a sign on trains: Doors will close half a minute before the designated time so the train can depart punctually. In America at some crossroads, the green lights for crossing the street flash numbers menacingly: ten more seconds to cross the street, nine . . . eight . . . In Japan, a train driver allegedly committed suicide for the shame of arriving one minute late. In Venice, funerals on the water, a poignantly beautiful and solemn tradition, are now given a definite time limit. In all countries, people are walking (and cars are driving) faster and faster. And so on. Time constructed like this becomes a trap. This is time-sickness, responsible for numerous pathologies, primarily hypertension.

Luckily there is another time, that of the agricultural societies, which is cyclic, approximate, and calmer: the time of day and night, the moon, the seasons, the cycles of the stars, which seem to move on the celestial vault. When we construct our time in this way, we feel more at peace, are open to what is truly important and beautiful, because we are not running after anything.

More important still, it is only when we are in this time frame, natural and tranquil, that we can glimpse eternity. While we are living in artificial time, dominated by the ticking of the clock, life is rougher and more constricted.

We cannot, of course, refuse altogether the relentless rhythm of our contemporary age. But it may be useful to realize what it does to us and what we can do about it. Also, we must face contradictions and ambivalences. On the one hand, precision is a sign of consideration and thoughtfulness. In my work I have always placed importance on punctuality. It seems to me a sign of respect toward others and oneself, as even one minute can be decisive. When you think about it, how long does an intuition take? A fraction of a second. When in a workshop I take a break, I say to the group, for instance: We will reconvene at three minutes past two. Everybody laughs, but at three minutes past two we are all there. Am I, too, victim of time-sickness? Certainly yes. Can we reconcile punctuality with a more serene and organic way of experiencing time? Perhaps, but we have to work on it.

In any case, nature's time is closer than contemporary time to transcendence and eternity. Eternity is not time that goes on forever. If you think about it, that would be a nightmare. Eternity is the suspension of time. We have all had an inkling of it. Our consciousness was totally absorbed in the moment: And so time stopped. This suspension of time is usually felt as a positive event. It is an experience of marvel, relief, and freedom. It is the closest thing there is to perceiving immortality.

In fact, when time disappears, fear of death does, too. We do not worry about what we still have to do, about being late, about time running short, about not knowing how to fill our time, or knowing too well but not having enough of it. Instead, the eternal now gives us the deeply regenerating and marvelous feeling of freedom.

Let us see the experience of a woman who found in transcendence a sense of calm invulnerability: "I was at the top of the Borobodur monument in Indonesia. It is a representation of the Buddhist path to nirvana. It is a sanctuary made of long steps, with more than six hundred life-sized statues, showing the whole life of the Buddha. At the first steps, you are in dark corridors, then gradually the walls fall away, so that when you reach the top, you are in the open. It is an extraordinarily beautiful place.

"When I went there, because of recent uprisings, there were no tourists. I was alone. Once at the top, I could see the jungle below me, before the sun came up, and from the jungle emerged the many sounds of tropical birds. I was surrounded by eight or nine statues which were under perforated bells. I was alone in the middle of nothing, yet I felt I was in the safest place in the universe."

At other times transcendence comes unexpectedly. No music, no architectural wonders, no starry sky, just ordinary life. A woman, after a painful divorce, left alone with her two children, is suddenly visited by timelessness: "I was sitting in the car at the street light, waiting for green. I looked to the other side of the street and saw a man: He was tall and walking slowly with a stick. He looked like he had had a stroke. Suddenly it was as if time had stopped. Everything slowed down, and I had a feeling of a veil opening to another dimension. I saw how this man was walking slowly, one foot tenta-tively after the other, bending on his stick. I saw so much truth and beauty in all this, I started crying. I was so moved by the gift this moment was giving me. Then the light turned green, and I moved on."

### Disintegration and Regeneration

These are memorable experiences. Unfortunately, things do not always go as they should. Transcendence can occur so suddenly and violently as to cause disorientation, confusion, or panic, instead of relief and serenity. This happens in the Stendhal syndrome. Imagine a person who has lived all his life moving between apart-ment, bank, and supermarket, in a commonplace contemporary environment. Put him on a tourist excursion bound for places far from his habits and culture, give him, perhaps, some serious jetlag, expose him suddenly to intense sights, such as cathedrals with stained-glass windows, statues and paintings depicting love, war, abductions, battles, miracles and nudity; and then also mosaics, vaulted ceilings, muted or echoing sounds, perfumes and song, angels and devils—all sensory experiences that can open him to beauty, but in a rather intense, almost violent way. That is tran-scendence in which an unprepared person loses himself because it is all just too much.

The Stendhal syndrome is a pathological caricature of the aes-thetic experience. It occurs when the structure of the personality is not strong, or not flexible enough. It is a fairly rare phenomenon.

Even so, anyone can feel beauty to be too intense, far grander than we are, to the point of being intolerable. Beauty then seems capable of disintegrating us. And if we let ourselves go, that is exactly what happens. But it is a positive event: For a short time the organization of our mental and emotional world is loosened, if not dissolved. We learn to transcend, to lift ourselves by our own bootstraps, and look beyond.

In fact, this is not such an uncommon event. We have been learning self-transcendence since we were children: The world is not all about me, me, me. Self-transcendence when we are adults is on a bigger scale. There is more stuff we have to transcend: More convictions, more emotional habits, more roles and imaginary constrains. At times, letting go of all that may feel scary: After all, it is what we have and can count on. And yet when we surrender to beauty, when we let ourselves be dazzled and transported by it, we experience relief, and we grow, since growth occurs only when we have the courage to abandon whatever in us is stale and obsolete. No cause for alarm—we will return to the familiar prison walls—that prison which, paradoxically, we love so much, because it gives us, not only oppression, but security and some degree of comfort as well. Yet at least we will know the world is bigger than we thought. We will feel nourished and renewed and less rigid. We will be a little more open.

Or perhaps a lot more open.

❧

# SIX

# SELF, NATURE, AND SOCIETY

# Abuse vs. Awe

In a small Tuscan town, the main square has been torn apart in the name of novelty and convenience. And within this open wound the builders will house the new council offices. The old square was fine. There was no need to touch a single stone; it had been that way for centuries. To me it seems a disgrace, one of the many signs of advancing ugliness.

When I look at the rip, I get the feeling it is a petrified cry of pain. As a psychologist, I think of all human expressions—a poem or graffiti, a fresco or a plate of pasta—as states of mind. And what this piazza expresses in my eyes is frozen misery, some sort of confused wretchedness no one is able to express in words. The problem is, now we all have to put up with it.

### Violated Beauty

If someone were to say this square is beautiful in the way it has been redone, I would make no comment, because I respect other people's taste. This is a basic condition for my work: People have the emotions they have—there is no right and wrong. Yet I do note my own reaction—here, one of dismay and pain. And I also think that travesties like these happen because beauty is not a priority. Other values supersede it: "development," efficiency, profit. For other times, harmony, sense of proportion, unity with nature, were the basic points of reference.

Still, it is possible for each of us to cultivate admiration of beauty in all its forms—not only in art, but, generally, in all the ways in which beauty has been expressed through the centuries. For example, a language like Italian, or English, or Chinese, is a masterpiece of ingenuity and aesthetics. It is the work of countless people through the centuries and allows us to express feelings and thoughts in amazing subtlety and an astonishing variety of nuances, variations, and metaphors. To reduce it to a few elementary words is an insult. A TV program that uses a vocabulary of four hundred words at the most, a newspaper article stuffed with foreign expressions and clichés, are a small ignominy. And what applies to language also applies to cooking, music, stories, traditions, clothes—all affected in one way or another by vulgarity, mass production, or oblivion. It would be a pity to lose these treasures forever. Beauty lies there, too.

This chapter is devoted to our relationship with the natural environment and the cultural environment (and by that I mean the world we humans create: outer—buildings, food, music, pictures, and inner—words, images, symbols). We shall see how this relationship defines our existence in the world and how sensitivity to beauty can influence it.

Let us straightaway consider an example: In a mountain region endowed with scenery of exceptional beauty, "progress" has struck again: A road carries busloads of crowds to a huge parking area, with ski lift, bar, restaurant, constant sounds to fill the mystery of silence. All is done in the fervent spirit of promotion and profit. This is a relationship based on the exploitation of the habitat.

Second example: In a Venetian square, a fourteenth-century stone well is covered with graffiti. This is a slur, but I do not think it is hostile nor exploitative. It is a need to declare: I have been here. It as a form of obtuse territorial control.

Third example: a freshly painted wall in a town building. You have all seen it: One day it is clean and new; the next, it is replete with obscene writing. Whoever the culprit, he has a hostile relation to the world, wants to vent anger, disfigure, and destroy.

Finally, fourth example: Roberto, a farmer I know, has a vegetable garden. It is a pleasure to watch him work. He grows lettuce, zucchini, fennel, celery, potatoes, tomatoes, green beans, peas, spinach, plus cherries, apples, apricots, and plums. His garden, with its tidy rows of vegetables, its staked tomato plants, its furrows ready for the seedlings, seems to me a masterpiece. Somewhere I have a photo of him holding in his hands a giant tomato. He holds it with tenderness and pride, as though it were a baby. While he is looking after the vegetable garden, his relationship with the environment is one of harmonious symbiosis.

### Protection of Nature

The way we relate to both inner and outer nature says a lot about who we are and how we live. The relationship is continuous and happens on many levels simultaneously—it involves the air we breathe, the smells we smell, the sounds we hear, the scenes we see, the foods we eat, the ground we walk on, the words we think and say. What is this relationship like? The answer describes our existence. Only if it is harmonious and fruitful can there be true physical and psychological health.

Perception of beauty can greatly influence our relationship to the environment. It can help us to feel well where we are, to preserve nature and scenery, to treasure and protect the heritage of our culture and that of others.

To be sure, this is not the whole story. Aesthetic intelligence is necessary but not sufficient: It would be naïve to think it were. The reality is, as always, complex and contradictory. Here is an example: I am on a plane bound for Australia (our family is half Australian). We are flying over coral atolls along the northeast coast. The colors are a dreamlike vision. It seems as if we were flying over opal in slow, constant change; the swirls are now dark blue, now white, now cream or reddish, now turquoise. Their phosphorescent lights appear to come from inside. Next we fly over the desert. The earth has the strong red color which is the trademark of this continent. The light is still radiant, and you can clearly see the dunes. The wind has left delicate, beautiful patterns on the sand. Finally, we arrive in Sydney. Despite the last few years' droughts, the impression, compared to the desert, is one of fertility, welcome, and the magnificent richness of nature. I see the gracious green curves of bays on the coastline, the sparkle of the water. Looking at this magnificence unrolling before my eyes, I am seized by awe. I think of our planet, of the infinitely beautiful jewel that has been entrusted to us. Who on Earth would want to spoil it? Seeing this spectacle, I wonder how we can manage to protect and preserve nature in every possible way, because it is not just our only source of nourishment and survival, but also a breathtakingly beautiful sight.

Then it occurs to me that at this moment while I am flying over Australia, I am on a plane that is pouring polluting gases into the atmosphere: One more contribution to global warming. My aesthetic experience is, after all, very costly.

Loving beauty is obviously not a sufficient condition for saving nature and protecting the planet. Each person has to play his or her part (and maybe that will not be enough either). You know the routine. Give up wasteful activities. Be aware of your carbon footprint and limit consumption. Save electricity, recycle as much as possible, use your car less, avoid waste, buy local foods rather than mummified imports from across the globe.

A practical attitude, a wish to cooperate, the right information—these are the minimum requirements if we hope to save the environment or to damage it as little as possible. Sensitivity to beauty is also a necessary element, because it generates a deeply felt motivation: You protect and preserve only what you love.

True, fear or duty may also motivate us. We will preserve nature if a catastrophe close to home forces us or the law effectively and persuasively obliges us to do so. But we can also do it out of love, because the beauty we see changes us so that we are horrified at the idea that we may harm living nature. Gregory Bateson, the great British anthropologist, said that it was a question of limits and identity. As long as I see a lake, for instance, as a separate entity, I will feel entitled to throw garbage and poisons into it. But the moment I understand that *I am* that lake, since I am part of nature just as that lake is, then throwing my garbage and poisons into it will seem to me just what it is: a self-inflicted damage.

How friendly, how intimate are we with nature? Our closeness to nature can be measured by an index: the connectedness with nature scale (CNS). It gauges how much we feel separated from nature or united with it. The more we feel connected, the more our sense of self expands, our behavior is respectful of the environment, and our subjective well-being increases.

### *Power Struggle, Love Relationship*

To the feeling of unity with nature, I would add aesthetic intelligence. If I appreciate the beauty of a lake—the rippled surface, the clouds mirrored in the water, the trees and flowers that frame it, the song of birds, and the clean, invigorating air—how can I possibly want to damage such a masterpiece? Beauty is capable of transforming a power struggle into a love relationship.

You preserve and protect beauty only if you see it and you love it. You feel it is a privilege to be living on such a beautiful planet. The same open, sensitive attitude applies to human landscapes and to art—in fact, to anything where beauty can be seen. If all of society appreciates the beauty of a landscape, or a building, or object, it will not tolerate any messing with it.

Luckily even one person's sensitivity can become a good example. Let us take the case of Gianna, a woman who for many years has lived in a town apartment. Her window overlooks a courtyard, which was supposed to belong to the building, but was sold separately by an absentminded, if not dishonest, administrator. That courtyard has gradually become a garbage disposal, filled with junk, scrap metal, car bodies, rubbish hurled from windows. At some point the condominium would have been able to buy the courtyard back. Gianna proposed to do so—she wanted to transform it into a communal garden. But her proposal was rejected. Finally she managed to buy her own three-by-ten-meter strip of the courtyard in front of her flat. Then she went to work: "I wanted to have some green and some flowers in front of my window. I started to plant and to water my strip. I took good care of it. Flowers, trees, climbers. It is a wasted little area next to a wall, then there is a gas station and a heavily trafficked road. Now if I look out, I see a green carpet, a thick bed of flowers, roses, and other plants, birds singing, and butterflies fluttering. I am happy. I feel I have realized a dream.

"The people in the condominium used to throw anything down there. Not anymore. I tell myself: Where you see ugliness and filth, it is like an invitation to throw more stuff. When we see beauty, we stop ourselves.

"In the season of greatest rose bloom, when a cascade of small white roses covers the gate between the old wall and the building, against the background of the deep red foliage of a tree, a passerby sometimes stops and looks at the beauty . . ."

The administrator had sent letters asking the tenants not to throw rubbish into the courtyard—with zero result. The beauty of the garden did it.

So we can say: Beauty redeems and dissuades from negligence and destructiveness. It may not be the only factor, but it is basic. If you see a boring, gray square, it is easy to decide to split it in two and construct a pile of cement offices: It is logical and profitable. If in that same square you see a delightful landscape that you love and admire, in which you can feel the presence of a living past, it does not cross your mind to touch it. If you just see any old beach, who cares if you drop cigarette butts, newspapers, peach stones, and empty bottles? If on this beach you see the beauty of fine sand shaped by the wind, clear turquoise water, the elegant forms of rocks, colored pebbles, and marvelous shells, then to spoil the sight seems a mortal sin.

We face a paradox here. Beauty is strong, since it can move and transform, redeem the world, save our life. But it is weak, because it can be forgotten or undervalued. It can be at the center of our attention. Or it can be ignored, and life goes on anyway in quiet desperation.

## Gratitude

So then: Beauty, when perceived, greatly improves our relationship with the environment—natural, urban, cultural, or interior. It evokes an attentive care that stems from unconditional love. It helps us find our deep connection with nature, which is our million years' inheritance. And it elicits the respect and involvement with memory, which in turn allows us to enjoy and protect our historical and artistic heritage.

Moreover, when we are in the presence of beauty, the fine qualities of awe and gratitude arise in us. Some years ago, in an unusually sunny January, I went to a country house of which I am very fond. A persimmon tree stands near a vegetable garden. The persimmon is one of my favorite trees. In autumn the show starts: The leaves are a range of colors from green to brick-red. Then they get redder still, and when they fall, they leave the fruits in full view—orange spheres hanging on dark branches, like balloons in a fairy tale. Most people do not care for them, and persimmons are regarded as a poor man's fruit. They cannot compete with, say, a glamorous pineapple imported from Africa. This is a mistake, as their flesh is extraordinarily sweet. If they are left on the trees, and no frost spoils them, persimmons get even better. They dry slightly, grow redder and sweeter.

I arrived one lovely afternoon in January, to find a few still on the tree. I ate one that had just fallen. It had an amazing taste. I felt a wave of gratitude for this tree, for nature nourishing us for free, like a capable and generous mother. I collected a few of the remaining persimmons. They were soft and delicate. Where would I put them? I looked in the house and found a few boxes. They were Gucci and Prada boxes, not mine, but those left by some friends who had stayed at the house and gone on a shopping spree at nearby outlet stores. Black boxes: true luxury containers. Then it occurred to me: Why not put the persimmons in them? So I did. Lining the boxes was some black tissue paper, I placed the fruits carefully inside, one by one, like beautiful designer jewelry.

They fit perfectly. I loved the idea, and days later it came repeatedly to mind. I wondered why the thought kept coming back. I realized it had been a symbolic act on my part. By placing the persimmons in boxes destined for high fashion clothing, I was treating them as quality items. People consider them a proletarian fruit and forget them on the branches. But they are nature's high fashion. In that moment of realization, my gratitude to nature grew even bigger. I had been given beauty, nourishment, amazing flavors, and textures. What else could I ask for?

# Beauty Is the Opposite of War

Proposal: A course for hunters.

A number of people like to shoot birds. They find it fun, claim it is useful, and consider it innate to human nature. Naturally, this explosive pastime is subject to controls and taxes. On top of that, I propose that hunters, in order to obtain their license, be asked to follow a course on birds. In this course they would probe the beauty of bird feathers under a microscope—they would look at all the wonderful, iridescent colors and multiform patterns that grace the feathers of many different birds. They would study the mechanics of flight—the exquisite architecture of a bird's wing and the miraculous feats of aerial evolution. Future hunters also would study birds in the history of art, from Leonardo da Vinci's notes and sketches to Audubon's loving portraits. Then they would devote time to birdsong and learn to recognize the nightingale, the lark, the finch. Having finished the course, they could hold the rifle and aim at a bird, the idea being to fill that living marvel with lead. And to kill it.

But will they still want to? Maybe not.

## The Disappearance of Armor

In this book we have seen that beauty helps us understand other people and other cultures, expands intelligence, breaks down stereotypes, gives joy. The result of this influence is as far as it can be from war and violence. Beauty inspires an open attitude, I would say almost one of defenselessness. We feel vulnerable. The center of our being is exposed in the presence of beauty, because we have no wish to defend ourselves against it, we just want to enjoy. This is an erotic attitude, one of nakedness and pleasure, foreign to calculation and exploitation of any kind. There can be no frenzy; the pace slows down. Competition and antagonism vanish. Instead of being hard and tough, we become soft, receptive, ready to be molded. Thus we also have a greater capacity for empathy and the understanding of other people's points of view.

This concept is perhaps best exemplified, as Elaine Scarry eloquently explains in her book *On Beauty and Being Just*, by the meeting of Ulysses and Nausicaä in the *Odyssey*. Ulysses is almost at the end of his ten-year journey, going back home to Ithaca after the Trojan war. He has met with dangers and tragedies of all kinds and is the only survivor among his men. He has been thrown on a beach by the waves after his self-made raft has been destroyed by the fury of the sea. He is naked, does not know where he is, has no identity or social role, and stands alone. His situation is symbolical: It represents a state in which we are free from all outer conditionings and inner structures that may in some way distort or repress what we are. The state of defenselessness. "It is as though"—writes Scarry—"one has suddenly been washed up onto a merciful beach: All unease, aggression, indifference, suddenly drop back behind one, like a surf that has for a moment lost its capacity to harm."

In this state Ulysses meets Nausicaä, a young princess playing ball on the beach with her servants, who all run away at the sight of Ulysses, leaving her alone. Nausicaä is exquisitely beautiful, and she greets him, as all beauty greets us when we meet it. Ulysses is struck by this vision and thinks for a moment she is a goddess. Later, when he arrives in Ithaca, he will have all the cunning and force he needs to kill his enemies, but now he is in a state of total openness.

This attitude of disarmament leads us to yet another dimension in which beauty may be fundamental: war and peace. On one point I hope we are all in agreement: the absurdity of war. It is the most inefficient, troublesome, costly, and painful method for solving problems. You do not need much reflection to agree.

And yet many people find war fascinating, even fun. Some time ago in London, a stadium hosted a big show in which soldiers from various countries marched in line, with all their regalia: weapons, uniforms, flags, and banners. Italy was represented by the Bersaglieri. Their trademark is the beautiful plumed hat, their specialty is running to battle (instead of marching) at the sound of a trumpet. When it was their turn in the show, the Bersaglieri immediately began to run. But, either by mistake, or because someone had played a dirty trick on them, they ran the opposite way, which meant that, prodded by a cheerful trumpet sound, they were running in retreat. The episode fit perfectly the cliché of the Italian bungler and coward. The whole stadium burst out laughing.

### The Absurdity of Violence

I, on the other hand, find nothing to laugh at. I am sorry for the embarrassment of the Bersaglieri, but I think the involuntary error was actually the best choice. Yes, we should all run as fast as possible away from war—from gratuitous killing, from the methodical materialization of hate, from bombs, rifles, and machine guns, from the cold contemporary videogame warfare, from the landmines that kill children, from the bombing of innocent people, from tanks razing towns to the ground, from incendiary or poisonous gases that exterminate bodies and souls, from technology that sees in the dark and destroys at night, from missiles that not only aim at you, but also chase you as you flee, from friendly fire that kills by mistake, from all the techniques of disseminating disinformation, chaos, and sedition in enemy communities, from the nuclear threat that could delete an entire people in less than a second. Or, do we really want to run happily toward annihilation? And blow our trumpet as well?

In Roman Polanski's film *The Pianist*, a Jewish pianist in Warsaw during the Second World War has to give up his work when his life is devastated by Nazi persecution. He loses his loved ones, escapes, and manages to survive. In the climactic scene, when Germany is already close to defeat, he hides in an abandoned building. There he meets a Nazi captain. He expects the captain to arrest him or kill him. But there happens to be a piano, and the captain asks him to play. The pianist plays Chopin and fills the destitute, dusty room with sublime melody. The captain listens. His face appears impassive, but gradually betrays a dawning realization. Although he is speechless, you understand perfectly what he is thinking: War, persecution, looting, are abominably absurd in the presence of beauty. Alongside beauty, war cannot seem but a ludicrous and tragic mistake. In the presence of beauty, killing becomes impossible.

### Being Unarmed

Can beauty truly stop war? It would certainly seem not. Can a swarm of mosquitoes stop a train speeding toward them at 150 km an hour? War, associated with such fearsome allies as high technology, age-old rancor, economic and territorial interests, and huge motives like hunger, thirst, conquest, wealth, seems immensely more powerful.

No one so far has found a remedy or a secret to persuade people not to kill one another. I will not even attempt here an analysis of the complex reasons for war, but will point out one crucial fact: The profound experience of beauty is incompatible with aggression. A society based on enjoyment of beauty would be less likely to be a warrior society.

Some studies show how beauty lowers the level of aggression. But the best proof is introspective. Try to think of an aesthetic experience. How did you feel looking at that flower, or on that beach along an exquisite coast, or listening to that music, or appreciating the perfect architecture of a poem? I would imagine you felt at peace. Open, and perhaps vulnerable. Not in the sense of weak, but unarmed, without the need to defend against anything, without erecting any barriers whatever. You had surrendered, yes, but to beauty. Above all, you felt happy.

Imagine you are feeling this way. Would you then want to act out revenge, hostility, or discrimination? I think not. Would you want to bomb, set fire, destroy, kill, torture, press the button that annihilates? Most probably you do not want this anyway, but in this case even less, because beauty accentuates the absurdity of war.

Consider an objection. Beauty unleashes in us the desire to possess, the worst territorial instincts, intense greed. You see something beautiful and straightaway you want to possess it. The Trojan war was fought over the fairest of women. How does that fit with the concept of beauty as the supremely nonbelligerent state? The answer is simple. Here we are looking at the aesthetic experience in its most profound and contemplative aspects. There is no enmity in the state of ecstasy. Also, it is a question of aesthetic range. If you can appreciate beauty in one item only, you risk becoming angry and fearful. But if you know and love many forms of beauty, the thirst for possession recedes to a vanishing point.

With these provisos in mind, consider beauty and war side by side. War is hard and metallic. We sharpen knives and put up swords. In the aesthetic experience, on the other hand, we lay down weapons, our innermost nucleus melts. All that is hard and sharp in us liquefies. To harm others is the farthest idea in our mind. Yes, beauty is the exact opposite of war.

There is little doubt that peace is in some way connected with beauty, especially with music. The cellist Vedran Smailović started playing in the streets of Sarajevo in 1992 during the war. The Opera theater had just been destroyed and some of his students had been killed by a bomb while standing in a breadline. When a CNN reporter asked him, aren't you crazy to play the cello while bombs are falling all around you, he replied: "You ask me if I am not crazy to play the cello. Why don't you ask me if they are not crazy to bomb Sarajevo?"

When the Berlin wall was falling, Mstislav Rostropovich, the great cellist who regarded music as "divine service," flew to Berlin on December 11, 1989, stood before the crumbling wall, and began to play a Bach Cello Suite. The Berlin wall was the epitome of suspicion and hostility, of division between peoples. Bach's music is a supreme form of unity and harmony. The images traveled around the world. Later Rostropovich said that in that moment he managed to unite the two parts of his existence that had been completely separate: His life in Russia before 1974 and his life in the West after.

The great pianist and conductor Daniel Barenboim has founded an orchestra of young Israelis, Palestinians, and Arabs from Egypt, Jordan, Syria, and Lebanon. Their base is in Seville in Andalusia, where Christians, Muslims, and Jews have been living peacefully for centuries. For Barenboim, music is a concrete demonstration of how apparently contrasting sounds, voices, themes can coexist in harmony.

It seems to me that what these musicians are saying is the same: Open yourself to beauty, stop fighting.

Do not think I am proposing we go to play the flute in front of advancing tanks. On the contrary, sometimes it is right that we be tough and know how to defend ourselves. At times we need to put on our armor, speak up, fight. The problem is when the armor becomes part of our muscle and bone, harshness and suspicion an abiding attribute of the soul.

So beauty has the peculiarity of dispelling or reducing hostility and fear in our life. Let us look at this unarmed state in a couple of examples. A woman writes: "I am magnetically attracted to certain men and I find myself observing their beauty, both inner and outer. After seeing them, the image of their faces and the memory of their voices come back to me. I am amazed at such beauty, and it makes me fall in love instantly. Also, newborns arouse in me a sense of veneration: glorious creatures who seem to be more in heaven than on Earth. I am struck by their tiny form, hands, feet, and when they are breast-fed by their mothers, I find that to be a very special moment."

Another woman, a primary school teacher, writes: "I have

thought of many occasions when I have experienced beauty. The strongest experience of all is watching first-grade schoolchildren learning to read and write: I do not think much can equal it in beauty. The feeling is of having captured for a moment a secret, of having found a pot of gold at the end of a rainbow, and of having at last widened my horizon. Reality seems to expand, reveal itself by magic, and while the outside perception broadens, the inner perception also expands: The children I watch are also inside me, and I feel myself opening as they open."

You read these words and you immediately grasp the idea that aggression, exploitation, destruction, hate, cannot coexist in us with beauty. Sometimes, however, beauty is forgotten, and violence wins. At other times, when beauty is truly perceived, violence and its ugliness are dissipated. In a story about an earlier Dalai Lama, a terrible Kung Fu master arrived in Tibet from China. He was so dangerous that when eight men opposed him, he killed seven, and only wounded the eighth in order that someone be able to go back and tell the story: A rustling was heard, and the master was so fast that no one saw his lethal moves; it seemed he had merely walked among the eight men. He appeared to be proceeding calmly, as if nothing were happening, but his rapid, invisible actions felled, in seconds, warriors of great strength and experience, as if they were lifeless puppets. The Kung Fu master was handsome, with long blue-black hair and leather armor hugging his lean, muscular body. He was very sure of himself, and all were terrified of him. Full of arrogance and spite, he presented himself to the Dalai Lama, who was at this time ten years' old. He said he wanted to destroy the ugliness in the world, but his voice did not sound truthful. The Dalai Lama claimed to know a superior master—a master of dance. He called for him, and a small and cheerful old man turned up. The Kung Fu master laughed calmly and dared the old man to hit him. They faced each other. Then the unthinkable happened. The master of dance brushed the eyes of the Kung Fu master, and it was as if a veil had fallen: Suddenly the scene all around him—the monks, the Dalai Lama, the master of dance himself—everybody appeared beautiful, irresistibly beautiful. The dance master brushed his nose with the delicacy of a butterfly and the Kung Fu master smelled the exquisite aroma of the tea the Dalai Lama was quietly drinking, the scent of spices drifting in the air from a faraway kitchen, the perfumes of the approaching spring. He brushed his genitals, and the Kung Fu master felt sexual desire arise in his body, heard the beautiful voice of a woman singing far away from a window, and fell in love.

He felt an amazing vibration in his whole body and began to sing a wondrous song. Then he took off his leather armor and danced. It seemed to him he had a thousand arms and legs. It was the most beautiful dance ever seen in that palace, and it lasted three days. Finally the Kung Fu master understood his true talent: Not to kill, but to inspire. Not to reek destruction, but to create harmony. The old dance master could now die, because he had found his best student at last. The rapture of beauty had prevailed over the madness of destruction.

# Conclusion

At the end of this book we are left with one question: How can we find more beauty in our life?

There is no general answer, no user manual. Beauty happens when it happens. It is a mystery.

And yet, we may make the experience of beauty more likely and more meaningful. We cannot say which road to take; we all have a different itinerary. But we can say how and in what spirit to travel.

*Beauty is spontaneous.* Like the shape of clouds, the flowers in the fields, a brilliant idea, a flash of lightning. We cannot say beforehand how it will be, and this is just what makes it special. Beauty comes when it will; it is up to us to be ready for it.

*We can remove hindrances.* Various blocks can hamper beauty: I don't deserve it, it's a waste of time, there are better things to think about, it is a luxury, I am not capable. It is a question of doing less, not more. Such ideas cost a lot of energy. Less thinking equals more beauty.

*Attention is nourishing.* Anything we give our interest to grows and develops. Anything we neglect or ignore atrophies. Attention is like a spotlight on a theater stage. It gives emphasis. The world is what it is, but we provide the accent. We look for beauty, give it our vital interest, create space for it. Then beauty will proliferate for us.

*Beauty is ineffable.* It is very hard, if not impossible, to put into words. Compare it with riding a bicycle. When we learn how, we can balance, but how can we describe that feeling? Beauty is difficult to pinpoint, but the more we cultivate it, the more we can find our own way in it.

*Beauty is everywhere.* We find it in music, poetry, a face. But we also find it in a wilted flower, moss on an old wall, rusted iron, a concert of croaking frogs.

A woman tells me: "When I was a child, my grandmother (whom I loved very much) used to get warm, radiant sunlight in her room. I saw the dust particles floating in the air and illuminated by the sun. I was in ecstasy. It was as though I had seen a miracle. At that moment, I knew what beauty was."

The world is full of beauty, both hidden and manifest. It is enough to be open, look around, be like a child again. And if we will only give it a little attention, we will find it, we will enjoy it, we will be saved by beauty.

# BIBLIOGRAPHY

## Introduction

Alberti, A. *Il Sé ritrovato*. Firenze: Giampiero Pagnini, 1994.

Armstrong, J. *The Secret Power of Beauty*. London: Penguin, 2004.

Cela-Conde, C., et al. *Activation of the Prefrontal Cortex in the Human Visual Aesthetic Perception*. www.jstor.org.

Di Dio, C., E. Macaluso, and G. Rizzolatti. "The Golden Beauty: Brain Response to Classical and Renaissance Sculptures," *PloS ONE* 2, 11 (2007): 1201.

Dissanayake, E. *Homo Aestheticus*. Seattle: University of Washington Press, 1992.

Donohue, J. O. *Beauty, The Invisible Embrace*. New York: HarperCollins, 2004.

Emerson, R. W. "Beauty." In *Essays and Lectures*. New York: The Library of America, 1983.

Freedberg, D., and V. Gallese. "Motion, Emotion and Empathy in Esthetic Experience," *Trends in Cognitive Science* 11(2007): 197–203.

Goguen, J., and E. Myin. *Journal of Consciousness Studies* 7, 8/9(2000).

Jacobsen, T., et al. "Brain Correlates of Aesthetic Judgment of Beauty," *Neuroimage* 29, 1(2006): 276–85.

Hillman, J. *La Politica della Bellezza*. Bergamo: Moretti & Vitali, 1999.

———. "The Practice of Beauty." In B. Beckley and D. Shapiro, *Uncontrollable Beauty* (New York: Allworth, 1998).

Kawabata, H., and S. Zeki. "Neural Correlates of Beauty," *Journal of Neurophysiology* 91 (2004): 1699–1705.

Maquet, J. *The Aesthetic Experience*. New Haven: Yale University Press, 1986.

Reber, R., N. Schwarz, and P. Winkielman. "Processing Fluency and Aestheitc Pleasure: Is Beauty in the Perceiver's Processing Experience?" *Personality and Social Psychology Review* 8, 4(2004): 364–82.

Rella, F. *L'enigma della bellezza*. Milano: Feltrinelli, 2006.

Sartwell, C. *Six Names of Beauty*. Abingdon: Routledge, 2006.

Turner, F. "How Beauty Evolves." *www.dallasinstitute.org*.

### Affirmation

Bygren, L. O., B. Benson Konlaan, and S. E. Johansson. "Unequal in Death: Attendance at Cultural Events, Reading Books or Periodicals, and Making Music or Singing in a Choir as Determinants for Survival: Swedish Interview Survey of Living Conditions." *British Medical Journal* 313(1996): 1577–80.

Johansson, S. E., B. Benson Konlaan, and L. O. Bygren. "Sustaining Habits of Attending Cultural Events and Maintenance of Health: A Longitudinal Study." *Health Promotion International* 16, 3(2001): 229–34.

Konlaan, B. B., et al. "Attendance at Cultural Events and Physical Exercise and Health: A Randomized Controlled Study." *Public Health* 114, 5(2000): 316–19.

Shaw, P. *What's Art Got to Do with It?* Arts Council England, 2003.

Stamatopoulou, D. "Integrating the Philosophy and Psychology of Aesthetic Experience: Development of the Aesthetic Experience Scale." *Psychological Reports* 95, 2(2004): 673–95.

Wikstrom, B. "A Memory of an Aesthetic Experience Transferred to Clinical Practice." *Education for Health* 16, 1(2003): 40–50.

———. "Older Adults and the Arts: The Importance of Aesthetic Forms of Expression in Later Life." *Journal of Gerontological Nursing* 30, 9(2004): 30–36.

### Beauty Is Everywhere

Plato. *The Symposium.* New York: Penguin, 1999.

Shapiro, J., A. Duke, J. Boker, and C. S. Ahearn. "Just a Spoonful of Humanities Makes the Medicine Go Down: Introducing Literature into a Family Medicine Clerkship." *Medical Education* 39, 6(2005): 605–12.

Shapiro, J., E. Morrison, and J. Boker. "Teaching Empathy to First Year Medical Students: Evaluation of an Elective Literature and Medicine Course." *Education for Health* 17, 1(2004): 73–84.

Shapiro, J., and L. Rucker. "Can Poetry Make Better Doctors? Teaching the Humanities and Arts to Medical Students and Residents at the University of California, Irvine, College of Medicine." *Academic Medicine* 78, 10(2003): 953–57.

### Fundamental OK

Hagman, G. "The Sense of Beauty." *International Journal of Psychoanalysis* 83, 3(2002): 661–74.

### Taste

Asch, S. E. "Opinions and Social Pressure." *Scientific American* 193(1955): 31–35.

LeBreton D. *La Saveur du Monde. Une Anthropologie des sens* (Paris: Editions Métaillé, 2006).

### Spontaneity

Otto, R. *The Idea of the Holy.* New York: Oxford University Press, 1958.

### The Reality of Reality

Korzybski, A. *Science and Sanity.* Fort Worth: Institute of General Semantics, 1995.

McGlone, M., J. Aronson, and D. Kobrynowicz. "Stereotype Threat and the Gender Gap in Political Knowledge." *Psychology of Women Quarterly* 30, 4(2006): 392–98.

### How Beauty Cures Us

Altenmüller, E., et al. "The Institute for Music Physiology and Musicians' Medicine." *Cognitive Processing* 8(2007): 201–6.

Baker, B. "The Art of Healing." *Washington Post*, August 17, 2004, p. HE01.

Cottrell, A. "The Role of Music and Sound in Healing from Cancer: Developing Your Own Sound Healing Practice." www.healingmusic.org.

Davis, J. "Psychological Benefits of Nature Experiences: An Outline of Research and Theory." www.johnvdavis.com.

Diette, G. B., et al. "Distraction Therapy with Nature Sights and Sounds Reduces Pain during Flexible Bronchoscopy." *American College Chest Physicians* 123(2003): 941–48.

Duncan, G. "The Psychological Benefits of Wilderness." http://ecopsychology.athabascau.ca/Final/duncan.htm.

Forgeron, N. "The Impact of Music Therapy on Alzheimer's Disease Patients." www.faculty.uccb.ns.ca/gcarre/courses/health/music.htm.

Friedrich, M. J. "The Arts of Healing." *Journal of the American Medical Association* 281(1999): 1779–81.

Hamilton, C., S. Hinks, and M. Petticrew. "Arts for Health: Still Searching for the Holy Grail." *Journal of Epidemiology and Community Health* 57(2003): 401–2.

Lawson, B. "Healing Architecture." *The Architectural Review* 211, 1261(2002): 72–75.

Leather, P., et al. "Windows in the Workplace." *Environment and Behavior* 30, 6(1998): 739–62.

Maas, A., et al. "Intimidating Buildings: Can Courthouse Architecture Affect Perceived Likelihood of Conviction?" *Environment and Behavior* 32, 5(2000): 674–83.

Owen, J. W. "Arts, Health and Wellbeing: A Third Way for Health?" *World Hospital Health Service* 35, 2(2001): 3–6.

Read, M., A. Sugawara, and J. Brandt. "Impact of Space and Color in the Physical Environment of Preschool Children's Cooperative Behavior." *Environment and Behavior* 31, 3(1999): 413–28.

"The Reading Cure." *The Guardian*, January 5, 2008, pp. 7–20.

Roszak, T. "Ecopsychology: Eight Principles." www.ecopsychology.athabascau.ca.

Shaw, P. "What's Art Got to Do With It?" www.artscouncil.org.uk.

Spencer, M. J. "Live Arts Experiences: Their Impact on Health and Wellness." Hospital Audiences, Inc., New York, 2000.

Taal, J., and J. Krop. "Imagery in the Treatment of Trauma." *www.imaginatie.nl*.

Ulrich, R. "View Through a Window May Influence Recovery from Surgery." *Science* 224, 4647(1984): 420–21.

### Creativity

Hagendoorn, I. G. "Some Speculative Hypotheses about the Nature and Perception of Dance and Choreography." *Journal of Consciousness Studies* 11, 3–4(2004): 79–110.

Pennebaker, J. *Writing to Heal*. Oakland: New Harbinger, 2004.

Ridenour, A. "Creativity and the Arts in Health Care Settings." *Journal of the American Medical Association* 279(1998): 399–400.

Stich, S., "Theater Gives Seniors an Outlet for Self-expression, Therapy, Socializing and Fun." *Time*, March 17, 2003.

Visser, A., M. Hoog, and J. Taal. "Assumer le Cancer par l'Expression Créative et l'Imagination." *Revue Francophone de Psycho-Oncologie* 19–24, 6(2004): 25–38.

### Nature and Music

Augé, M. *Non-lieux, Introduction à un anthropologie de la surmodernité*. Parigi: Editions du Seuil, 1992.

Clift, S., et al. "Choral Singing and Psychological Well-being: Findings from English Choirs in a

Cross-national Survey Using the WHOQOL-BREF." International Symposium on Performance Science, Porto, Portugal, 2007.

Clift, S., et al. "The Perceived Benefits of Singing." *The Journal for the Royal Society for the Promotion of Health* 121, 4(2001): 248–56.

Danon, M. *Ecopsicologia*. Milano: Apogeo/Urra, 2006.

Dorfles, G. *Horror pleni*. Roma: Castelvecchi, 2004.

Hilliard, R. E. "Music Therapy in Hospice and Palliative Care: A Review of the Empirical Data." *eCAM Advance Access* 2, 2(2005): 173–78.

Krout, R. E. "The Effects of Single-session Music Therapy Interventions on the Observed and Self-reported Levels of Pain Control, Physical Comfort, and Relaxation of Hospice Patients." *American Journal of Hospice and Palliative Medicine* 18, 6(2001): 383–90.

Maler, T., et al. "Description of Musical Expression and Initial Results of the Lubeck Music Therapy Model." *Psychotherapie, Psychosomatik, medizinische Psychologie* 44, 3–4(1994): 122–27.

National Park Service, "Effects of Noise." U.S. Department of the Interior.

Nelson, D., and R. Weathers. "Necessary Angels: Music and Healing in Psychotherapy." *Journal of Humanistic Psychology* 38, 1(1998): 101–8.

Pacchetti, C., et al. "Active Music Therapy in Parkinson's Disease: An Integrative Method for Motor and Emotional Rehabilitation." *Psychosomatic Medicine* 62(2000): 386–93.

Richards, R. "A New Aesthetic for Environmental Awareness: Chaos Theory, the Beauty of Nature, and Our Broader Identity." *Journal of Humanistic Psychology* 41, 2(2001): 59–95.

Wells, N. "At Home with Nature." *Environment and Behavior* 32, 6(2000): 775–95.

Werhan, P. O., and D. G. Groff. "Research Update: The Wilderness Therapy Trail: Wilderness Therapy Can Help Provide Personal Growth and Physical Health Benefits." *Parks & Recreation*, November 2005.

Wignall, A. "Keeping Body and Soul in Tune." *The Guardian*, August 26, 2008, p. 16.

### The Invisible Ally

Angyal, A. *Neurosis and Treatment*. New York: John Wiley, 1965.

### The Beauty of the Soul

Carlson, E. "Physical Beauty Involves More than Good Looks." www.sciencedaily.com.

Etcoff, N. *Survival of the Prettiest—The Science of Beauty*. New York: Anchor Books, 1999.

Etcoff, N., S. Orbach, J. Scott, and H. D'Agostino, "The Real Truth About Beauty." www.campaignforrealbeauty.com.

Langlois, J. H., et al. "Maxims or Myths of Beauty? A Meta-analytic and Theoretical Review." *Psychological Bulletin*, 126, 3(2000): 390–423.

"Beauty and Success: To Those That Have, Shall Be Given." *The Economist*, December 19, 2007.

### The Good and the Beautiful

Anderson, C., N. Carnagey, and J. Eubanks. "Exposure to Violent Media: The Effects of Songs with Violent Lyrics on Aggressive Thoughts and Feelings." *Journal of Personality and Social Psychology* 84, 5(2003): 960–71.

Brodsky, J. Nobel Lecture in Literature, 1987.

Brodsky, J. *On Grief and Reason*. New York: Farrar Straus and Giroux, 1994.

Hill, M. "The Effects of Heavy Metal Music on Levels of Aggression in College Students." www.apa.org.

Hillman, J. *The Thought of the Heart and the Soul of the World*. Milan: Adelphi, 2002.

Mithen, S. *The Prehistory of the Mind*. London: Thames and Hudson, 1996.

————. *The Singing Neanderthals*. London: Weidenfeld & Nicolson, 2005.

North, A., M. Tarrant, and D. Hargreaves. "Effects of Music on Helping Behavior." *Environment and Behavior* 36, 2(2004): 266–75.

Witherspoon, G. *Language and Art in the Navajo Universe*. Ann Arbor: University of Michigan Press, 1971.

## Beauty Is Primary

Dissanayake, E. *Art and Intimacy*. Seattle: University of Washington Press, 2000.

Dutton, D. "Aesthetics and Evolutionary Psychology." In *The Oxford Handbook for Aesthetics*. Edited by Jerrold Levinson. New York: Oxford University Press, 2003.

————. "Hardwired to Seek Beauty." *The Australian*, January 13, 2006.

Enquist, M., and A. Arak. "Symmetry, Beauty and Evolution," *Nature* 372, 6502(1994): 169–72.

Grammer, K., et al. "Darwinian Aesthetics: Sexual Selection and the Biology of Beauty." *Biological Reviews of the Cambridge Philosophical Society* 78, 3(2003): 385–407.

Haidt, J., et al. "Body, Psyche, and Culture: The Relationship between Disgust and Morality." *Psychology and Developing Societies* 9, 1(1997): 107–31.

Jacobsen, T. "The Primacy of Beauty in Judging the Aesthetics of Objects." *Psychological Reports* 94, 3 Pt. 2(2004): 1253–60.

Kaplan, G., and L. Rogers. "Elephants That Paint, Birds That Make Noise." www.dana.org.

Martindale, C., P. Locher, and V. M. Petrov. eds. *Evolutionary and Neurocognitive Approaches to Aesthetics, Creativity and the Arts*. Amityville, N.Y.: Baywood Publishing, 2007.

Miller, G. *The Mating Mind*. New York: Anchor Books, 2001.

Rhodes, G. "The Evolutionary Psychology of Facial Beauty." *Annual Review of Psychology* 57(2006): 199–226.

Rhodes, G., et al. "Attractiveness of Facial Averageness and Symmetry in Non-Western Cultures: In Search of Biologically Based Standards of Beauty." *Perception* 30, 5(2001): 611–25.

Zaidel, D. W., S. M. Aarde, and K. Baig. "Appearance of Symmetry, Beauty, and Health in Human Faces." *Brain and Cognition* 57, 3(2005): 261–63.

## Mind and Beauty

Catteral, J. "Critical Links: Learning in the Arts and Student Social and Academic Development." www.aep-arts.org.

Chipongian, L. "Can Music Education Really Enhance Brain Funtioning and Academic Learning?" www.brainconnection.com.

Coomaraswamy, A. K. *The Dance of Shiva, Essays on Indian Art and Culture*. New York: Dover, 1985.

————. *The Transformation of Nature in Art*. New York: Dover, 1956.

Daumal, R. *Rasa, or Knowledge of the Self*. New York: New Directions Books, 1982.

Dickinson, D. "Learning Through the Arts." www.newhorizons.org.

Freeland, C. "Teaching Cognitive Science and the Arts." www.uh.edu.

Gruhn, W., N. Galley, and C. Kluth. "Do Mental Speed and Musical Abilities Interact?" *Annals of the New York Academy of Sciences* 999(2003): 485–96.

Hagendoorn, I. "The Cognitive Neuroscience of Dance Improvisation." www.ivarhagendoorn.com.

Huntley, H. E. *The Divine Proportion*. New York: Dover, 1970.

Gilbert, A. G. "Movement Is the Key to Learning." www.newhorizons.org.

Jenkins, J. S. "The Mozart Effect." *Journal of the Royal Society of Medicine* 94(2001): 170–72.

Matsumoto, K. "The Nature Journal as a Tool for Learning." www.newhorizons.org.

Millis, K. "Making Meaning Brings Pleasure: The Influence of Titles on Aesthetic Experiences." *Emotion* 1, 3(2001): 320–29.

Portowitz, A. "Music Activities as a Cognitive Tool for the Enhancement of Analytical Perception, Comparison, and Synthesis for the Blind Learner." www.newhorizons.org.

Root-Bernstein, R. S. "Aesthetic Cognition." *International Studies in the Philosophy of Science* 17, 1(2002): 61–77.

Spelke, E. "Effects of Music Instruction on Developing Cognitive Systems at the Foundations of Mathematics and Science." www.dana.org.

Washington State Arts Commission Newsletter, Winter 2003. "Stimulating the Brain and Sense Through Art."

Winner, E. "Effects of Instrumental Music Training on Brain and Cognitive Development in Young Children: A Longitudinal Study." www.dana.org.

Zull, J. "Arts, Neuroscience and Learning." www.newhorizons.org.

### Revelation

Bullitt, J. T. "Deep Earth Dome." www.jtbullitt.com.

Emoto, M. *The Hidden Messages in Water*. Hillsboro: Beyond Words, 2005.

Jenny, H. *Cymatics*. Basel: Basilius Presse AG, 1966.

Lu, P., and P. Steinhardt. "Decagonal and Quasi-Crystalline Tilings in Medieval Islamic Architecture." *Science* 315, 5815(2007): 1106–10.

Ramachandran, V. "The Science of Art. A Neurological Theory of Aesthetic Experience." *Journal of Consciousness Studies* 6(1999): 6–7.

Schwenk, T. *Sensitive Chaos*. London: Rudolf Steiner Press, 1965.

Takahashi, R. "Project Development." www.mimg.ucla.edu.

Wade, D. *Li: Dynamic Forms in Nature*. New York: Wooden Books, 2003.

### Secret Echoes

Bargh, J. "What Have We Been Priming All These Years? On the Development, Mechanism, and Ecology of Nonconscious Behavior." *European Journal of Social Psychology* 36(2006): 147–68.

Carey, B. "Who's Minding the Mind?" *The New York Times*, July 31, 2007.

Hassin, R., J. Uleman, and J. Bargh. *The New Unconscious*. New York: Oxford University Press, 2005.

### Transcendence

Dossey, L. *Time Space and Medicine*. Boston: Shambala, 1982.

### Abuse vs. Awe

Mayer, S., and F. McPherson. "The Connectedness to Nature Scale: A Measure of Individuals' Feeling in Community with Nature." *Journal of Environmental Psychology* 24(2004): 503–15.

### Beauty Is the Opposite of War

Brodsky, J. *One Grief and Reason*. New York: Farrar, Straus and Giroux, 1994.

Choi, A., L. M. Soo, and J. Lee. "Group Music Intervention Reduces Aggression and Improves Self-esteem in Children with Highly Aggressive Behavior: A Pilot Controlled Trial." *eCAM*, doi:10.1093/ecam/nem182.

Scarry, E. *On Beauty and Being Just*. London: Duckworth, 2000.

Piero Ferrucci is a psychotherapist and philosopher. He has been a student of and collaborator with Roberto Assagioli, the founder of psychosynthesis. He is the author of *The Power of Kindness*, *What We May Be*, *Inevitable Grace*, and *What Our Children Teach Us*, as well as the editor of *The Human Situation*, a book of Aldous Huxley's lectures. He lives near Florence, Italy, with his wife and two sons.

# TIMELESS WISDOM FROM

## PIERO FERRUCCI

### THE POWER OF KINDNESS

A classic bestseller that reveals the surprising secret to enjoying a happy life and navigating a world that has become anxious, difficult, and fearful: Behaving with kindness.

### INEVITABLE GRACE

This classic handbook on achieving breakthrough transpersonal experiences explores how exceptionally creative and talented individuals grow capable of their remarkable feats, and teaches the techniques and inner attitudes that put these breakthroughs within anyone's grasp.

### WHAT WE MAY BE

The widely acclaimed and uniquely accessible introduction to psychosynthesis—both a psychology of self-actualization and a philosophy of the art of living.